RETHINKING JOURNALISM AGAIN

It's easy to make a rhetorical case for the value of journalism. Because, it is a necessary precondition for democracy; it speaks to the people and for the people; it informs citizens and enables them to make rational decisions; it functions as their watchdog on government and other powers that be...

But does rehashing such familiar rationales bring journalism studies forward? Does it contribute to ongoing discussions surrounding journalism's viability going forth? For all their seeming self-evidence, this book considers what bearing these old platitudes have in the new digital era. It asks whether such hopeful talk really reflects the concrete roles journalism now performs for people in their everyday lives. In essence, it poses questions that strike at the core of the idea of journalism itself. Is there a singular journalism that has one well-defined role in society? Is its public mandate as strong as we think?

The internationally renowned scholars comprising the collection address these recurring concerns that have long defined the profession and which journalism faces even more acutely today. By discussing what journalism was, is and (possibly) will be, this book highlights key contemporary areas of debate and tackles ongoing anxieties about journalism's future.

Chris Peters is Associate Professor of Media and Communication at Aalborg University's Copenhagen campus. His research explores how people get and experience news and information in everyday life, and the sociocultural impact of transformations in the digital era. His publications include *Rethinking Journalism* and *Retelling Journalism*.

Marcel Broersma is Professor of Journalism Studies and Media, and the director of the Centre for Media and Journalism Studies at the University of Groningen. He has published widely on historical and current transformations in journalism. His publications include *Form and Style in Journalism*, *Rethinking Journalism* and *Retelling Journalism*.

RETHINKING JOURNALISM AGAIN

Societal role and public relevance in a digital age

Edited by Chris Peters and Marcel Broersma

Routledge
Taylor & Francis Group

LONDON AND NEW YORK

First published 2017
by Routledge
2 Park Square, Milton Park, Abingdon, Oxon OX14 4RN

and by Routledge
711 Third Avenue, New York, NY 10017

Routledge is an imprint of the Taylor & Francis Group, an informa business

British Library Cataloguing in Publication Data
A catalogue record for this book is available from the British Library

Library of Congress Cataloguing in Publication Data
A catalog record for this book has been requested

ISBN: 978-1-138-86085-8 (hbk)
ISBN: 978-1-138-86086-5 (pbk)
ISBN: 978-1-315-71624-4 (ebk)

Typeset in Bembo Std
by Out of House Publishing

CONTENTS

NOTES ON CONTRIBUTORS

Stuart Allan is Professor and Head of the School of Journalism, Media and Cultural Studies at Cardiff University. Much of his research revolves around different aspects of war, conflict and crisis reporting, including his authored book *Citizen Witnessing: Revisioning Journalism in Times of Crisis* (Polity Press, 2013). He is particularly interested in the evolving relationship between professional and amateur or citizen news photographers, ranging from the mid-nineteenth century to the digital photo-reportage of today. He is currently writing a book on this topic, as well as conducting research on mobile technologies and civic engagement.

Pablo J. Boczkowski is Professor and Director of the Master of Science in Leadership for Creative Enterprises at Northwestern University. His research examines the transformation of print culture in the digital age. He has written three books, most recently *The News Gap* (co-authored with Eugenia Mitchelstein, MIT Press, 2013), and over 20 journal articles and 50 conference presentations.

Marcel Broersma is Professor of Journalism Studies and Media at the University of Groningen and the Director of its Centre for Media and Journalism Studies. His research examines emerging forms and styles of journalism, the use of social media in journalism and politics, shifting patterns of news use, and the epistemology of journalism. He is the author of numerous journal articles and book chapters. His books include *Form and Style in Journalism* (Peeters, 2007), *Rethinking Journalism* (Routledge, 2013), *Retelling Journalism* (Peeters, 2014) (the latter two co-edited with Chris Peters) and *Redefining Journalism in the Era of the Mass Press 1880–1920* (Routledge, 2016, co-edited with John Steel).

Matt Carlson is Associate Professor of Communication at Saint Louis University, where his research examines the changing conditions of contemporary journalism, with a particular interest in metajournalistic discourse and the production of meanings about the news. He is author of *Journalistic Authority* (Columbia University Press, 2016) and *On the Condition of Anonymity* (University of Illinois Press, 2011), editor of *Boundaries of Journalism* (Routledge, 2016) with Seth C. Lewis and *Journalists, Sources, and Credibility* (Routledge, 2011) with Bob Franklin, and has published numerous journal articles and book chapters.

Mark Coddington is Assistant Professor of Journalism and Mass Communication at Washington and Lee University. He studies networked journalism and the sociology of news amid changing informational and technological environment. He is a contributor to the Nieman Journalism Lab at Harvard University, where he wrote a weekly piece from 2010 to 2014. His research has been published in journals including *Mass Communication and Society*, *Journalism & Mass Communication Quarterly*, *Journalism Studies* and the *International Journal of Communication*.

Nick Couldry is Professor of Media, Communications and Social Theory, and Head of the Department of Media and Communications at the London School of Economics. His work has drawn on, and contributed to, social, spatial, democratic and cultural theory, anthropology, and media and communications ethics. His analysis of media as 'practice' has been widely influential. He is the author or editor of 11 books, most recently *Media, Society, World* (Polity, 2012), and many journal articles and book chapters.

Mark Deuze is Professor of Media Studies at the University of Amsterdam. His research is concerned with the way our life takes place increasingly in the media. He is the author of seven books on journalism and media, including *Media Work* and *Media Life* (Polity Press, 2007 and 2012). As a visiting professor, he has lectured at various schools and departments in the fields of journalism, communication and media in the Netherlands, Belgium, Germany, Finland, Norway, Denmark, Portugal, South Africa, Australia, New Zealand, the UK and the USA.

Yigal Godler is a doctoral candidate at Ben-Gurion University of the Negev. His research interests include the sociology and epistemology of journalism. He is a co-author of *The Skeptic in the Newsroom* (Israel Democracy Institute, 2016) and his work has appeared in *Journalism*, *Journalism Studies* and *Journalism Practice*.

Kaori Hayashi is Professor of Media and Journalism Studies at the Graduate School of Interdisciplinary Information Studies, University of Tokyo. She has also served as a member of the Broadcasting Ethics and Program Improvement Organization (an independent self-regulatory organization of the broadcasting industry in Japan) and is a board member of the Deutsches Institut für Japanstudien (German Institute for Japanese Studies). Her English articles have been published in journals including *Journalism Studies* and *Media, Culture & Society*.

Avery E. Holton is Assistant Professor and Humanities Scholar at the University of Utah, where he is the co-founder of the Communication, Health, and Social Media Lab and operates within the Immersion Lab. His research emphasizes the evolving roles of digital technology in media engagement, identity maintenance and health communication. His work has appeared in *Communication Theory, Mass Communication & Society* and *Journalism Studies,* among others.

Seth C. Lewis is the Shirley Papé Chair in Electronic and Emerging Media in the School of Journalism and Communication at the University of Oregon and a visiting fellow at Yale Law School. His research explores the digital transformation of journalism, with a focus on conceptualizing human–technology interactions and media innovation processes. He is co-editor of *Boundaries of Journalism* (Routledge, 2015) and editor of *Journalism in an Era of Big Data* (Taylor & Francis, 2017). He is a two-time winner (2013, 2016) of the Outstanding Journal Article of the Year in Journalism Studies Award from the International Communication Association.

Eugenia Mitchelstein is an Assistant Professor and Director of the Undergraduate Communications programme in the Department of Social Sciences, Universidad de San Andrés. Her research examines the interaction between new media, political communication and civic engagement. She is the author of *The News Gap: When the Information Preferences of the Media* and *the Public Diverge* (MIT Press, 2013, with Pablo Boczkowski). Her current major project, undertaken jointly with Pablo Boczkowski and Ignacio Siles, is an ethnographic study of the demise of print newspapers in Chicago, Paris and Buenos Aires, as a window into larger dynamics of institutional decay.

Rasmus Kleis Nielsen is Director of Research at the Reuters Institute for the Study of Journalism in the Department of Politics and International Relations at the University of Oxford. His research deals with political communication, campaign practices, and media institutions and their ongoing transformations. His first monograph, *Ground Wars* (Princeton University Press, 2012), won the American Political Science Association's Doris Graber Award in 2014 for the best book in political communication in the previous ten years. He has edited five books, written numerous articles and book chapters, and serves as Editor-in-Chief of the *International Journal of Press/Politics.*

Chris Peters is Associate Professor of Media and Communication at Aalborg University's Copenhagen campus. His research investigates the changing experiences, conceptions and spatiotemporal uses of information in a digital era, and the sociocultural transformations associated with this in everyday life. His publications include *Rethinking Journalism* (Routledge, 2013), *Retelling Journalism* (Peeters, 2014) (both co-edited with Marcel Broersma) and *The Places and Spaces of News Audiences* (Routledge, 2016), as well as numerous journal articles and chapters.

Zvi Reich is Associate Professor in the Department of Communication Studies at the Ben-Gurion University of the Negev, Israel and a former journalist. His research interests include journalism studies, news sources, technology use among journalists, epistemology and authorship. He is the author of *Sourcing the News* (Hampton, 2009) and one of the contributing authors to *Participatory Journalism* (Wiley-Blackwell, 2011).

Jane B. Singer is Professor of Journalism Innovation at City University, London. She previously held faculty posts at the University of Iowa and Colorado State University in the US, and served as Johnston Press Chair in Digital Journalism at the University of Central Lancashire in the UK. A former print and online journalist, her research has traced the evolution of digital journalism since the mid-1990s, with a focus on journalists' changing roles, perceptions, norms and practices.

John Steel is Lecturer in Journalism Studies at the University of Sheffield. His research focuses on the history and theory of debates concerning the relationship between journalism and democracy and free speech, censorship and the freedom of the press. His publications include *Journalism and Free Speech* (Routledge, 2012), the *Routledge Companion to Media History* (Routledge, 2015, co-edited with Martin Conboy) and *Redefining Journalism in the Era of the Mass Press 1880–1920* (Routledge, 2016, co-edited with Marcel Broersma).

Karin Wahl-Jorgensen is Professor in the Cardiff School of Journalism, Media and Cultural Studies at Cardiff University, and also serves as Director of Research Environment and Development in the school. Her research focuses on journalism and citizenship, and she has authored or edited five books, including most recently *Disasters and the Media* (Peter Lang, 2012, with Mervi Pantti and Simon Cottle) and *Handbook of Journalism Studies* (Routledge, 2009, co-edited with Thomas Hanitzsch). She is currently working on *Emotions, Media and Politics* for Polity Press. She has authored more than 40 journal articles and 20 book chapters.

Silvio Waisbord is Professor in the School of Media and Public Affairs at George Washington University. His books include *Media Sociology: A Reappraisal* (Polity Press, 2014), *Reinventing Professionalism: Journalism and News in Global Perspective* (Polity Press, 2013) and the co-edited compilation *Global Health Communication* (Wiley, 2012). He is Editor-in-Chief of the *Journal of Communication* and former Editor-in-Chief of the *International Journal of Press/Politics*. He has published articles on news and politics, journalism, global health communication, communication and social change, and media policy.

Tamara Witschge is Rosalind Franklin Fellow at the Centre for Media and Journalism Studies, University of Groningen. Her research explores the ways in which technological, economic and social change is reconfiguring journalism. She is co-author of *Changing Journalism* (2011, Routledge) as well as numerous journal articles and book chapters. She is the principal investigator on the NWO Vidi project 'Entrepreneurship at Work: Analysing Practice, Labour, and Creativity in Journalism' and a member of the editorial boards of *New Media & Society*, *Social Media + Society*, *Platform: the Journal of Media and Communication* and the German edition of the *Global Media Journal*.

INTRODUCTION

Towards a functional perspective on journalism's role and relevance

Marcel Broersma and Chris Peters

Notions of life and death hold a prominent place in our metaphorical repertoires. As oppositional pairs go, there are few more stark and palpable, and this is probably why it's not only tempting but also persuasive to present the claim for journalism's worth in similar terms. If journalism is indeed the 'lifeblood of democracy' and all this implies, societies with an unhealthy press are evidently at risk. Pleas for solutions to improve journalism's conditions therefore tend to go hand in hand with doomsday scenarios about the broader losses for society if journalism-as-we-know-it should cease to exist. While such thinking may not always be put in austere terms, it is nonetheless a constitutive part of the discourse that surrounds journalism as well as the basis for many concerns over its future.

Journalism has long and successfully claimed to be 'the primary sense-making practice of modernity' (Hartley, 1996, p. 12). While it has always been one sense-making practice among many interrelated others, its value to society has been and still is widely acknowledged, not least by journalists, politicians, and journalism scholars. In the course of its modernist professional project, journalism carved out a specific place and function in democratic societies, fulfilling distinctive needs for citizens. This period, which took hold over the course of the twentieth century in much of the Western world, witnessed the rise of the mass press as well as the appearance of many of the paradigmatic claims about journalism's value and necessity (Broersma, 2007), which still hold sway to this day. This was a time of grand theories and strong normative stances, and for the most part, such claims seemed laudable and worth striving towards, albeit challenging to realize in practice.

While admittedly fairly complicated and nuanced, it nonetheless remains that a key characteristic of this period was the appearance of durability and predictability when it came to many social institutions, forms of and approaches to knowledge (Beck, Giddens and Lash, 1994), including those associated with journalism. However, as we move beyond modernity – late, reflexive, liquid, post, or otherwise – this stability is increasingly challenged. Public trust and reliance on the 'expert' forms and institutions that modernity helped create is now continually being re-assessed as people turn to emerging alternatives. In addition, the development of personal media devices, 4G telecommunications, and Web 1.0, 2.0 and (soon) 3.0 fundamentally disrupt previous patterns of information provision and circulation. With this backdrop, it is no wonder that the tenor of post-millennial discussions about the news industry has been characterized by an emphasis on change. Technological advancement and economic models are the typical culprits identified in terms of how they are disrupting journalism practice and the news, and impacting journalisms ability – both positively and negatively – to deliver on its historical promises.

From rethinking to rethinking again

As we argued in the introduction to *Rethinking Journalism*, which can be seen as a precursor to this collection, such changes are not merely incremental or simply discursive; they are structural and strike journalism at its core. Whereas modernist discourses tend to anticipate change in terms of adaptation and subsequent progression, this now seems increasingly untenable (Broersma and Peters, 2013). Two intertwined trends have profoundly disturbed the relationship between journalism and its publics, who are, of course, also its customers. The de-industrialization of information and de-ritualization of audiences in contemporary digital media environments challenge not only what news is, but also what it can be.

In this sense, the rise of the mass press in modernity was less about the inherent value of its sense-making properties as it was a result of the logic of industrialization being brought to information. The 'trick' of journalism's business model was getting mass audiences to pay for a product (through their presence as consumers for advertisers, members of the tax and licence fee-paying public, or actively via subscriptions), which often contained little information they needed and which they couldn't see in advance. However, the product as a whole, 'the news', performed a host of worthwhile informative and social functions that became part and parcel of daily life. It did everything from conveying information about current affairs, social issues, weather reports, and where to find jobs and housing to providing topics for conversation, putting one in touch with one's community, and structuring and giving meaning to everyday life. In short, journalism connected audiences within democratic market societies. With the decline of mass media monopolies, this industrial logic of journalism seems to be outdated, its core functions for people gradually eroded (Broersma and Peters, 2013).

Whereas the authors in the previous collection (Peters and Broersma, 2013) offered profound insights into what this means for longstanding ideals surrounding trust, participation and engagement with the news, this book, comprising an almost entirely different line-up of communication, media and journalism studies scholars, refocuses discussions more closely on the object itself. When we thought up the focus of this volume, we invited the authors, somewhat provocatively, to move beyond the established rhetoric in scholarship and journalism practice. For all its seeming self-evidence, how much affinity does this talk share with the concrete functions journalism performs, or could perform, in the digital age? And what about journalism as a cultural form itself? Is there a singular journalism that has a well-defined task in democracy and society? Specifically, we challenged the contributors to critically reconsider not only journalism's essential social role but also its associated public relevance. Journalism studies as a field of media and communication research is a child of journalism itself; as a result, changes are typically looked at from journalism's point of view. This is an understandable focus given that our academic business is analysing journalism and the natural extension of this is that any perceived disruption within the object itself is cause for our attention. However, allowing journalism practice and the industry to act almost as a centripetal force for our scholarship leads to a somewhat predictable approach.

Specifically, it seems as though when it comes to *arguing for the value of journalism*, many of us studying the news, and journalists and the public themselves too for that matter, look back to familiar rhetoric – the aforementioned grand normative theories or updated editions thereof – to do so (Peters, 2015). At the same time, inherent to the past decade and a half of scholarship about journalism has been a recognition that the affinity between the rhetorical claims of journalism and its ability to realize these are growing apart. When it comes to *accounting for change in the industry*, however, the focus typically shifts to technological advancements and their possible implications. A brief glance at recent international academic conferences, prominent reports, journals shaping the field and book titles (including arguably this one) illustrates this tendency toward being a future-focused, one might even say obsessed, discipline. The obvious conclusion, but one that is hardly ever explicitly drawn given the persistence of the dominant rhetoric underlying the doxa of the field, might be that many of the theoretical frameworks in use no longer (completely) match the empirical studies into 'new' journalistic practice they aim to conceptualize. Although we acknowledge that the normative underpinnings of journalism and journalism studies are worthwhile, we have to conclude (somewhat gloomily) that it is challenging for historical propositions and forward-based technological forecasting to align.

Over the last couple of years, we have continued to wonder whether or not rephrasing familiar rationales about the purpose of news was serving to bring journalism studies forward. If our common sentiment is a wish that journalism in some form remains sustainable and worthwhile, how then might we better approach scholarship and our object of study to help enable this viability? While we suspect at least some authors in this collection and readers may disagree with our proposal, the remainder of this introductory chapter takes up these familiar discussions to try to begin a conversation anew. Our thinking in this respect is guided by a common sentiment prevalent throughout the chapters, as well as the afterwords, which is that most authors acknowledge that something meaningful is changing in journalism, but are still grappling over whether this necessitates updating previous concepts and paradigms to gain explanatory purchase over these changes or if entirely new vocabularies and approaches are needed.

Inspired by them, we take up the implicit challenge we read contained within these works, namely to begin to initiate a way forward for understanding and analysing journalism's contemporary status in a manner that encompasses historical premises, current practices and future change. We begin by discussing the first part of this collection's subtitle, namely journalism's societal role and relevance, to critically interrogate the stability of our traditional understandings of its purpose. While many of these familiar notions may have made some sense in journalism's formative period, we question the extent to which they hold up now. This brings us to the next section, which parallels the latter portion of the subtitle. In it we look to the place of journalism within a broader digital informational ecology to see how technological development impacts our scholarship. We argue that this metaphor alerts us to the competitive realities of the knowledge economy and helps to de-centre journalism without slipping into relativistic scholarship. In the final section, the chapter introduces the idea of a functional approach to studying the news, arguing that it offers the possibility of taking both latent and manifest functions of contemporary journalism and folding these into a relational framework grounded in everyday life. We hope it can offer a nuanced, substantiated and situational analytical lens that helps us to avoid all-or-nothing pronouncements on what journalism has been and can be by encompassing multiple temporal prisms. Only then can we understand what journalism 'is'.

Societal role and relevance

Constituting a collection centred around the societal role and relevance of journalism might seem somewhat self-evident in light of the dominant emphases in journalism studies scholarship. Crisis talk (Zelizer, 2015), the prominence of a democratic paradigm when conceptualizing and evaluating journalism (Josephi, 2013), and the aforementioned tendency toward forward-looking scholarship intersect to form a persuasive nexus for justifying the necessity of news as well as formulating longstanding normative arguments for the value of journalism. The gravitational pull created by such thinking is hard to escape and for academics orbiting journalism as an object of study, the tendency to be pulled in is understandable. It may, in fact, be definitional. The rise of journalism studies as a prominent sub-field of media and communications research has paralleled – one might even say been premised on – the 'decline', in many ways, of its definitional object of study. In such a climate, the idea of change, and especially forward-looking change, gains almost paradigmatic status. The result is a scholarly discipline whose very existence, paradoxically, is oftentimes tied to an object many fear is disappearing for good or changing beyond recognition.

Such thinking is not unique to academics. Journalists and industry observers are similarly forthcoming with pronouncements on the societal 'need' for thorough and independent journalism, and it is frightfully easy to find panels, think tanks and public declarations in recent years from within the industry stating that many trends of the digital era are taking news in a transformative direction (e.g. Kirkland, 2014; Cassidy, 2015). The technological tools bequeathed to audiences allow participation, interaction, crowdsourcing and many other seemingly beneficial endeavours, but searching questions remain about fragmentation, information overload and economic models to underwrite the news. As with the academic tendency above, when asked why this all matters, it is easy to fall back on familiar refrains which operate at a macro level. Much of the modernist project of journalism was founded around the premise, and indeed promise, of providing information to the masses and being legally (if not constitutionally) fundamental to democracy because of this. In short, the unifying function of mass media was implied if not strived for, and by advancing the illusion of trying to be everything for everyone, journalism's discourse became tied to a number of assumptions about its societal role and relevance that were not only advanced but also codified in law, reflected in news organizations' mottos and advertising slogans, and gradually internalized as central to public discourse around the profession.

These ideas are as familiar as they are potentially determinative: information source, watchdog, public representative, mediator for political actors and similar notions (for useful overviews, see Schudson, 2008; McNair, 2012). Despite the fact that the rhetorical functions by which we discuss the necessity of news might not have ever been taken up as we might think (or wish), and notwithstanding our understanding that these metanarratives tend towards overgeneralization, they nonetheless offer succour, as the absence of these things, we assume, is problematic. However, we benefit from critically interrogating such assumptions. For instance, the changing digital landscape and participatory options available to audiences challenge our understanding and invocation of the grand normative theories that have defined journalism (Peters and Witschge, 2015). This in turn relates to a reconfiguration of collective versus individualized understandings of its professional and democratic functions. In terms of these latter two ideas, we can further query how the unrelenting emphasis on democracy (Zelizer, 2013), or for that matter the essential claim of professionalism itself (Donsbach, 2014), frame enquiries around familiar lenses which may blind us from seeing what journalism is being, or has become, in a new media environment. Many other fruitful possibilities exist – from considering journalism in terms of its (shifting) boundaries (Carlson and Lewis, 2015) or (reconfigured) gatekeeping practices (Vos and Heinderyckx, 2015) – to seeing whether we can adapt 'old' paradigms to continue to explain the role of news and its institutional status, or whether we need completely new approaches to understand its societal position in the digital era.

As we embark on such conceptual journeys, it is worth sounding a slight note of caution. It seems increasingly evident to us that when we look to many intended functions or desirable social outcomes of journalism, the construction of these appears centred on cultural expectations more than everyday consequences. Such normative thinking is both ubiquitous and hard to test empirically, and for these reasons leads to stirring soundbites, philosophies and mission statements, but not necessarily to robust, testable conceptualizations. This miscasting impacts the utility of both public- and commercial-based understandings of journalism's contemporary purpose and our certainty over its need. In this respect, it is important to keep in mind that many of our hopes for journalism are founded on a public ethos that may bear little affinity to actual collective practices and prerequisites. This is unlike, say, infrastructure or education – more conventional public goods in the sense that they produce positive externalities that, albeit difficult to measure, are services everyone will need to make use of at some point. For these, relevance is built into the core of the object itself (we likely won't stop needing and using roads and schools anytime soon, and trying to think of widespread alternatives emerging to replace them is tricky at best).

However, the same cannot be said for journalism, and many have already moved on, if they were there in the first place. In addition, it is questionable whether journalism has ever been financially supported to the extent needed to fulfil the public services it claims to perform. Moreover, when we go beyond the definition of the object itself and its position in the broader field of cultural knowledge production, we get to relevance. But here too we find challenges. For instance, the investigative watchdog function sounds hard to replace, but whistleblowers and auditors are not in short supply and perform many similar societal roles. Similarly, public, commercial and non-governmental organizations as well as citizens' groups continue to find meaningful ways to circumvent journalism to distribute their message, meaning that the mediating, informational and representational functions served by news, while still useful, are no longer exclusive. Moving away from politics and current affairs (i.e. the purview of traditional 'hard' news), it is also easy to see how the 'softer' functions of journalism are being even more rapidly usurped, often by private enterprises better positioned to thrive in a new informational ecology where specialization abounds. This is evident for things like classified ads, travel advice, film and arts reviews, sports and the like.

The point isn't that such shifts aren't potentially problematic and worrisome, and that the societal consequences aren't meaningful – they are. Nor are we claiming such changes happen overnight; stability has a role to play when it comes to the role and relevance of journalism, discursively and materially through long-established practices, artefacts, institutional structures and legal texts which still exist and undoubtedly have tangible impacts going forth. In this respect, perhaps change is the right idea but the wrong emphasis. Including historical, contemporary and future perspectives together shifts the focus from forward-looking, discrete change to the pace and particularities of structural transformations. In this light, the caveat noted above about conceptualizing relevance based on normative expectations simply alerts us to the possibility that familiar discourses may be quite disconnected from what's happening on the ground. In this respect, if we want to advance persuasive claims for journalism's societal value or, equally pressingly, figure out robust funding models going forth, looking to the media environment may prove a fruitful starting point. For if we expect journalism's potentialities to align with its lived everyday functions, viewing it as one of many knowledge producers in a broader informational ecology may prove a more accurate representation of its possible worth than the traditional aspirations assigned to the Fourth Estate.

Informational ecology

With its well-known historical discourse and associated assumptions, trying to come to grips with what journalism 'is' becomes understandably Janus-faced. The historically grounded rhetoric discussed in the previous section typically moulds discussions around purpose and thus tends towards the familiar. Conversely, attempts to account for change mainly tend towards the manifest technological developments of the current digital era and their economic consequences; when practices are a focal point, the emphasis naturally shifts to emergence rather than stasis. Technological change undoubtedly shapes how journalism is produced, the forms it takes, its distribution and consumption, so it would be odd if academics didn't emphasize these aspects when 'doing' what is accurately and increasingly – although somewhat superfluously – called digital journalism studies (see Franklin and Eldridge II, 2016; Witschge *et al.*, 2016). This particular stress is understandable as, much like journalists chasing a scoop, the pressure to 'innovate' in scholarship is inherently forward looking. This tendency is reinforced by funding agencies that demand that academics predict the prosed societal worth of a project before it is conducted, institutions that brand around revolutionary research and future-proof degree programmes, and journals constantly in search for the next cutting-edge topic. This is not problematic per se, as the opposite of innovation is stagnation, which is an undesirable goal for a discipline. However, this focus on technological change and its implications can become potentially problematic if it is employed too narrowly or in isolation.

A central observation in the area of media ecology is that technologies tend to be perceived as most disruptive at the outset, before gradually becoming expedient and increasingly unnoticed devices in everyday life through processes of rationalization (Meyrowitz, 1985). In this regard, despite being a metaphor drawn from science, its understanding is intensely cultural, pointing us towards the forces of change in terms of technological emergence and subsequent integration, control and habitualization. This emphasis is crucial, for it moves us away from focusing on individual technological developments to instead consider how they interact culturally, institutionally and – most importantly – relationally. This is easy to lose sight of, as the pace of change in the media ecology has been exceptionally rapid these past couple of decades, which means that disruption can appear to be constant.

The technologically inspired foci of a decade's worth of journalism studies scholarship points to a news ecosystem that barely comes to grip with one technology, if it does at all, before the next appears. We have seen a constant flow of scholarship focusing on the newest technological features with accompanying rising practices, such as blogs, chat, online news, produsage, citizen journalism, user-generated content, mobile media, convergence, audience participation, social media, transmedia, networks, crowdsourcing, cross-media, click rates, big data, algorithmic journalism and on and on. Trying to piece this together becomes overwhelming and it is quite reasonable that many try to maintain focus amidst all of this change by considering specific impacts within the walls of what we might still call journalism practice. This is a reasonable limitation but limiting it is, nonetheless.

The concept of ecology as a metaphor to explain the interconnection of different media environments is not accidental and leads to a number of useful observations. For one, ecologies are interdependent and relational. Shifts at one level are (potentially) far-reaching, if gradually felt. What started as an email distribution list to inform friends of local events in San Francisco in 1995 and became a web-based service a year later foretold the demise of the classified ad as a secure source of revenue. Craigslist (now active in 70 countries) and equivalent web services worldwide are evidently part of the same informational ecology as news organizations, and while this may not have been obvious in 1995, it quickly became so. Media archaeologists would undoubtedly be able to trace the first ripple in the pond even more precisely in terms of the history of necessary technological development.

While it is but one example, it is a useful one to make the point – if we only focus on how technology impacts journalistic practice and texts rather than communicative flows and informational cultures more broadly, we may be caught unawares. It also raises another key insight. While some dislike the ecological metaphor as they feel it implies a system that strives for homeostasis, we feel this is an odd interpretation. Ecologies, while potentially beautiful from far away, are far more like a Hobbesian worldview when one looks closely, and the lives of individual organisms within them can certainly be nasty, brutish and short. Similarly, seemingly small changes on a micro level (a mutated virus or different bacterial strand, the decline of krill in the Antarctic) can wipe out entire populations. Species become extinct. Polluted areas don't necessarily grow back. While we're not trying to fall into doomsday 'crisis speak' by invoking this metaphor, we also don't want to run the risk of falling into what amounts to informational climate change denial by ignoring ecological shifts.

In this regard, we have sympathy with the growing chorus of media scholars who warn against taking a media-centric approach to scholarship (see Morley, 2009; Couldry, 2012), as this surely alerts us to being receptive to influences outside what we might consider our traditional object of study. Even when journalism studies has taken an ecological approach, it tends to focus on journalistic production (who are the new players in the ecology and how do they relate to the established agents?) and news texts (what new features are facilitated by new technology to distribute information and tell stories?). But paradoxically, when we want to understand the structural changes in journalism, we have to zoom out and study it as only one phenomenon in the informational ecology among many others that are just as meaningful. In this regard, what we are curious about in terms of journalism studies is trying to figure out what makes for a robust organism. How are the functions that journalism traditionally has for people now being fulfilled and to what extent does journalism-as-we-know-it play a part in this? How could journalism adapt and transform now that tasks and functions are redistributed? In a cut-throat media ecology, what survives and adapts are things which fulfil a well-described, well-defined, well-defended position within it.[1]

A functional perspective

If we want to understand how and why journalism's position in the informational ecology is changing, we should look not at what it could or should do *to* people, but what it does *for* them instead. Considering the role and relevance of journalism in a digital era accordingly means looking to its ongoing status in everyday life and, in this regard, the functions it provides for people within the broader informational ecology. This implies that we should not depart, either explicitly or tacitly, from grand normative theories that by definition mould journalism into a predefined democratic framework, but take a bottom-up approach instead. Starting from daily practices, rituals, routines and habits allows us to carefully examine which functions journalism (still) fulfils in people's daily lives and what practices it intersects with (if it does). This is necessary to tease out what people's 'needs' are and to critically interrogate how journalism 'fits' – or could fit – within. Contrasting this with what different media offer allows us to analyse which functions are complimented by journalism and which are fulfilled better by alternatives, and are thus either already being done or taken over by other players. It may also alert us to what functions are being served poorly, or not at all, which journalism might exploit. Stretching the point to what might seem its most commercial interpretation, although one equally applicable to its public service mandate we would argue, it might even encourage thinking of how to tender a worthwhile function even when people cannot yet clearly articulate such a want or need. This dialectics of confronting manifest and latent needs with supply is especially challenging for journalism studies (and might actually be an important reason for its focus on production and content) because, as Bird (2011, p. 490) argues, 'when one moves away from definitions of news that are producer oriented, and begins with the consumer, the very understanding of what constitutes news begins to blur, thus making it harder to conceptualize the relationship between news and audience'. In other words, when one starts with the informational needs of users and later 're-centres' media and journalism to say something meaningful about them, doing research might become almost as complicated and confusing as the current transformations in the informational ecology.

But if we want to understand why in an ecology some species come up and blossom while others face extinction, we cannot study journalism in isolation. We have to think relationally. This links up to a major trend we've previously signalled, namely the corruption of the industrial logic that traditionally guided journalism both economically and organizationally as the former mass media paradigm is slowly but surely being complemented and maybe even replaced by a networked paradigm of communication (Broersma and Peters, 2013). Whereas media institutions in the past had a monopoly on the distribution of current information in the broadest sense, ranging from breaking news to the weather report and next week's sales, the power and capacities to fulfil these informational needs have been or are being redistributed to a range of new institutions and individual agents, whether they define themselves as journalists, information workers, product managers, citizens or consumers. Contemporary informational flows mean we are now just as likely to get updates through friends, social media or directly from weather companies, department stores, government agencies and the like than from journalism. Of course, we realize that interpersonal communication has always been around, that reliable information needs to be produced by someone before it can be curated and that established media organizations have strong positions. But these caveats aside, the 'old' mass media logic now undeniably interacts with a 'new' networked logic which challenges our understanding of traditional public functions afforded to journalism and 'the news'. In the current hybrid informational ecology, a broad range of agents 'create, tap, or steer information flows in ways that suit their goals and in ways that modify, enable, or disable others' agency, across and between a range of older and newer media settings' (Chadwick, 2013, p. 4).

Whereas both the business model and normative underpinnings of mass media presupposed that every medium and media organization fulfilled all functions for all people, we now observe a redistribution of tasks among multiple agents. On the production side, it has become hard if not impossible to monopolize and monetize the value chain as journalism has long been able to do: it produced the news, sold advertisements, printed or broadcasted the news product and distributed it among audiences. What we have observed in the past decade or so is that journalism's control over the value chain has been slipping. On the internet, news is now increasingly distributed through social platforms such as Facebook's 'Instant Articles' or Snapchat's 'Discover'. Advertisements are sold by specialized companies that are able to sell personalized desires of consumers in a split second to advertisers. News is now produced by a range of agents that might label themselves as journalistic or not, but still satisfy the information hunger of people. This points to the fact that the informational ecology is also a monetized, typically capital-based ecology in which the industrial logic of controlling the value chain has become increasingly obsolete for most news organizations and is unlikely to be regained.

On the consumption side, in the digital information ecology, users create their individual media repertoires in which different media are more easily interchanged for different purposes and in which the use of platforms is dependent on each other (Hasebrink and Domeyer, 2012). Accordingly, people have the opportunity to choose a supplier that best fulfils a specific need, or creates a new one, as well as to pay for a certain service that has a specific function in their daily life instead of buying the whole package. This means that players in the informational ecology have to be aware of what purpose they serve for people and how to cater these. What is the job-to-be-done, to frame it in the jargon of disruptive innovation (Christensen, Skok and Allworth, 2012)? Traditionally, journalism had the luxury of not having to think about this and, when forced, unfortunately wasn't particularly good at it either. Partly, this is because key to journalism's modernist professional project is its normative framework that centres around the concept of independence. It postulates that journalism should not only be independent from politics and business, but – especially when it comes to 'quality' journalism – also from its audience. The conception of the 'public' as a monolithic and abstract category has placed users effectively at a safe distance. In the trustee model, professional journalists decide what citizens need to know to be able to function in democracy. So while people are certainly invoked, it is but indirectly. Conversely, when journalism reaches out to the hearts and underbellies of individuals, such as in the case of tabloid journalism, the issue whether or not this is still journalism or mere entertainment is quickly raised. All to say, time and again we are reminded that journalism's discourse is less functional than it is functionalist.

A functional rather than functionalist perspective

At this point, it is worth addressing a potential misinterpretation of our argument. Putting forth the idea of a 'functional' perspective likely raises eyebrows, sure as it is to evoke the ghosts of functionalism. Similarly, aligning a functional approach so closely with an interpretation of the digital media landscape as ecology has echoes of functionalism's tendency towards modelling a positivist social science. Perhaps the idea of 'function' in the humanities and social sciences has been irrevocably tarred by its apparent semantic association with functionalism. Nonetheless, we feel the positives gained from deploying it in a bottom-up articulation, as we propose here, is well worth the risk of trying to re-appropriate the term. Moreover, when we think through what a functionalist interpretation of media actually entails, it quickly becomes clear that this is already dangerously close to what we have been critiquing from the outset and what is frequently done when discussing journalism – in essence, falling back on familiar claims to define its societal role and relevance.

As it pertains to communication and journalism scholarship, functionalism offers a theory that tries to explain the role of media in society in terms of societal and private needs. It emphasizes both the importance and agency of media organizations, and asserts that journalism should contribute to the common good of a healthy and sustainable society. Although disregarded for both its conservative character preserving the societal status quo and its inadequacy to go beyond the descriptive and commonsensical, functionalism still 'offers a language for discussing the relations between mass media and society and a set of concepts that have proved hard to replace' (McQuail, 2010, p. 98). Indeed, the functions that are attributed to media, news and journalism in functionalism will sound familiar to many precisely because these have been conceptualized in close relation to the normative rhetoric of the profession. Journalism monitors events and developments to provide relevant news and information to foster an informed citizenship. It is a watchdog or Fourth Estate which, as an instrument of surveillance, controls and corrects the powerful in society. It offers a podium on which citizens can voice their opinions and thus fosters public debate. It advocates the interest of certain groups in society. And, added to the list more or less unwillingly because it aligns so poorly with the normative expectations of journalism, it entertains the people.

Although we acknowledge that functionalism might be useful on the rhetorical level and might even be hard to escape, we do wonder if it resonates (and has ever resonated) or lives up to the possible interrelated functions of news in the everyday lives of people. We argue that we cannot explain social institutions by the effects they are said to have post hoc. To understand changes in journalism and anticipate a possible future for it, we should study functions at the micro level without lapsing into functionalism and its predefined, top-down conceptions. In other words, if we want to understand which functions news and information have in the daily lives of people, and consequently which suppliers fulfil these, we have to start from everyday practices, habits, routines and experiences of users. How is news integrated in the banal and ever-changing sequences of social encounters, responsive behaviour and daily – and, as such, insignificant – events that translate into the patterns which structure our daily existence? We argue that we should first study these functions and then see if this can actually leverage up to macro-level perspectives and theorizing.

In this regard, uses and gratifications theory, which looks specifically at how media meet different individual needs, might at first sight seem useful (cf. Ruggiero, 2000). However, there are two problems here. First, it is infused with the same normative rhetoric that is omnipresent in journalism research and predefines gratifications that build upon it. Second, it embarks from assumptions of rational behaviour and categories of manifest needs: it presupposes that people are clearly aware of their desires and how they can gratify these by anticipating the affordances of specific media. But in daily practice, media use seems in most cases not to be based on active and conscious choices. It is so intimately integrated with other social practices that it almost becomes a background activity instead of a deliberately performed act. Moreover, paradoxically, people use media they do not like while they do not use what they actually prefer (Swart, Peters and Broersma, 2016).

Thus finding issue with both functionalism and uses and gratifications theory, we argue that we need to embrace a cultural approach to study the redistribution of functions and tasks traditionally performed by journalism to get a grip on the changes in the informational ecology. This still happens too little, as Bird (2011, p. 491) has argued: 'journalism scholars rarely tackle the reception of news in other than quantitative, text-response ways, and cultural studies scholars and anthropologists continue to focus primarily on entertainment genres'. When it comes to journalism, the ritual function of mass media has been emphasized: people have their own daily habits and routines for media consumption, and these might not be primarily geared towards the content of news, but are situated in other activities and needs. Historically, fixed moments of news consumption not only structured the day – whether it was the morning paper or the evening news broadcast – but also united individual people as a public that consumed the same news simultaneously, thus constructing a similar frame of reference (Carey, 1975; Anderson, 1983). However, now that news is available wherever and whenever users want it, a de-ritualization, and at the same time potentially a re-ritualization, of news use takes place. We not only need to study which new news habits are emerging if we want to understand why journalism is suffering from a (potential) loss of functions and how it can anticipate this, but we must also develop a new conceptual vocabulary (or renovate old ones) to describe and conceptualize this.

In this regard, it might be useful to distinguish between manifest and latent functions that news media supply for people and how these functions are folded into everyday life. Interestingly, what would be a manifest function for one person could be a latent function for another, and vice versa. For example, a manifest function would be supplying relevant information that enables people to make sense of the world around them and engage in daily conversation and activities. Obviously this is the key function journalism claims to provide: it is the go-to place for an encompassing, and nowadays ongoing, update of what is happening in the world and how we should interpret that. However, when we start from the perspective of the user, things look different. When people are interested in something informationally specific, they will most probably go to a search engine. When it's less specific 'news' one is after, aggregation sites that curate local or topical news or organize content based on continuous, mostly hidden, feedback and information from the user are trying to push to the fore. In itself, these are dramatic changes, but even to focus on them risks overlooking what's happening. Increasingly (the) news is not something you go to or that comes to you, but a commodity that finds you in an often semi-personalized way through continuously refreshed social networks like Facebook, Twitter, YouTube or LinkedIn. The opportunity for each and every one to publish stripped journalism of one of its most important functions: gatekeeping. Nowadays it is not only news organizations that determine which topics and arguments enter and circulate in the public sphere. Recent developments show that 'non-journalistic' platforms increasingly try to keep the user on their own domain by offering content that loads quickly in users' timelines instead of referring them via links to the original news websites. This is problematic for most news organizations because nowadays, search and social generate the large majority of the traffic they need to fund their business.

When we move on to more latent functions, such as providing quick and convenient access to services, social networks and mobile apps have effectively invaded the informational ecology. Through partnerships with other companies, whether they offer opportunities for entertainment, shopping, personal services or social interaction, Facebook in particular has developed into the dominant channel for identifying oneself and logging in. Although at first sight this might seem trivial and unrelated to what journalism traditionally does, it pushes journalism to the periphery of the information ecology by, at least partly, stripping it from its referral function, while at the same time making it dependent on others. Most successful 'beasts' in the new information ecology have managed to capture, combine and marry different informational flows (comparing prices, reviewing products and services, providing maps and traffic updates, etc.) with different cultural functions (shopping, cooking, occupying leisure time, commuting and so forth), and then lever this influence to try to stabilize these correlations and build pathways to more permanent relationships.

When it comes to another latent function of journalism, structuring daily life through a range of usually materialized and embodied ritual practices, journalism even runs the risk of becoming obsolete. Waking up with radio news and sifting through the morning paper or watching a news show over breakfast are for older generations still rituals that contribute to their mental and social well-being. Although research is scarce, it suggests that they pay just as much for the experience as for the news itself (Bentley, 2001; Swart, Peters and Broersma, 2016). However, younger generations seem far less willing to pay for the news or to value this particular experience. They start the day with checking their smartphones in bed, doing a checking cycle of a few apps that are usually not primarily focused on news; it is hard for news organizations to infiltrate these cycles (Costera Meijer and Groot Kormelink, 2014). Social networks and messenger services in this sense serve their rituals better than previous media, or at least afford more control over this structuring and its associated meanings. In this regard, while we are not trying to join in the common chorus that laments journalism's disappearing youth demographic (often conservatively implying a lack of civic engagement), when we view such changes from a functional perspective, it does point at concerns for journalism's future that we would be foolhardy to ignore.

Our aim in this introduction is not to scrutinize the changes in the informational ecology by extensively examining the various functions journalism has. But we do hope that through these few examples we have illustrated that there might be a discrepancy between journalism's rhetoric and the tasks it fulfils in the daily lives of individuals and society at large. This does not imply an all-or-nothing approach. We can still find instances where classic democratic functions are fulfilled by journalists, news organizations and the news. But from a broader perspective, task allocations are changing in the informational ecology and, in many cases, journalism might be (permanently) displaced. To better understand the current and future societal role and public relevance of journalism, if any, we suggest that it is fruitful to study what journalism does *for* people, how this relates to their needs and what others in the informational ecology offer. This re-orientation of scholarship on what journalism *does* instead of what it *is* and *aspires to be* will hopefully change the way we pose questions – and will make for challenging but potentially more grounded research questions. It opens up the playing field of scholarship to a broader range of questions. Are there (still) such things as acts of journalism? And, if so, what are they? And who performs these acts for people? If journalism had to invent itself in the current timeframe, would it then be journalism?

Conclusion

Introductions to collections such as these often have modernist expectations built into their form and structure; that is, they try to summarize and combine many strands from the chapters which comprise the book together. Instead, in the spirit of the collection, we've tried to sketch a way forward for understanding and analysing journalism's contemporary status in a manner that encompasses historical premises, current practices and future change. The point we have tried to make is that journalism isn't there primarily for journalists or to serve the interest of media corporations. Nor is it to stagnate in well-intentioned, but in the face of change increasingly hard-to-achieve historical rhetoric of working for the common good and in the interest of the public. In the age of connectivity which allows people to redistribute tasks and functions that were traditionally part and parcel of journalism, this rhetoric falls short. If journalism isn't 'the primary sense-making practice' of society anymore and companies like Google, Facebook and many others have eroded journalism's claim to comprehensively serve the public, what is journalism still good for?

A functional perspective, as we envision it, urges journalism scholars to move away from news production and news texts. In a sense, it urges academics to de-centre journalism and to start at the other end: with the functions journalism fulfils or could fulfil in the daily lives of ordinary people. This implies a move away from the grand normative theories in which both research and the societal claims of journalism are usually framed. At the same time, any profession or individual organization needs a normative framework to legitimize its place in society and to communicate its use for people. Departing from a bottom-up approach that carefully situates the functions of journalism in lived experiences would allow both journalists and journalism scholars alike to develop a new vocabulary to understand – and potentially advocate – new frameworks to conceptualize the place of journalism and its role versus individuals and society at large.

The chapters in this volume set out to do so, but not necessarily in the way we have laid out in this introduction. The first part of the book focuses on the societal role of journalism and how we can rethink this in the light of the current transformations in the informational ecology. The six chapters in this part engage with questions of journalism's expertise, authority and filter function, how this relates to the grand normative frameworks of journalism's role in democracy, and our conceptual scaffolds for making sense of its performance and responsibilities. The second part asks if and how journalism can retain its public relevance. The authors argue that we should move beyond newsrooms, that entrepreneurship, reciprocity and caring for communities could be workable solutions, and point at the gaps between what journalism offers, how it talks about itself and what its public wants. The two afterwords frame the chapters in each part in a broader perspective, using the themes therein as inspiration for conceptual exploration and directions for future scholarship and research. First and foremost, the aim of *Rethinking Journalism Again* is to offer inspiration and new directions to reflect on how the societal role and public relevance of what we have come to call journalism are changing. How can we conceptualize journalism beyond modernity, taking into account its historical premises and current practices, while anticipating future change? Even if journalism-as-we-know-it would become inadequate and disappear, it is worthwhile trying to figure out how to hold on to what it has come to represent, to ensure the functions it fulfils for people and for society remain.

Note

1 If ecology is not one's academic cup of tea, one might also sense resonances of Bourdieu's field theory in what we are outlining, in terms of taking a relational approach that looks to status and power via positions within the field and external forces from associated fields without.

References

Anderson, B. (1983). *Imagined communities. Reflections on the origins and spread of nationalism.* London: Verso.

Beck, U., Giddens, A., & Lash, S. (1994). *Reflexive modernization: Politics, tradition and aesthetics in the modern social order.* Stanford, CA: Stanford University Press.

Bentley, C. (2001). No newspaper is no fun – Even five decades later. *Newspaper Research Journal, 22*(4), 2–15.

Bird, S. E. (2011). Seeking the audience for news: Response, news talk, and everyday practice. In V. Nightingale (Ed.), *The handbook of media audiences* (pp. 489–508). New York: Blackwell.

Broersma, M. (2007). Form, style and journalistic strategies. An introduction. In M. Broersma (Ed.), *Form and style in journalism. European newspapers and the representation of news, 1880–2005* (pp. ix–xxix). Leuven, Paris and Dudley, MA: Peeters.

Broersma, M., & Peters, C. (2013). Introduction. Rethinking journalism: The structural transformation of a public good. In C. Peters & M. Broersma (Eds.), *Rethinking journalism: Trust and participation in a transformed news landscape* (pp. 1–12). London: Routledge.

Carey, J. W. (1975). A cultural approach to communication. *Communication, 2*, 1–10, 17–21.

Carlson, M., & Lewis, S. C. (Eds.). (2015). *Boundaries of journalism: Professionalism, practices and participation.* London: Routledge.

Cassidy, J. (2015, 28 September). The Financial Times and the future of journalism. *The New Yorker.* Retrieved from http://www.newyorker.com/news/john-cassidy/the-financial-times-and-the-future-of-journalism.

Chadwick, A. (2013). *The hybrid media system: Politics and power.* Oxford: Oxford University Press.

Christensen, C., Skok, D., & Allworth, J. (2012). Breaking news. Mastering the art of disruptive innovation in journalism. *Nieman Reports, 66*(3), 6–20.

Costera Meijer, I., & Groot Kormelink, T. (2014). Checking, sharing, clicking and linking: Changing patterns of news use between 2004 and 2014. *Digital Journalism, 3*(5), 664–679.

Couldry, N. (2012). *Media, society, world: Social theory and digital media practice.* Cambridge: Polity Press.

Donsbach, W. (2014). Journalism as the new knowledge profession and consequences for journalism education. *Journalism, 15*(6), 661–677.

Franklin, B., & Eldridge II, S. (Eds.). (2016). *The Routledge companion to digital journalism studies.* London: Routledge.

Hartley, J. (1996). *Popular reality: Journalism, modernity and popular culture.* London: Arnold.

Hasebrink, U., & Domeyer, H. (2012). Media repertoires as patterns of behaviour and as meaningful practices. A multimethod approach to media use in converging media environments. *Participations, 9*(2), 757–779.

Josephi, B. (2013). De-coupling journalism and democracy: Or how much democracy does journalism need? *Journalism, 14*(4), 441–445.

Kirkland, S. (2014, 30 July). 8 digital media lessons from Poynter's 'Journalism and the web @ 25' panel. Poynter. Retrieved from http://www.poynter.org/news/mediawire/260794/8-digital-media-lessons-from-poynters-journalism-and-the-web25-panel/.

McNair, B. (2012). *Journalism and democracy: An evaluation of the political public sphere.* London: Routledge.

McQuail, D. (2010). *McQuail's mass communication theory* (6th ed.). London: Sage.

Meyrowitz, J. (1985). *No sense of place: The impact of electronic media on social behavior.* Oxford: Oxford University Press.

Morley, D. (2009). For a materialist, non-media-centric media studies. *Television & New Media, 10*(1), 114–116.

Peters, C. (2015). Evaluating journalism through popular culture: HBO's *The Newsroom* and public reflections on the state of the news media. *Media, Culture & Society, 37*(4), 602–619.

Peters, C., & Broersma, M. J. (2013). *Rethinking journalism: Trust and participation in a transformed news landscape.* London: Routledge.

Peters, C., & Witschge, T. (2015). From grand narratives of democracy to small expectations of participation: Audiences, citizenship, and interactive tools in digital journalism. *Journalism Practice, 9*(1), 19–34.

Ruggiero, T. (2000). Uses and gratifications theory in the 21st century. *Mass Communication & Society, 3*(1), 3–37.

Schudson, M. (2008). *Why democracies need an unlovable press.* Cambridge: Polity Press.

Swart, J., Peters, C., & Broersma, M. (2016) Navigating cross-media news use. Media repertoires and the value of news in everyday life. *Journalism Studies.* doi: 10.1080/1461670X. 2015.1129285.

Vos, T., & Heinderyckx, F. (Eds.). (2015). *Gatekeeping in transition.* London: Routledge.

Witschge, T., Anderson, C. W., Domingo, D., & Hermida, A. (Eds.). (2016). *The Sage handbook of digital journalism.* London: Sage.

Zelizer, B. (2013). On the shelf life of democracy in journalism scholarship. *Journalism, 14*(4), 459–473.

Zelizer, B. (2015). Terms of choice: Uncertainty, journalism, and crisis. *Journal of Communication, 65*(5), 888–908.

PART I
Journalism and its societal role

1

RECONSTRUCTING JOURNALISM'S PUBLIC RATIONALE

Nick Couldry

For a century or more in so-called developed democracies, it has not been necessary to build a rationale for the public value of 'journalism'. By 'journalism' I mean for this purpose the institutionalized production of facts, information and reference points of common interest for public circulation. Debates have raged about whether *particular* aspects of journalistic practice meet the standards that society expects (notably and recently, the recent UK phone-hacking scandal). Such debates often rely on the notion of a 'free press', but always assume that journalism will continue *to exist*. It is quite another matter to build normative arguments as to why journalism *in general needs* to exist and, how, in order for it to exist over the long-term, it should be funded in some form. But that is today's challenge, and it involves rethinking journalism not so much in its practical implementation, but, more fundamentally, as part of the infrastructure that healthy societies need. The warm glow cast by the principle of a 'free press' is insufficient in itself as an argument to *re-create* a free press in a digital age when, as I will explain, an older model of journalism is under threat.

The legal theorist Edwin Baker captured the sense of vertigo appropriate when discussing such questions in the following passage, whose first version was published back in 1998: 'democracy is impossible without a free press. At least courts and commentators tells us so ... This consensus, however, floats above crucial, but more controversial matters. What *type* of free press does a democracy need and why does democracy need it? And if governmental policy correctives are necessary ... what interventions would promote a more "democratic press" – that is, a press that properly serves a society committed to democracy?' (Baker, 2002, p. 125). Yet the digital age will almost certainly require us to build precisely such normative arguments rather than float above them. The specific reason derives from recent developments in the advertising industries and the data mining sector that has grown up to support them: those developments are having profound effects on journalism's *potential* social role in a digital age.

Joseph Turow (2007) has, in the past decade, carried out pioneering work on the increasing niche specialization of the advertising industry; importantly, in his most recent book *The Daily You* (2012), he has uncovered how the value of audiences to advertisers is increasingly being redefined, in particular in the USA. A new model of advertising has emerged whereby no longer do audiences represent the speculative value of an aggregate of viewers paying simultaneous attention to mass-targeted advertising content (while really intending to watch something else); audience value becomes the precisely weighted value of *the data* that can be gleaned about an individual consumer by sending a particular (often customized) advertisement to them at a particular moment when they are online *for any purpose whatsoever*. The index of advertising cost, and thus of the value of advertising to its sellers, has become less and less the cultural context of mainstream audiences' collective media consumption, and more and more an instantaneous data-point which lacks *any* context in the contents that media industries have historically produced. If that is right, the basic economic rationale for advertisers' historic cross-subsidy of large-scale media content is destined over time to evaporate – at least in the USA and in other countries where, albeit possibly within a different balance between public and private subsidy, the same underlying dynamic of data-driven tracking of audiences is developing. If so, in order to survive longer-term, journalism practices as we know them must either become directly profitable in their own right (something which, with the exception of specialist outlets like the *Financial Times*, they have not recently been) or must receive new forms of *subsidy* from other, as yet undiscovered, sources – hence the need for a new public rationale for journalism that can convince all citizens, not just journalists and advertisers, of its necessity.

This issue is something in which, as a citizen, I have become increasingly concerned. So, with due humility as a non-specialist in journalism studies, I want to explore in this chapter how we might build the normative arguments that can reinforce older rationales for the public subsidy of journalism (where they exist) and support new rationales (where they do not).

Background

We are looking here at the unintended side-effects for democracy of advertisers' fundamental revision of the subsidy that their industry has long provided to media firms. The argument is not that this revision has occurred universally or is destined to do so, but rather that it has a dynamic which challenges us to rethink the public rationale for journalism in a new and more robust way. But how can we start to get a grip on this problem?

Democracy depends on *some* effective form of participation, and media institutions have played a major role in sustaining that over the past two centuries. Take Robert Dahl's (1989) classic theory of 'polyarchy', which means the various frameworks that in large societies are necessary before we can have anything like a working democracy in place. For Dahl, polyarchy requires political relations between the state and its citizens based on 'broad, equal, protected and mutually binding consultation' (Tilly, 2007, pp. 13–14). But such consultation in turn requires the common circulation of facts, themes and reference points as background to the issues for consultation. Such shared public reference points go well beyond news (Williams and Delli Carpini, 2011); it will be no part of my argument to assume that it is only highly 'rational' journalistic content that is needed (nor indeed will I rely at all on public sphere models, which have often argued exactly that).

In diagnosing the dangers facing contemporary media institutions, it is unhelpful to romanticize their past. No one is pretending that journalism of the mass-media age was perfectly socially representative or served democratic needs without fault or without significant cost: there was no golden age. What matters are quite specific shifts in the operating conditions of today's journalism, which may be undermining journalism's role as a source for common reference points of both contention and mutual acknowledgement. It is those reference points that enable us to recognize each other as members of the same social and political space. The post-structuralist political theorist Chantal Mouffe (normally quoted for her emphasis on the conflictual nature of democracy) notes in her book *The Democratic Paradox* that democracy (if it is to be more than disguised violence) requires that social and political adversaries must share some 'commitment to a system of reference … a way of living, or of assessing one's life' (Mouffe, 2000, pp. 74, 97). But how is such a shared commitment sustainable over the longer term when advertisers and marketers are driven by the need for, and professional content producers are increasingly oriented to offering, the *personalization* of content in ways that *mark off* one consumer from another?

These concerns go far beyond earlier concerns about the segmentation that came with challenges to public broadcasters due to TV channel multiplication or the early rise of the internet (Katz, 1996; Gitlin, 1998). Today we are potentially seeing a *deep* personalization: content whose selection has already been *decided for* citizens on the basis of criteria unknown to them and calibrated not to their actual selection decisions, but to big data-generated *assumptions* about where those citizens would want to focus their attention or where marketers need those citizens' attention to be focused. Concerns about something like this have already emerged in the political field regarding the segmentation of information in political campaigns (Bennett and Iyengar, 2008). But the concern here is actually wider: it is the adoption in *all* public communication of individualized information targeting as an *overriding*, not an occasional, principle. This development is not the result of a conspiracy to remove people from collective experience or democratic participation. It is just an accidental result – a *negative externality*, as economists call it – of how the relations and mutual interdependencies between advertising, big data and media content production have developed over the past two decades. And note that it is personalization at the level of news *production* (in the source of inputs to news circulation) with which I am concerned. I acknowledge entirely that personalization is not the only force at play at the level of news consumption, where the *sharing* of news is a huge trend.

The key point[1] is expressed in a quotation from Joseph Turow's book *The Daily You:* 'Marketers haven't *ever* wanted to underwrite the content industry', Rishad Tobaccowala, a high-ranking Publicis strategy executive, told Turow in 2010. 'They've been forced' (Turow, 2012, pp. 111–12). This implies that once advertisers are no longer so forced because they can reach audiences another way, they will cease to do that underwriting. This danger has been noted by commentators on the future of the newspaper form, most trenchantly by Clay Shirky (2009; see also Anderson, Bell and Shirky, 2012). But I hope to show that the concern here goes *much wider* than a concern for the future of newspapers as particular media formats.

If that quote from a top marketing executive – named recently by *Time* magazine as one of its five leading 'marketing innovators' worldwide – expresses the new direction of travel, its implementation takes a number of potential forms, as Turow and I explain in more detail elsewhere (Couldry and Turow, 2014; see also Anderson, 2013; Carlson, 2013). The *first* dynamic is the most dominant to date and involves publishers working with advertisers to personalize the signals consumers receive when they encounter particular editorial matter. Using a growing number of data points, marketers and publishers vary their messages according to the types of people, and even the individuals, being targeted. The *second* dynamic has emerged during this decade and is known as *native advertising*. A native ad is any form of content that supports the aims of an advertiser (who also pays for it) while mimicking the style of the publisher carrying it – hence the word 'native'. It is advertising masquerading as something native to the journalistic domain. The *New York Times*' new website design seeks to quarantine it within a boundary labelled 'paid post', but it is unclear how long this boundary will be meaningful and what the impact will be of a large percentage of what readers see being marketing content of this sort. What if one result is that readers lose their capacity to notice the boundary?

These first two forms of personalized content-creation are advertiser-driven. So far, publishers have not moved so much to change the agenda of material *they* show visitors or to change the content itself based on what they believe they know about their visitors, but there are signs that this is under way, as Turow (2012) notes. As publishers become used to advertisers' micro-targeting and as native advertising becomes a part of their everyday landscape, it is easy to see how publishers might develop this third dynamic. They may begin to vary their own material based on their sites' visitors and what they know about the visitors. We are not there yet, but it is the growing tendency that is of crucial importance. It is captured by this quotation from the industry-oriented newsletter *PaidContent* (January 2013):

> Twitter's gotten better and better at what's called 'entity extraction' – identifying a person, place, or thing, then associating behaviors and attributes around that thing … *Real time entity extraction* crossed with signals like those described above is the Holy Grail. This is fundamentally the same goal that

both Google and Facebook are focused on as well: *how do you show users only things that are relevant to them, and hide those that aren't* – in real time?

(Quoted in Couldry and Turow, 2014, p. 1717, emphasis added)

Note the comment 'relevant to them'. No one is suggesting, incidentally, that personal relevance will become the only dynamic shaping the news that reaches individuals; indeed, it will always be relevant to individuals to know *something* of what is relevant to others, just because they must live and compete with others over scarce resources. Rather, the issue is a shift in the balance of forces that influence journalism as it is performed on a daily basis.

Three dynamics are at work here: targeted messaging, embedded ads and content producers' gradual personalization of content. We can predict that at some point in the not too distant future, they will begin working together, and marketers and publishers will routinely start showing different constructions of reality to people that they categorize differently. People may not realize they are being treated differently and may not understand the reason even if they do. Indeed, the logic (expressed by the PaidContent writer) of 'hiding' in advance from individuals what is less 'relevant' to them *must* automatically also conceal the fact that it is operating. Marketers and publishers will try to reduce tensions over this situation by claiming a service of increased – indeed, more 'personal' – relevance to their customers. After a while, people may take such personalization for granted as the filter through which they must try to understand the world (compare Pariser, 2011).

For sure, most media institutions have always competed on the basis of targeting audience segments, hoping to offer what seems to suit those segments' tastes, at least at a generic level. And, to be sure, some pressures today still run counter to personalization. Large media will for the foreseeable future continue to make claims that they speak to the wider population; indeed, governments rely on them to make such claims if there is to be a space of appearances in which politics can visibly get done. As noted above, even personal relevance dictates to some extent that such presences remain. Meanwhile, mega-events do manage to draw people through their own distinctive advertising and marketing dynamics. Indeed, not only media institutions but also many other institutions depend on media's claims to be 'central' social institutions: such claims will not simply disappear (Couldry, 2012, Chapter 1). But such rhetoric will increasingly be undermined by forces oriented *specifically* at individuals and at the data value those individuals represent.

So (and this is the starting point for the rest of my argument), we may have to get used to our societies becoming spaces that lack any institution whose intrinsic purpose is to provide common information flows in the way that journalism classically sought to do, often with the explicit aim of supporting democracy. We certainly cannot assume that internal forces within journalism will be strong enough to resist this shift. Not even premium content sites are immune from these pressures: when *The Atlantic* was challenged about its editorial team letting past a native ad for the Church of Scientology, its response was not to say this should never happen, but to apologize for how it was handled (Stelter and Haughney, 2013). Meanwhile, the basic economics of increased competition for declining audiences mean fewer professionals (whether at newspapers or news agencies) have the time, resources and standing to resist such challenges to basic journalistic values.

Reconstructing journalism's rationale – first stage

If all this is right – and you may of course want to dispute my starting points, but then you must also dispute the relevance of the empirical universe that Turow's US-based fieldwork opens up – then over time, and across an increasing range of media systems, we can expect a drastic fall in the subsidy that advertising gives to content production and/or (it is likely to be a combination) a shift in the rationale of such subsidy so that it becomes *conditional* on the increasing involvement of marketing organizations in determining such content. The latter is deeply problematic, which suggests that journalism in the sense with which I started, if it is to survive, needs new forms of subsidy. That in turn will require a renewal, in a cross-national context, of journalism's public rationale. So where do we start in rebuilding journalism's rationale under such pressure?

The first step must be to go back to journalism's relationship to democracy. It doesn't matter what form of theory of democracy you espouse: journalism matters for democracy.[2] Elite democracy theory, the least democratic of democratic theories, depends on the assumption that knowledge is diffused in some *sufficiently* effective way among the population, even if it relies, more than other theories do, on the determining role of expert elites. The relationship between the press and popular sovereignty has seemed fundamental to all defenders of democracy for two centuries. As Tocqueville put it: 'when the right of every citizen to cooperate in the government of society is acknowledged, every citizen must be presumed to possess the power of discriminating between the different opinions of his contemporaries, and of appreciating the different facts from which inferences may be drawn. The sovereignty of the people and the liberty of the press may therefore be looked upon as correlative institutions' (2002, p. 210). But what happens when the common system for knowledge distribution starts being organized on a different principle: that of circulating what merely *passes for* common knowledge among its receivers in order to generate for advertisers better data on individual consumers? What if that trend is something media companies, because they face harshly reduced returns on direct online advertising, lack the powers in all but the most exceptional cases to resist?

Once again, I am bracketing out here the very different starting points as regards public media of different countries, for example, between the USA and the UK or the Netherlands. Rather, the point is about how the argument for constructing and sustaining a free and effective press would proceed in principle – clearly such arguments would proceed more easily if what was involved was building on an existing strong structure of publicly funded journalism, as with the BBC. But it is problems with the underlying nature of such arguments with which I am principally concerned in this chapter and which I want to move beyond.

You might argue that it is unhelpful to draw such drastic and broad conclusions from Turow's diagnosis. However, before you dismiss what follows, I would insist that Turow's empirical evidence for the US case is very strong and the dynamics he exposes have plenty of potential to be replicated – wherever, that is, the options for media consumers' attention are rapidly expanding and new forms of data tracking are available to reach individuals *whatever* media they are consuming at a particular moment. In any such context, whatever its history of public subsidy for journalism (or the lack of it), the appeal to the consequences for democracy and democratic values is insufficient in itself. The recent shift in the advertising industry's relations to content producers is deeply embedded in the struggles of each for *survival* in drastically changed business environments. They will not be deterred from their survival strategies just because of the speculative side-effects on something as abstract as democracy. In any case, the relationship between media industries and democratic culture has *never* been straightforward or direct, and there is no prospect of it becoming so now. No one would say that the advertising subsidy was anything other than a fortunate accident (that is, in economists' terms, a positive externality). Ed Baker noted that good journalism is a positive externality of commercial media operations, and positive externalities (a loose 'social responsibility' to make nice things happen) have never made for legally enforceable obligations; indeed, it would be an abuse of state power to force institutions to make such things happen (Baker, 2007, p. 34). And remember: that argument is even harder in the case we are addressing, where advertisers (and others involved in data mining) are being asked to promote positive externalities in *another* sector, a sector they (quite plausibly) say was never part of their purpose to subsidize or promote. It follows that a *simple* appeal to the values of democratic functioning is insufficient to bring our problem into focus.

One way to strengthen the appeal to democratic values is to complicate the account of democracy with which we work. No institution should be uniquely charged with implementing or underwriting democracy: democracy, as Pierre Rosanvallon (2011, p. 225) points out, is a multidimensional and multi-institutional process involving civil society, the workings of a particular political 'regime', a 'form of society' and an overall mode of government. The best accounts of media's contribution to democracy must be similarly complex. Ed Baker proposed a model of 'complex democracy' which valued both pluralism (the diverse expression of individual and group perspectives) *and* the production of common ground (1998, p. 335); such a complex democracy in turn required, he argued, *both* segmented media and general media, that is, media 'that support a search for general societal agreement on "common goods"' (1998, p. 344). Joseph Turow (2012, p. 193) and, much earlier, James Curran (1991) argued for something similar; so too does Habermas.

So the problem is not that the shift in advertising subsidy encourages particularism and niche marketing, but that this is becoming its *only* (or at least its dominant) logic, which must in the long run override everything else. Nor is the problem that journalism no longer (if it ever did) produces consensus, picturing 'society' as a coherent whole that never existed; the problem is that journalism risks becoming oriented to doing precisely *the opposite* of producing consensus, that is, producing *difference*. Here Rosanvallon's detailed insights are useful. For him – he was not discussing the media directly – the challenge for contemporary societies that aim to be democratic is to generate 'an ensemble of actions and discourses for commonality and making the system of social interactions both more legible and more visible' (Rosanvallon, 2006, p. 250). That is needed if contemporary societies are to recover what Rosanvallon argues we have lost over many decades: 'a practical experience of the general will', that is, a way of figuring out together solutions to difficult problems of interdependence (2008, p. 313). Indeed, democracy needs a symbolic territory, as Rosanvallon puts it, of 'shared trials, similar situations and parallel histories' (2011, p. 183). The key word here is 'shared'. However contentious or disputatious it becomes, democracy requires, for its basic operations, *some* sharing of experience across a range of social locations, some basic flow of information and argumentation, empathy and imaginative reference, otherwise its members will barely recognize each other as part of the same space. Yet deep personalization in advertising, which may be starting to colonize journalism too, is pushing in another direction. This is troubling.

Reconstructing journalism's rationale – second stage

However, 'troubling' is not enough to stop advertisers doing what they are otherwise disposed to do. Even though he died in 2009 and wrote before the advance of the trends Turow discusses, Ed Baker already sensed a worrying tendency. In his last book *Media Concentration and Democracy*, he noted that 'the consumer shift to Internet access to news could reduce the [financial] resources available to support serious commercial journalism' (2007, p. 116) because of failing offline readerships and failing average revenues from online ads. Worse, 'the Internet [may be] drawing down the relatively fixed pot of advertising revenue, potentially *dramatically* reducing advertisers' support of traditional media' (2007, p. 117, emphasis added). He already feared a shift from advertising money supporting journalists to supporting the 'distributors of online content' (2007, p. 118) such as search engines. Turow in his later work has begun, as we saw, to discuss a much more extensive shift around the data mining industry and those who work closely with it. But in any case, as Baker also pointed out, if the costs of producing serious journalism remain *constant* while the cost of other types of content production *fall*, then there is *already* an economic disincentive against the production of serious journalism within the operations of content producers (2007, p. 120).

If so, there is a problem with the whole new environment of journalism and advertising. It is not a matter of convincing particular institutions to think more democratically. The whole system of incentives and rewards is becoming skewed away from operations that might benefit democracy, creating a built-in democratic *deficit* that is environmental in terms of its scope and scale. Metaphor may work better here to alert us than formal argument.

My fear (compare Couldry and Turow, 2014) is that we are unwittingly creating a landscape *cleared* of one basic element of democratic life: the reliable exchange of ideas and facts about matters of common concern. The information landscape of future democracies may be rich in continuous updates to individuals on the issues closest to them, interrupted by occasional grand news spectacle and a regular flow of curiosities, but it will be thin in the shared reference points that orientate people to a common public world. It will be short, to use a term that I have employed in earlier work, of resources for 'public connection' (Couldry, Livingstone and Markham, 2010).

The metaphor of 'clearance' comes from the drastic transformation of the economy of the Scottish Highlands in the eighteenth century (Prebble, 1968), when a previous form of agriculture – and the people who lived it – were cleared from the land to make way for sheep. Only sheep generated enough profit for the distant landlords with their large metropolitan property bills to pay. The Scottish Highlands now is almost empty. It takes a considerable amount of imagination to recover any sense of the dense lifeworlds that once filled those empty valleys. This reminds us that epochal change can happen for reasons very distant from the practices of those most affected. Could today's crowded landscape of news production be 'cleared' over the next decade or two to suit the goal of rationalizing the advertising industries' new business models? And if this is a serious risk, how do we address it?

By using an environmental metaphor, I am trying to shift the debate into the realm of the social imaginary (to use Charles Taylor's phrase): can we imagine being happy living in a future democracy cleared in the way I have described? Can we fail, whoever we are, to recognize the dangers to us all from such a transformation? The metaphor of an environment implies a common need for action, such as emerged in the 1960s to 1980s around the threats to the physical and biological environment (Jonas, 1984). Just as our ethical understanding of the relationship between man, nature and technology was transformed when we started realising that man's continuous uses of technology might, through their side-effects, damage nature and so change irrevocably our relations *with* nature, and in turn change us, so in the same way we can argue that the relationship to democracy of journalism as an institution for the production of facts-in-common – so intrinsic a relationship that during the past two centuries in some places we have never needed to defend it – is part of the soil from which democracy itself grows; if it is damaged, our relationship to democracy becomes damaged and *we too* are damaged.

But even this does not get us far enough. Metaphor may appear to conjure up a common responsibility for action, but advertisers can refuse to accept it. Indeed, why should *they, in particular*, stop doing what they are doing when the problem, despite affecting us all, is an accidental byproduct of what, for them, is perfectly legitimate practice? The fact that the problem is a common one does not mean that the solution should be borne by particular parties, unless, perhaps, we can be clearer on what is the damage *done* by those corporate powers, as we have become clearer with polluters of our rivers. And this means, in turn, being more explicit about how exactly we understand the practice of journalism and why it is a practice vulnerable in particular ways, just the ways that are of intrinsic importance to democracy.

Reconstructing journalism's rationale – third stage

This is where we get to the heart of the issue. For at this third stage of the argument, we have to state more directly what we see the point of journalism to be and why we might think something like a native ad directly undermines the basic purpose of journalism, or metaphorically 'pollutes' it as an environment. Discussions about the principle of a free press emerged historically out of something broader: the defence of the freedom of individual speech, from Milton onwards. Milton interestingly used a pollution metaphor himself, drawing on a passage in the Psalms to talk of 'the streaming fountain of Truth' which would be 'turned to a muddy pool of conformity and tradition' if freedom of speech (and therefore of thought) were constrained (1974, p. 231).

By the time of Thomas Paine, understanding of the complexity of modern societies had developed, and generated a *knowledge* problem that representative democracy itself was in part designed to address. The point for Paine of the 'representative system' (and therefore of the free press that might serve it) was to 'diffuse such a body of knowledge throughout a nation, on the subject of government, as to explode ignorance and preclude imposition' (1937, p. 157). For rule in large societies, according to Paine, requires 'an assemblage of factual knowledge which no individual can possess', thus ruling *out*, on *cognitive* grounds, monarchy and aristocracy as forms of government (1937, p. 152).

Half a century later, for Tocqueville, as we saw, this equation of working democracy with a working free press had become almost automatic, but on cognitive grounds consistent with Paine; that is, that the press enable citizens to appreciate the 'different facts' from which they can infer their opinions and make their judgements, and so participate in the workings of popular sovereignty (2002, p. 210). Turn forward to late twentieth-century democratic theory, as I noted earlier, and the even distribution of knowledge and resources for interpreting knowledge, is proposed as one of democracy's key preconditions (Dahl, 1989).

Of course, the distribution of common factual information and reference points is not the only thing that media do or should do, and this plurality of media purpose (as Baker and Turow stress) is vital. We can easily distinguish four 'functions' of media institutions that serve democracy, some less obviously cognitive than others: speaking up to power in a coordinated way; witnessing for individuals and groups; operating as vehicles of civil society organization; and providing a specialist information resource (at least for elites). However, all depend, as their background, on the existence (somewhere in the media sector) of those who perform the more basic role of knowledge diffusion. Otherwise, why bother to witness the lives of others or to speak up for organizations or interests? Otherwise, how and on what basis could the press *aim* to speak up to power?

So, if a process can be seen to run directly counter to this basic role of the press – the gathering and circulation of facts-in-common – the basic workings of democracy and the distribution of power within it are affected. Even here, however, whatever advertisers' private loyalty to democracy, it may not be enough to dissuade them from pursuing their corporate interests. Thus, once again, we must broaden the focus and consider the role of this cognitive aspect of journalism in something wider: in the sustaining of *social order* in an era of complex interdependency.

Whether or not we are explicitly building a democracy, can we argue that the effective running of government and society now depends on the reliable exchange of information (accurate information, not promotional puff) throughout society? Journalism on this stripped-down reading becomes a means of filtering basic knowledge for general social awareness, not just government knowledge. The link to *general* awareness is crucial, since government as an institution cannot survive without the cooperation in some part of the population, and governments by them-selves might be quite happy to survive on feeding their populations a diet of illusion. Without these basic information-filtering and disseminating functions being fulfilled, there is risk of society lapsing back – for reasons of sheer complexity rather than only the drive towards brutish violence that Hobbes emphasized – into what he called 'the confusion of a disunited Multitude' (1985, p. 229), a confusion which will undermine business as much as democracy.

Here we can move to a more fundamental reference point: the contemporary theory of human development. This is philosopher Amartya Sen's (1999) *double* argument for democracy and political voice: as something intrinsically good (as an enactment of political freedom, a key dimension of human freedom), but even if that is not persuasive, as also a *necessity* if one wants human development rather than just stagnation. In order to aim at them, people need to be able to construct what their development needs are, and that in turn requires the flow of common information about actualities and possibilities, which Sen in turn argues requires a free media. Sen's discussion implies the basic roles of journalism that I mentioned earlier: speaking up to power and witnessing suffering, for example, to challenge the failure of governments to deal with famine; making demands on behalf of social groups (as he says, rather optimistically, 'in a democracy, people tend to get what they demand': 1999, p. 156); and the provision of information necessary to fuel what he calls 'the evaluative need for public discussion' (1999, p. 110).

According to Sen (and contrary to the realpolitik of market fundamentalists), eco-nomic needs always to *add to*, rather than subtract from, political needs (1999, p. 148). In other words, Sen *regrounds* the argument for effective journalism not in democratic ideals, but in broader goals of human development at which economic and all other social activities should be aimed. Most crucially, he helps us shift the argument about journalism away from the seemingly unresolvable wrestling bout between long-term democratic goals and short-term corporate interest, to consider what *economic* growth would be if its side-effect was to undermine the key means of supporting political freedom, and so to undermine the wider goal of human development.

You will notice that I have not relied at any point in my argument on public sphere theory (Habermas, 1996). That is because of my scepticism about any argu-ment based, as Habermas' always are, on the supposed demands of rationality itself. That, in my view, is slippery territory and particularly unhelpful when there are *com-peting* 'rationalities' at stake: corporate and economic rationalities on the one hand, and democratic and public rationalities on the other. Our best chance of getting on to solid ground comes, following Sen, when we try to articulate an overarching, and to some degree inherently pluralistic, goal, such as human development, which gives us a vantage point on both economic and political freedoms, and the practical relationship between them. This helps us to see that human development itself, on any coherent account, *requires* the sustaining of institutions free to carry out the fundamental information-sharing role of journalism from which I began.

You might, however, still object that I have only got round the problem of subsidizing democracy (and journalism) by placing it in a larger context. But it is this detour that is precisely the point. The point of Sen's argument is to show us that the defence of democratic practice (and therefore of free journalistic practice) *is* part of the wider aim of human development which also encompasses economic growth. As Sen has done in his work ever since 1987 – the book *On Ethics and Economics* – we can and must always relate economic goals to wider *ethical* aims; that is, the achieving of a good life in common.

Conclusion

It is at this point, as you may already have realized, that the real argument comes into view, and it takes a double form. First, it is necessary to persuade a *widening range* of institutions (including, though of course indirectly, governments and perhaps universities too) that they must start subsidizing journalism in new ways if they want to promote rather than hinder human development. And, second, perhaps even harder given the acute financial pressures that they face, it is necessary to persuade media institutions that they must *refuse* subsidy, whether direct or indirect, from the advertising industries whenever the price is to align journalism more closely with the aims of maximizing data that matters to *advertisers* and less closely with the production of facts that matter to us in common as citizens of a shared world. Within the term 'advertisers' for this purpose, perhaps we should include any social actor trying to promote a specific message for instrumental ends: non-governmental organization (NGO)-funded news may well be better than no news in the short run, but in the long run it can become problematic too.

It is obvious that such large-scale arguments are a collective task, a task of decades, and not the stuff of a single book chapter. Such work, given the global focus of the concept of human development itself, needs to be comparative, drawing as much as possible on the best theoretical resources. It is important to acknowledge that the horizon is not entirely negative: the perspective may, for example, look very different in Brazil, where a long history of newspapers and big media too close to power makes the new beginning for journalism that a network of committed political bloggers might provide attractive (de Magalhães and de Albuquerque, 2014). It is also important to allow for the possibility that audiences for journalism may make a significant contribution to practically address the concerns raised here (Peters and Witschge, 2014). The outcome need not be to invent a new kind of journalism; it is surely enough to sustain the best of what journalists already do by clarifying our rationale for why it matters.

Acknowledgements

Thanks to the organizers and audiences at the Rethinking Journalism II conference at the University of Groningen in January 2014, as well as events at the University of Leicester in March 2014 and the University of Colorado, Boulder in April 2014, where earlier versions of this argument were given, in the last case as the Faculty of Journalism and Mass Communication's annual Ralph L. Crosman Lecture. Thanks very much to my LSE colleague Charlie Beckett for his comments on an earlier draft of the argument. Thanks also to Anthony Kelly for research assistance.

Notes

1   I am hugely indebted to Joseph Turow for the inspiration and insights that generated the discussion in the following paragraphs and indeed throughout this chapter. The argument draws in places on Couldry and Turow (2014), but I take responsibility, of course, for the particular formulations here.
2   Note that it is no part of my argument to claim that journalism is definitionally tied to democracy; indeed, it is important to see that democracy is not a sufficient condition for the existence of journalism, and that journalism can occur outside democracies (Josephi, 2013). But there remains a relation between journalism and democracy, which is based in underlying principles that, as we shall see, go beyond democracy itself.

References

Anderson, C. (2013). Towards a sociology of computational and algorithmic journalism. *New Media & Society*, *15*(7), 1005–1021.
Anderson, C., Bell, E., & Shirky, C. (2012). *Post-industrial journalism: Adapting to the present*. Center for Digital Journalism. Retrieved from http://towcenter.org/wp-content/uploads/2012/11/TOWCenter-Post_Industrial_Journalism.pdf.
Baker, C. E. (1998). The media the citizens need. *University of Pennsylvania Law Review, 147*(2), 317–408.
Baker, C. E. (2002). *Media, markets and democracy.* Cambridge: Cambridge University Press.
Baker, C. E. (2007). *Media concentration and democracy: Why ownership matters.* Cambridge: Cambridge University Press.
Bennett, L., & Iyengar, S. (2008). A new era of minimal effects? The changing foundations of political communication. *Journal of Communication, 58*, 707–731.
Carlson, M. (2013). Journalistic change in an online age: Disaggregating visibility, legitimacy, and revenue. *JOMEC Journal: Journalism, Media and Cultural Studies, 3.*
Couldry, N. (2012). *Media, society, world: Social theory and digital media practice.* Cambridge: Polity Press.
Couldry, N., Livingstone, S., & Markham, T. (2010). *Media consumption and public engagement.* Basingstoke: Palgrave Macmillan.
Couldry, N., & Turow, J. (2014). Advertising, big data, and the clearance of the public realm: Marketers' new approaches to the content subsidy. *International Journal of Communication, 8*, 1710–1726.
Curran, J. (1991). Mass media and democracy: A reappraisal. In J. Curran & M. Gurevitch (Eds.), *Mass media and society* (pp. 82–117) (2nd ed.). London: Edward Arnold.
Dahl, R. (1989). *Democracy and its critics.* New Haven, CT: Yale University Press.

De Magalhães, E., & de Albuquerque, A. (2014). Jornalistas sem jornal: A 'blogosfera progressista' no Brasil. Paper given to: *The 23rd Annual COMPOS Meeting, Belem, 27–30 May.*

De Tocqueville, A. (2002). *Democracy in America.* New York: Bantam (original work published 1835).

Gitlin, T. (1998). Public sphere or public sphericules? In T. Liebes & J. Curran (Eds.), *Media ritual and identity* (pp. 168–174). London: Routledge.

Habermas, J. (1996). *Between facts and norms.* Cambridge: Polity Press.

Hobbes, T. (1985). *Leviathan.* Harmondsworth: Penguin (original work published 1651).

Jonas, H. (1984). *The imperative of responsibility.* Chicago: University of Chicago Press.

Josephi, B. (2013). How much democracy does journalism need? *Journalism, 14*(4), 474–489.

Katz, E. (1996). And deliver us from segmentation. *Annals of the American Academy of Political and Social Science, 546,* 22–33.

Milton, J. (1974). Areopagitica. In *Selected prose* (pp. 196–248). Harmondsworth: Penguin (original work published 1644).

Mouffe, C. (2000). *The democratic paradox.* London: Verso.

Paine, T. (1937). *The rights of man.* London: Watts & Co (original work published 1791).

Pariser, E. (2011). *The filter bubble.* New York: Penguin.

Peters, C., & Witschge, T. (2014). From grand narratives of democracy to small expectations of participation. *Journalism Practice, 9*(1), 19–34. doi: 10.1080/17512786.2014.928455.

Prebble, J. (1968). *The Highland clearances.* Harmondsworth: Penguin.

Rosanvallon, P. (2006). *Democracy past and future.* New York: Columbia University Press.

Rosanvallon, P. (2008). *Counter-democracy.* Cambridge: Cambridge University Press.

Rosanvallon, P. (2011). *Democratic legitimacy.* Princeton: Princeton University Press.

Sen, A. (1987). *On ethics and economics.* Oxford: Blackwell.

Sen, A. (1999). *Development as freedom.* Oxford: Oxford University Press.

Shirky, C. (2009). Newspapers and thinking the unthinkable. Retrieved from http://www.shirky.com/weblog/2009/03/newspapers-and-thinking-the-unthinkable.

Stelter, B., & Haughney, C. (2013, 15 January). *The Atlantic* apologizes for Scientology ad. *New York Times.* Retrieved from http://mediadecoder.blogs.nytimes.com/2013/01/15/the-atlantic-apologizes-for-scientology-ad/.

Tilly, C. (2007). *Democracy.* Cambridge: Cambridge University Press.

Turow, J. (2007). *Niche envy: Marketing discrimination in the digital age.* Cambridge, MA: MIT Press.

Turow, J. (2012). *The daily you: How the new advertising industry is defining your identity and your worth.* New Haven, CT: Yale University Press.

Williams, B., & Delli Carpini, M. (2011). *After broadcast news.* Cambridge: Cambridge University Press.

2

REAPPRAISING JOURNALISM'S NORMATIVE FOUNDATIONS

John Steel

To literally 'rethink journalism' requires a commitment to critically re-engage with some of the central ideas about the role and function of journalism today and what they pertain to. Much current debate about journalism's role has revolved around its significance to politics and, in particular, to those democratic processes that require transparency and accountability, and that provide critical feedback to those in positions of power. As journalism is experiencing significant structural and social transformations, given the ways in which the economic environment is impacting on journalism's practices and products, it is worth considering these central normative positions afresh. In doing so, I argue that in responding to the task of rethinking journalism, one must confront some of the key normative claims that have underpinned journalism historically and that continue to feed into our contemporary understanding of the purpose and role of journalism today. I suggest for the purposes of theory building that critically confronting journalism's normative foundations, particularly within the context of its purported democratic significance, is a necessary though not sufficient step in the right direction.

To be sure, the ideas that fuel contemporary thinking about journalism emerged from particular historical contexts and contingent values. Despite significant social and political crises, particularly during the twentieth century when journalism sustained autocratic, totalitarian, fascist and other less than democratic systems, we still accept that journalism fuels democracy. Indeed, amidst the complexities of our contemporary political world, it may be that we are simply asking too much of journalism in the present, given the dramatic historical shifts and political transformations that have occurred since the burgeoning public sphere of the seventeenth and eighteenth centuries from which its normative core has been shaped. It is this sense of a growing lack of fit between the contemporary political context and those founding ideals of an informed and lively public sphere that is the motivating concern for this chapter.

Rather than attempting to rethink journalism normatively from a virtual *tabula rasa*, I suggest that we look to the realms of political and democratic theory as a necessary precursor to any reformulation of journalism's normative core. The reason for this is that it was in the realm of ideas, most significantly political ideas involving debate and deliberation of an ever-expanding political community, where the normative expectations we have of journalism today were shaped. As such, in developing this argument, I will focus my attention on the deliberative aspect of journalism's normative core and its central role in nourishing democracy, as this element is one of its most enduring and resilient elements. In stressing the centrality of the deliberative component of journalism's democratic functioning, I emphasize the rich historical legacy of journalism that has contributed to our contemporary expectations about what journalism should be today. From this I go on to examine the ways in which journalism is largely seen to be failing in its democratic mandate from different ends of the political spectrum. This is seen either in terms of its relative inability to engage and stimulate a deliberative civic sphere or because of the constraints placed upon it by so-called over-regulation and market interference. Finally, I offer two very different theoretical analyses of democracy and particularly democratic deliberation that provide a useful counterpoint to the contemporary discussion about democracy and which I suggest provide an innovative addition to the enterprise that motivates this volume.

Journalism, deliberation and the political sphere

The basis of my argument stems from an understanding of the key elements that underpin journalism's claims to a specifically democratic function – to hold power to account and to provide a voice for the public within the broader civil and public sphere. My focus on journalism's democratic role is not to dismiss or undervalue the range of other sources that have contributed to the development of journalism as I have pointed out elsewhere (Steel, 2009), but it is arguably journalism's service to the political and specifically liberal democratic polities that is the most resonant and robust of journalism's core claims today. Ironically it is these very features, or rather normative ideals, that seem increasingly out of kilter with the contemporary world. I am, of course, talking here about the model of a deliberative rational public sphere facilitated in its democratic goals by diverse and representative media of which journalism is a key component. Such a deliberative ideal can be traced in the USA to the Founding Fathers' commitment to representative government and the Madisonian compulsion to protect free speech and freedom of the press so as to breathe life into the public. This ideal was articulated by Dewey in *The Public and its Problems* (1927), the Hutchins Commission (1947) and more recently by scholars such as Sunstein (1995), Dryzek (2002) and Haas (2007), who have all stated the significance of a deliberative democratic environment nourished by vibrant and representative forms of journalism (Steel, 2012). Within the European context, of course, we have the legacy of Habermas (1989) and his conception of the democratic public sphere that became corrupted by capitalism's propensity towards the atomization and fragmentation of the public. The present neo-liberal era, such as it is, seems more than ever to have limited the possibilities of a dynamic, rich and deliberative rational public sphere despite the rapid technological transformations in the communications ecology.

Attempting to re-engage with the normative foundations of journalism's democratic functions requires a brief summary of their claims. The overarching principle here is that within a representative liberal democratic polities the public must have access to the processes of government in order for this same government to have legitimacy. To borrow from Jeremy Bentham, journalism provides 'security against misrule' by ensuring that elected representatives in government are exercising their power in the interests of the people that they represent and not in their own narrow self-interests. Journalism then provides a check on power and it is this element of journalism's rational core that has remained a constant feature since the birth of democratic institutions in Europe and North America in the late eighteenth and nineteenth centuries (Copeland, 2006). However, transparency is not a sufficient condition of democratic government and journalism's democratic credentials require that it perform another equally important function – that of serving as a proxy for the public, scrutinizing government *and* holding it to account on behalf of the wider community. As Dahlgren has suggested, 'journalism lays claim to accurate and impartial renderings of a reality that exists independently of its telling' and 'serves as an integrative force and as a common form for debate' (2009, p. 41). He continues: 'even if journalism in the real world has never operated quite in this way, this paradigmatic model of how it should be has guided our understanding and expectations of it' (2009, p. 41). The claims of impartiality and holding power to account are particularly problematic, as this is where journalism is often seen as failing. At best, it is selective in shining light on 'bad government', while at worst, it colludes with the very powers that it purportedly holds to account.

Whilst there is insufficient space here to delve into debates about ownership, influence and journalistic autonomy, it is necessary for the purposes of this argument to look more closely at this idea that government should be held to account by journalism and that journalists should somehow facilitate or represent forms of public response to the actions of their political representatives. Holding government to account involves journalists, on behalf of the public, having the ability to both scrutinize the practices and performance of government and the power to censure those in power. The *principle* of freedom of the press then provides the moral framework for journalists to censure government on behalf of the public without fear of sanction. Yet it is this expectation that journalism represents the interests of the people in the political realm that generally exposes its weaknesses. In other words, though journalism might at certain moments expose corruption and highlight the wrongdoing of those in public office, thereby facilitating the legitimation of its political power, its ability to reflect and represent the interests of the public has long been open to question.

Historically the relationship between journalism and the public has revolved around the so-called Lippmann–Dewey debate and variations of this polemic have remained constant throughout the twentieth and into the twenty-first centuries (Schudson, 2008). The main questions it generates are: should the public have the journalism that it wants – sensational, trashy, entertaining yet exposing public officials if they step out of line, or should journalism aspire to do more than entertain and fill the coffers of the multinational owners and conglomerates? Shouldn't journalism be more than about making money and protecting vested interests, and be motivated by a desire to represent the diversity of public opinion? Indeed, shouldn't journalism engage the public and stimulate a more rational democratic civic space as envisaged by so many? From the Hutchins Commission in the USA in the mid-twentieth century through to the various Royal Commissions, Calcutt Reports and the Leveson Inquiry in the UK (Steel, 2012, 2013), this polemic, which argues that journalism either gives the public what they want or serves the democratic, deliberative aspects of public life, has been prominent. It has specifically been the debate about journalism's role in stimulating and cultivating a more inclusive democratic culture that has arguably been core to some of the more critical analyses of journalism (Curran and Seaton, 2010; Keane, 1991; Muhlmann, 2010). Yet this deliberative ideal has also been the most problematic for those wishing to reform the corroding influences on an idealized version of journalism as it *should* be. Though the seeds of this deliberative component are varied, we only need to look at two examples from opposing ends of the political spectrum to see just how powerful and influential such a focus on the importance of public deliberation has been. Indeed, it is within these contributions that the limitations of our current normative expectations might be exposed, as much of our understanding of public deliberation and its rational power stems from these two sets of ideas. The two thinkers that I'd like to highlight are John Stuart Mill and Jürgen Habermas.

To focus on a discussion of democratic deliberation by highlighting the work of John Stuart Mill might seem a strange choice, especially given that he was not convinced that all members of society, at that juncture in history, had the intellectual capacity to understand and embrace the complexities of Victorian political life. As such, he is not someone who might be signalled as the most obvious proponent of the sort of democratic values that underpin some of journalism's more salient deliberative ideals today. However, Mill certainly saw the power of deliberation as an essential requirement for any mature society to progress. His treatment of the role of the press is crucial as it signifies how debate and discussion within a broader public sphere facilitated social and political progress within advanced liberal democratic societies (Wishy, 1959). Contained within his so-called 'truth argument' and its contextualization in *On Liberty* (1992), Mill envisages a public space in which individuals are protected against infringements against their autonomy from the state and, importantly, from each other. *On Liberty* therefore sets up the context in which the deliberative power of an unfettered press provides the space within which the public can express their concerns and opinions freely as a component of their individual autonomy. Furthermore, Mill's so-called 'truth argument'

(Haworth, 1998; Schauer, 1982) emphasizes just how important the 'liberty of thought and expression' is in sustaining a progressive and dynamic society. Despite the fact that Mill was seen by his contemporaries as more of a radical than a liberal (Reese, 1985), it is his contribution to contemporary liberalism and democratic theory that is worth emphasizing as it is via his understanding of individual autonomy and of the safeguards required to protect the individual from both the state and the incursions of wider public opinion on individuals, that we appreciate the separation of public and private spheres within which an enlightened deliberative public would thrive. *On Liberty* is significant because the limits required to protect individual freedom also serve the wider public good, as these provide scope for a deliberative public space through which rational discourse and progressive politics can thrive. Journalism's contribution to this public space, as in the early nineteenth-century era of the unstamped radical press, as Hollis (1970) and Chalaby (1998) have pointed out, would be varied and representative of a wide variety of interests and constituencies within society.

In a similar vein, Habermas (1989) idealizes a rational discursive realm in which open and representative democratic discourse enriches a political sphere where citizens consult, debate and deliberate on matters of social significance and importance. For Mill, it was the lack of education amongst the majority of the population and the stifling effects of public opinion that damaged the deliberative capacity of the people and thereby rendered them largely unable to engage with the political process. For Habermas, it is the corrupting influence of capital and the priorities of self-interest that polluted the deliberative context required for genuine democratic citizen engagement and participation. If it ever genuinely existed, journalism's era of public representation was, as Chalaby (1998) has pointed out, eventually eroded by the development of the industrial press and the imperatives of profit. Rather than embodying public facing values, journalism became commodified and any inclusive, representative and democratic core was diminished. Thus, the 'invention of journalism' heralded a simultaneous dilution of the public's deliberative capacity. Though never fully realized, this ideal of a deliberative active citizen engagement in matters of politics and public affairs continues to be seen as an important element of democratic life and one which requires journalism to play a significant role (Dahlgren, 2009). Both of the thinkers above, though at different ends of the ideological spectrum, envisage a deliberative space for members of society which is stimulated by journalism and which furnishes democracy with an engaged and lively citizenry.

Broken journalism and the degraded public sphere

Thus far in this chapter I have sketched out some of the features that contribute to journalism's normative heart by emphasizing the key value of deliberation. In this section I would like to develop my argument and assert that it is because of an uncritical acceptance of these cherished norms and core values that journalism is left requiring such a fundamental reconsideration. In this respect my argument resonates with those who suggest that we 'de-couple' journalism and democracy altogether (see Josephi, 2013; Nerone, 2013; Zelizer, 2013) as the link between the two concepts has become stale and in need of re-appraisal. Indeed, in Zelizer's view, democracy needs to be 'retired' from the equation altogether (Zelizer, 2013). To put it another way, the expectations that we have placed upon journalism to deliver the deliberative democratic nirvana that social and political theorists have promised us for generations are at the root of the problem of journalism today.

But what *is* the problem of journalism? If we look at attempts to reform journalism into something that would enable it to become more representative, deliberative and democratic, we immediately see the problem. Journalism simply does not stimulate an informed and active participatory culture. It does not represent all of society's constituent parts. It is precisely journalism's failure to deliver an informed, engaged and active participatory democratic public sphere that is generally understood to be at the root of its problems and maybe even partly responsible for problems of political dissatisfaction and disengagement more broadly (Hay, 2007). These problems are emphasized by journalism's cosy relationship to the same political authority that it ideally should be far more distanced from. If we look at the controversies surrounding the various attempts to reform journalism along more democratic, deliberative and representative lines, then we see the scale of the problems confronting the task of truly rethinking journalism. The aim of making our media more democratically accountable and journalists more responsible to the public is laudable and one with which I have much sympathy. The Leveson Inquiry report (2012) in particular highlighted not only the unethical depths to which some journalists have gone to in attempting to secure an exclusive story, but also the intimate and uncritical relationship that journalism can and does have with political and economic power. It also exposed a raw nerve in relation to how journalism might be reformed. The problem of 'fixing' broken journalism brings with it the issue that has plagued it from its earliest inception: that in order to remain independent and serve the public in scrutinizing government, it should be detached from government and free from the constraints of regulation. Whilst the debate about the pros and cons of the Leveson recommendations for press reform continue, I suggest that those who aspire to reform journalism in a way that makes it more accountable, representative and deliberative generally subscribe to the very same normative ideals as those who they are arguing against. This, as I will suggest below when highlighting the work of Dean (2009), makes progression unlikely.

Those wishing to reform journalism and encourage it to become more deliberative and democratically responsible of course provide important critical spaces and pressure points that highlight where and how the commercial imperatives of media organizations stifle democratic deliberation and representation. Organizations such as the Campaign for Press and Broadcasting Freedom and the Media Reform Coalition gain intellectual substance from a long tradition of important critical scholarship into media systems, structures and processes and their impact on democratic life. Yet in their aspirations to 'reform' media and journalism, in particular to make it more *accountable*, *representative* and *diverse*, such groups draw from essentially the same normative well as their adversaries; rather than imagining new bases for rethinking journalism, they tend to re-tread familiar ground. Likewise, the staunch neo-liberal 'Fourth Estatists', proprietors such as Rupert Murdoch, editors such as Paul Dacre as well as advocacy organizations such as the 'Freespeech Network' protest against 'attacks' on freedom of the press via so-called state regulation or media monopolization. The ongoing debate about media regulation highlights the opposing ideological positions of the debate, yet both positions essentially draw from the same intellectual sources that feed the familiar normative claims about what journalism should do, as highlighted above. Such positions, however, are dependent upon a decrepit conception of political culture and democratic participation which sees journalism as a facilitator of democratic politics and guardian against tyranny, but cannot deliver either because of the priorities of profit or because of an overly regulatory media environment. My own position falls well within the tradition of critical media scholarship; however, in continuing to draw from this traditional normative basis, we are missing the opportunity to move the debate on in more meaningful ways.

Within critical journalism studies we see various areas of scholarship that look to examine journalism in ways that directly or indirectly re-affirm these normative foundations. Whether scholars are discussing media systems and political influence or the broader political economy of journalism and the media more generally, they generally do so from a familiar normative standpoint. The implicit and explicit normative claims that are made in areas of journalism studies scholarship that analyse media systems and structures in ways that emphasize, or more critically expose their inefficiencies and limitations with regard journalism's 'proper functioning', tend to stress journalism's relative inability to fulfil its democratic deliberative obligations, given the range of structural impediments it has to cope with, be they an over-dependence on advertising, a lack of editorial independence from owners, political influence or the various 'filters' and production practices news goes through before it is consumed (Herman and Chomsky, 2008; Klaehn, 2005; McChesney, 2004; Szántó, 2007), and tend to prioritize, at least implicitly, a specific normative aspiration about journalism's core values (see also Berry and Theobald, 2006). As noted, this is generally drawn from a rich intellectual heritage, which, as I have stated, prioritizes a deliberative ideal. Greater media plurality, accountability and enhanced media representation are articulated in order to challenge, or at least highlight, the commercial imperatives of large media corporations and stress the 'democratic deficit' that contemporary business models of journalism promote (Phillips and Witschge, 2012).

It is not solely in analysing journalism's structures that we find this narrative, as scholarship on the practice of journalism and those who 'do' journalism is also significant. Work on journalism's role perceptions of course builds on the work of Donsbach (1993, 2010) and focuses on the lived experiences, perceptions and motivations of those working within journalism. The research highlights the ways in which journalists articulate and experience their work and the role, whether ideal or otherwise, that they play. This research is particularly valuable as it provides an insight into just how powerful and resonant the normative ideals of journalism are and the ways in which they are internalized by news workers (Eldridge II, 2014). Within such work, we see expressions of (idealized) normative claims of journalism and its purported democratic functioning, within a reflective framework that highlights the contradictions and tendencies within the production of news and amongst newsworkers themselves. In contrast to the aforementioned more structural analyses, this work tends to draw on the lived experiences of those practising to explore issues of identity and democratic functioning from the perspective of journalists and media workers themselves (Deuze, 2005, 2007; Shapiro, 2010). Though offering a valuable insight into the workings and changing dynamics of 'journalism' in different contexts, and providing accounts of the power of the established normative narrative, I suggest that this work suffers in much the same way as that which details the problematic structures or political economy of media in that it has the tendency to implicitly claim or at least draw attention to the idea that democratic culture is something that requires rehabilitation *and* that the media and journalism practice in particular are important sites for such rehabilitation.

This journalistic *praxis* is gauged in relation to what I would argue are a degraded set of democratic ideals and aspirations as they are no longer fit for purpose. However, in mining the lived experiences of journalism with a view to exposing the contradictions and tensions of the world that journalists inhabit, we have not interrogated with sufficient vigour the purportedly self-evident democratic values and contexts in which the journalists themselves are positioned and grapple with on a day-to-day basis. Such work tends to be divorced from a rigorous engagement with important concepts and debates, such as the nature and character of political deliberation (for example), the substance of political culture or, indeed, the character of democracy itself.

The crux of my argument therefore tallies with the sentiment expressed by Strömbäck, when he concludes by stating that:

> only by specifying what kind of democracy we are referring to when using the term, and by specifying its normative implications for media and journalism, that we can fully understand how media and journalism affect democracy.
> (Strömbäck, 2005, p. 343)

However, where I differ from Strömbäck is that I advocate developing new ideas about democracy from which new normative bases for journalism might spring. While helpful in signalling how different models of democracy – procedural, competitive, participatory and deliberative – might require journalism's normative bases to reflect these differences and be developed into a standard, his analysis fail to move us into new realms of politics.

Alternative normativity

It is all very well criticizing the normative claims, implicit or otherwise, that are made in the name of journalism, but what alternatives do I offer to counter the malaise that I have attempted to signal? Ironically, I suggest that we mine the very same realms of thought and inquiry that proved so fruitful in the establishment of our earlier visions of journalism. I am not, however, suggesting that we return directly to the ideals of Madison, Mill and Dewey to re-imagine conceptions of engagement and political participation, but rather that we look to their legacy within political theory and begin to rethink the nature of public deliberation and citizen engagement itself.

One example might be the work of political theorist Jeffrey Green, who, in his book *The Eyes of the People: Democracy in an Age of Spectatorship* (2010), challenges the essentially deliberative foundations of our contemporary political culture, arguing instead for more realistic expectations of what we understand political participation to be. Green criticizes the largely deliberative or 'vocal' claims that are made about political engagement and participation, noting that such deliberation rarely involves the wider public and is instead largely confined to an elite few. Green fundamentally questions the notion of genuine democratic participation and engagement as emerging from a discursive or deliberative base as envisioned by political theorists and media scholars alike. Returning to John Stuart Mill, Green (2010, p. 96) notes that the author of *On Liberty* and *Considerations on Representative Government* had far too much faith in the power of journalism in particular in bridging the gap between government and representation. Mill was essentially 'hyperidealistic' in thinking that the then:

> modern technologies of public opinion formation (journalism) were sufficient to return to the People the very legislative power that representative government – with its division between active and passive citizens – otherwise appeared to have sacrificed.
>
> (Green, 2010, pp. 96–7)

Green develops the idea of a 'plebiscitary' form of democratic participation and engagement that does not prioritize speech and dialogue over other forms of 'engagement'. He instead emphasizes the power of the public gaze, the act of looking and the politicians' never-ending public exposure as providing a realistic and sustainable form of political participation and legitimacy. Drawing on the work of Max Weber, Green suggests that Weber's conception of:

> the People's gaze, in effect, creates a stage – and the stage was a device whereby leaders would be both elevated (empowered to speak in the name of the People or at least directly to the People) yet constrained by the very condition of publicity.
>
> (Green, 2010, p. 156)

Echoing some of the disciplinary functions of the Panopticon (see Ball, 1994; Petley, 2013), politicians on the public stage are both empowered by and rendered subject to the People's gaze as they 'are compelled to appear in public under conditions they do not [always] control' (Green, 2010, p. 207). It is under these conditions of significant and constant scrutiny, removed from politicians' ultimate control, that Green calls the politics of candour. It is here then that Green develops the idea of a 'plebiscitary' democracy, where the power of the people is vested not in their contribution to the discursive realm of politics, but in the People's power to force political leaders to appear in public under the conditions of candour.

Though critics might charge Green with positing an essentially passive electorate, he is aware that, for the most part, most of us do not have much influence over the decisions that govern our lives. Yet, of course, he is aware that:

> when the People is invoked, as it is after all by journalists and within popular culture, it is identified with the electorate that votes on election day and responds to opinion polls – a usage that is triply alienating vis-à-vis the everyday citizen insofar as it refers to the extraordinary and rare moment of election rather than the everyday, *silent* experience of politics; assumes that the citizen is part of the majority that wins elections rather than the minority that loses; and presupposes that the citizen identify with substantive opinions and decisions, even though on most particular issues citizens do not possess clear or stable preferences.
>
> (Green, 2010, p. 209, emphasis in original)

The extended quote above emphasizes Green's understanding of the objective reality that under the conditions of liberal democracy, the People at large cannot hope to exercise their deliberative power in a way that secures their particular interests and objectives. Rather, political power resides more broadly in the capacity of the People – all of them rather than a select few – to ensure that under the conditions of candour, 'popular sovereignty ought to be reserved for – and revitalized through – the eyes of the People' (Green, 2010, p. 210).

As we have seen, democratic deliberation is one of the cornerstones of journalism's rationale, at least as envisioned by many who wish to reform and revive journalism's democratic spirit. Yet Green's book is an important contribution to the debate about journalism's normative foundations, as it challenges the very same idealized deliberative model of democracy that is so engrained within our democratic and journalistic culture; a model of democracy that is clearly far from realization. What Green offers instead is a form of political pragmatism that builds on the reality of liberal democratic constitutional arrangements and the People's relationship to and with these arrangements. For journalism studies, the normative expectation that deliberation is superior to 'merely' observing is severely challenged by Green's thoughtful analysis as he pays attention to our capacity to make political decisions based on the visibility of our political representatives. His analysis does not therefore place the heavy burden of deliberative politics on the public and, likewise, possibly offers a more pragmatic basis for, and expression of, political engagement.

Another challenge to the security of our normative conventions within journalism, albeit from a much more radical perspective, emerges through the work of Jodi Dean (2010). Dean analyses how various public challenges to power, for example the worldwide protests against the Iraq War in 2003 and the anti-globalization movement, are essentially articulated from within an ethical and technological framework that at the same time as providing space for critique also limits its capacity for effective change. Dean's work attempts to rehabilitate a Marxian analysis which grapples with the complexities of contemporary capitalism in ways that offer new opportunities for understanding the very basis of democratic culture and critical politics. More specifically, Dean's analysis of 'communicative capitalism' orientates us towards thinking about how neo-liberalism in particular has co-opted much of the moral capital from the Left and incorporated it into its own language and power. She suggests that:

> communicative capitalism designates the strange merging of democracy and capitalism in which contemporary subjects are produced and trapped. It does so by highlighting the way networked communications bring the two together. The values heralded as central to democracy take material form in networked communications technologies. Ideals of access, inclusion, discussion, and participation come to be realized in and through expansions, intensifications, and interconnections of global telecommunications.
>
> (Dean, 2009, p. 22)

Drawing on Zizek and Mouffe, she demonstrates that the communicative and deliberative opportunities provided by our new communication environment are ultimately subsumed into the politics and culture of neo-liberal individualism in ways that block out the social context and our connection to the wider social world. In doing so, within this neo-liberal media context, opportunities to move outside or beyond our current predicaments are limited. Journalism and the new deliberative opportunities afforded by new media therefore reflect and reinforce the narrowing of our interpretative horizons. Similarly to Green, Dean (2009, p. 91) takes aim at the ideals of deliberative democracy and suggests that deliberation is essentially a process that ignores the fact that political decisions have to be made, and that solving problems that deliberated decisions give rise to tend to be 'solved' by more deliberation. As such, democratic deliberation, as formulated by theorists such as Gutmann and Thompson (1996, 2004) is self-justifying as a process. When decisions are made, usually at the expense of one set of ideals and perspectives, the problem is resolved by more and more deliberation and negotiation. The point that Dean is making is that democratic deliberation is in itself a process of delaying decisions or deferring responsibility from an equal plane of influence. This is simply not the case as politics requires that decisions be made, thereby making alternative possibilities or outcomes not possible, until of course the consensus-based process of deliberation is revived once again.

Ultimately, theorists who place too much weight on the democratic power of deliberation fail to see its limitations as a tool of political decision making – a function of politics. For those of us concerned with how Dean's analysis of deliberation might contribute to normative foundations of journalism's democratic functioning, the outlook may seem grim, as it suggests we are condemned to stasis, seemingly unable to step outside of neo-liberalism's force. Yet Dean's analysis is progressive as it helps us understand how the corrosive capacity of neo-liberalism has usurped the very language and tools that are fundamental to challenging the status quo. For scholars and journalists looking to build new normative horizons, Dean's work is a fruitful starting point as it alerts us to existing barriers and the 'entrapment of psychotic politics' that cannot seem to transcend the present condition (2009, p. 18). As she concludes, we may 'have an ethical sense. But we lack a coherent politics, primarily because we remain attached to our present values' (2009, p. 175).

Conclusion

The main aim of this chapter should be clear: rather than focusing on an expectation that journalism should stimulate an essentially deliberative ideal in its nourishing of democracy, it asserts that journalism studies scholars in particular might do well to leave aside some of these more cherished notions of journalism's normative heart and dare to go beyond some of the core assumptions central to our contemporary understanding of what journalism should do. In doing so, I have argued that for journalists and scholars of journalism, new perspectives on democracy and democratic agency might refresh our notions of what journalism might do in a time when the changes affecting journalism are so pronounced. It may not be that the link between democracy and journalism needs to be 'retired', as Zelizer (2013) suggests; rather, it may be that the limitations of journalism should be seen in the context of the limitations of present democracy itself. As someone who has, in previous work, sought to re-articulate and re-state claims about journalism's democratic obligations and the essence of its democratic heart, I write this chapter as critical of myself as of others. In highlighting alternative sources of intellectual creativity by citing the contributions of Dean and Green as just two examples, I have attempted to prompt scholars of journalism to begin to step back and to re-assess some of these core ideals, in much the same way that Green and Dean, albeit from very different political perspectives, have sought to do in relation to democracy and participation. These two very different analyses of democracy, political agency and culture are examples of work from political theory which do not shy away from asking difficult questions about the nature of democratic life, political participation and particularly the ideals of democratic deliberation. I suggest that we, as scholars of journalism studies, would do well to do the same.

References

Ball, T. (1994). *Reappraising political theory: Revisionist studies in the history of political thought.* Oxford: Oxford University Press.

Berry, D., & Theobald, J. (Eds.). (2006). *Radical mass media criticism*. Toronto: Black Rose Books.

Chalaby, J. (1998) *The invention of journalism*. Basingstoke: Macmillan.

Copeland, D. (2006). *The idea of a free press*. Evanston: Northwestern University Press.

Curran, J., & Seaton, J. (2010). *Power without responsibility*. London: Routledge.

Dahlgren, P. (2009). *Media and political engagement: Citizens, communication and democracy*. Cambridge: Cambridge University Press.

Dean, J. (2009). *Democracy and other neoliberal fantasies: Communicative capitalism and left politics*. Durham, NC: Duke University Press.

Dean, J. (2010). *Blog theory*. Cambridge: Polity Press.

Deuze, M. (2005). What is journalism?: Professional identity and ideology of journalists reconsidered. *Journalism, 6*(4), 442–464.

Deuze, M. (2007). *Media work*. Cambridge: Polity Press.

Dewey, J. (1927). *The public and its problems*. London: Allen & Unwin.

Donsbach, W. (2010). Journalists and their professional identities. In S. Allen (Ed.), *The Routledge companion to news and journalism* (pp. 38–48). London: Routledge.

Donsbach, W., & Klett, B. (1993). Subjective objectivity: How journalists in four countries define a key term of their profession. *International Communication Gazette, 51*(1), 53–83.

Dryzek, J. (2002). *Deliberative democracy and beyond: Liberals, critics, contestations*. Oxford: Oxford University Press.

Eldridge II, S. (2014). *Interloper media: Journalism's reactions to the rise of Wikileaks*. (PhD Thesis). University of Sheffield.

Green, J. (2010). *The eyes of the people: Democracy in an age of spectatorship*. Oxford: Oxford University Press.

Gutmann, A., & Thompson, D. (1996). *Democracy and disagreement*. Cambridge, MA: Belknap.

Gutmann, A., & Thompson, D. (2004). *Why deliberative democracy?* Princeton, NJ: Princeton University Press.

Haas, T. (2007). *The pursuit of public journalism*. New York: Routledge.

Habermas, J. (1989). *The structural transformation of the public sphere: An inquiry into the category of bourgeois society*. (T. Burgher, Trans.). Cambridge: Polity Press.

Haworth, A. (1998). *Free speech*. London: Routledge.

Hay, C. (2007). *Why we hate politics*. Cambridge: Polity Press.

Herman, E., & Chomsky, N. (2008) *Manufacturing consent: The political economy of the mass media*. London: The Bodley Head.

Hollis, P. (1970). *The pauper press: A study in working-class radicalism of the 1830's*. Oxford: Oxford University Press.

Hutchins Commission. (1947). *A free and responsible press*. Chicago: University of Chicago.

Josephi, B. (2013). How much democracy does journalism need? *Journalism, 14*(4), 474–489.

Keane, J. (1991). *The media and democracy*. Cambridge: Polity Press.

Klaehn, J. (Ed.). (2005). *Filtering the news: Essays on Herman and Chomsky's propaganda model*. Montreal: Black Rose Books.

McChesney, R. (2004). *The problem of the media*. New York: Monthly Review.

Mill, J. S. (1992). *On liberty*. Oxford: Oxford University Press (first published 1859).

Muhlmann, G. (2010). *Journalism for democracy*. Cambridge: Polity Press.

Nerone, J. C. (2013). The historical roots of the normative model of journalism. *Journalism, 14*(4), 446–458.

Petley, J. (2013). *Media and public shaming: Drawing the boundaries of disclosure*. London: I.B. Taurus.

Phillips, A., & Witschge, T. (2012). The changing business of news. In P. Lee-Wright, A. Phillips & T. Witschge (Eds.), *Changing journalism* (pp. 3–20). London: Routledge.

Reese, J. (1985). *John Stuart Mill's On liberty*. Oxford: Clarendon Press.

Schauer, F. (1982). *Free speech: A philosophical inquiry*. Cambridge: Cambridge University Press.

Schudson, M. (2008). The 'Lippmann–Dewey debate' and the invention of Walter Lippmann as an anti-democrat 1986–1996. *International Journal of Communication, 2*, 1031–1042.

Shapiro, I. (2010). Evaluating journalism: Towards an assessment framework for the practice of journalism. *Journalism Practice, 4*(2), 143–162.

Steel, J. (2009). The idea of journalism. In W. Eadie (Ed.), *21st century communication: A reference handbook* (pp. 583–591). Thousand Oaks: Sage.

Steel, J. (2012). *Journalism and free speech.* London: Routledge.

Steel, J. (2013). Leveson: Solution or symptom? Class, crisis and the degradation of civil life. *Ethical Space, 10*(1), 8–13.

Strömbäck, J. (2005). In search of a standard: Four models of democracy and their normative implications for journalism. *Journalism Studies, 6*(3), 331–345.

Sunstein, C. (1995). *Democracy and the problem of free speech.* New York: The Free Press.

Szántó, A. (2007). *What Orwell didn't know: Propaganda and the new face of American politics.* New York: Public Affairs.

Wishy, B. (1959). *Prefaces to liberty: Selected writings of John Stuart Mill.* Boston: Beacon Press.

Zelizer, B. (2013). On the shelf life of democracy in journalism scholarship. *Journalism, 14*(4), 459–473.

3

ESTABLISHING THE BOUNDARIES OF JOURNALISM'S PUBLIC MANDATE

Matt Carlson

Can journalists talk themselves into being socially relevant? Perhaps not. Prone to platitudes, journalists espouse their democratic utility while warning of the consequences of their profession's demise. Even if the arguments underpinning journalists' normative rhetoric have not, in the abstract, become invalidated in contemporary social and political life, problems with journalism's self-definitions are clear and well rehearsed: a normative vision fixed on democratic self-governance is too singular and limited, accounting for only a sliver of what journalism does; journalists' truth claims draw scepticism; and lofty rhetoric leaves too much room for easy disproval when examining actual news content and practices (Dahlgren, 1992). Dismissing talk about journalism as removed from what is actually occurring in the newsroom or from news audiences' experiences is easy. Derogatorily, we call it navel-gazing.

This chapter prods us to take public arguments about journalism seriously. If journalism is not static or a fixed entity, if it can be said to change and adapt over time and if it is prone to competing visions, then these narratives cannot be ignored. Instead, their role in the larger struggle over the evolving practices and meanings of journalism deserves clarification, elaboration and engagement both from scholars and from the larger public. In many places around the world, the social role and continued relevance of contemporary journalism are subject to scrutiny. In this environment of uncertainty, even the most hackneyed normative appeal to the value of journalism – trite as it may sound to critical ears – is an expression of a felt belief presented as a justification for the continuing power of journalists to represent reality back to us. Non-journalistic voices need to be included as well, given the ample discourse produced about news performance – including from journalism scholars. The news does not exist in isolation, but as a discourse embedded within a larger metadiscourse seeking to make sense of journalism.

The suggestion that journalism requires a public mandate raises all kinds of important analytical questions about the form this mandate should take. In one sense, 'mandate' denotes official sanctioning. But this statutory definition does not suffice when describing a voluntary ascription to journalism as a way of knowing about events in the world. Journalism's public mandate must instead be understood in a cultural sense. There is nothing innate about particular forms of journalism. Instead, journalistic practices accrue legitimacy through the public negotiation of particular practices, organizational structures, normative espousals and textual forms as valid and appropriate – or as unsatisfactory. Moreover, the stability of this mandate can never be assumed or total; it is always being remade and transformed in response to the changing context in which the news is produced and circulated. Clearly, this is not a neatly defined process, but a messy array of competing practices and ideas.

This chapter takes up the problem of how to make sense of the discursive terrain of talk about journalism and its relationship to journalism's public mandate. To interrogate this type of discourse and to theorize about how it works and why it matters, three interlinked concepts that the author has individually developed elsewhere are brought together: metajournalistic discourse (Carlson, 2016a), boundary work (Carlson, 2015a) and journalistic authority (Carlson, 2016b). The connections between these three concepts both shed light on how journalism comes to have shared meaning and provide an analytical tool for examining how the image of journalism is being worked out in the contemporary media landscape. Ultimately, they help us to map the consequences of the competition over journalism's public mandate.

In the end, 'rethinking' is not an internal mental task, but an external discursive exercise resulting in texts that are carefully presented for public consumption. We should then ask what this rethinking entails and, just as importantly, who participates in it. As the conclusion argues, to account for this type of talk, care must be taken not to accord journalism scholars the same position of objective observer regularly critiqued when applied to journalists. Instead, all talk about journalism is situated, and needs to be recognized as such. There is no place to stand outside of such discussions.

Metajournalistic discourse

The first concept to be plumbed is 'metajournalistic discourse', a category denoting public discussions of news practices, normative commitments and the interaction with legal, political and economic issues pertaining to journalistic institutions (Carlson, 2016a). This term both corrals a universe of topically oriented discourse and suggests its role in delineating how journalism can be talked about (more on this below). The core theoretical contention is that the news cannot exist independent of the webs of meaning in which it is enveloped. Even the very recognition of a text as news – or, just as powerfully, the rejection of a text as not-news – rests on pre-existing shared understandings of what constitutes news. Beyond recognition, metajournalistic discourse encompasses criss-crossing narratives about news, from critiques of stories as sensationalistic, politically biased or motivated by commercial interests to the lauding of journalism as necessary for democracy and a watchdog acting on behalf of publics. These claims exist side-by-side in public, emerging out of specific contexts and circulating among different audiences.

Examples of journalist-driven metajournalistic discourse are not hard to find. All collectives engage in talk about themselves, a point made clear in many of the references below in the literatures on professions and on boundary work. Yet, whereas other professions must often work through journalists to reach outsiders, journalists are uniquely situated to talk directly to the public about themselves in spaces normally reserved for reporting on external events. This type of talk appears embedded within news texts alongside other stories or isolated in public spaces – journalism reviews, conferences, memoirs, award ceremonies, etc. It includes a wide range of occasions, including anniversaries of notable events (Kitch, 2002; Zelizer, 1992), retirements (Usher, 2010), commemorations of deceased colleagues (Carlson, 2006, 2007; Carlson and Berkowitz, 2012), the winning of awards (Zelizer, 1993), episodes of deviance (Berkowitz, 2000; Carlson, 2014; Hindman, 2005; Reese, 1990), changes in the news industry (Carlson, 2012; Haas and Steiner, 2002) and so on. Many large news organizations task reporters to cover media (Haas, 2006) or to self-monitor (Nemeth, 2003). Moreover, the exposure elite journalists receive helps them attain fame (Meltzer, 2009) or even the status of being a cultural icon (Carlson and Berkowitz, 2012). This celebrity increases their reach. Finally, to this list we should add the voices of those outside of journalism that publicly speak about the news, from irritated politicians to amateur bloggers.

Clearly, the cultural negotiation of journalism's public mandate belies easy categorization. Talk about journalism occurs in many places. Any thorough accounting of metajournalistic discourse requires attending to an extensive field comprising disparate actors, texts and sites (Carlson, 2016a). Bringing conceptual order to this discourse requires first attempting to identify its central tendencies. To this end, metajournalistic discourse warrants the scrutiny of three intertwined issues: context, content and scope.

First, statements about journalism need to be recognized as inseparable from the context of their creation and circulation. Utterances about journalism cannot be disconnected from the economic, political and cultural conditions in which they occur. For example, journalists engaging in public self-criticism about their own work or the work of their organization confront competing pressures. Opening up about reportorial uncertainties or deficiencies risks alienating both audiences that rely on this news and advertisers who wish to associate with journalism's credibility as well as its reach (Haas, 2006). Conversely, journalists are also forced to confront pressing questions of how a transforming media environment affects their work (Carlson, 2012). It is hard to ignore the troubles plaguing the news industry. This complicated context is marked by the twin imperatives of maintaining credibility and acknowledging that changes in news should be recognized when looking at how journalists speak about their work.

To account for context, the lens of performativity helps by providing a situated perspective for examining discourse. An emphasis on metajournalistic discourse as performance accentuates the strategic aims of social actors that produce it

(Broersma, 2010).The analysis of performative acts involves both the utterance and the conditions in which it is produced – e.g. the goal of the speaker, the space in which it occurs and the position of the audience. Anther contribution of performativity to metajournalistic discourse is its sensitivity to how recurring statements that may not communicate new information come to have ritualistic significance for a community. The repetition of core principles is itself meaningful. This is also true for critics outside of journalism or proponents of emerging news forms who have their own strategic aims regarding how they position news texts and the journalists who create them.

Thinking through the consequences of metajournalistic discourse also requires close attention to its content. Representing journalism through language necessitates the selection and privileging of certain aspects at the expense of others. Utterances about journalism mix explicit declarations with implicit assumptions. Often this can be seen in how such talk flattens journalistic difference into a coherent whole. Through a subjunctive tone, various actors claim that 'journalism should do X' or 'journalism should be Y'. The haziness of defining journalism will be taken up in the section below on boundary work, but suffice to say that the label 'journalism' is a difficult referent, applicable to a craft, an institutional understanding, a set of normative commitments, a type of cultural output and a profession. It is not a fixed object, even as it is treated as one in metajournalistic discourse. Accepting this statement requires careful attention to how various actors homogenize journalism by attributing – or disavowing – specific norms or practices as core elements of journalism. A parallel issue involves the representation of temporality. Statements describing journalism are necessarily time-bound in that they privilege particular moments as noteworthy while ignoring other patterns. For example, contemporary talk about journalism often suggests an unprecedented degree of dynamism within the present news environment while assuming a past stasis. This view distorts the longer history of journalistic transformation (Schudson, 1982).

Actors' attempts to impose a cohesive definition can be examined through Bourdieu's (1993) concept of intrafield competition. For Bourdieu, all fields of cultural production are structured between poles of heterodoxy and orthodoxy. The power to define the field is the power to establish its orthodoxy. Unsurprisingly, such efforts engender intense internal competition that can lead to the transformation of a field as once marginal actors gain social capital. Bourdieu (2005) considered journalism to be more heteronomous than autonomous, but this perspective nonetheless contributes to an understanding of what metajournalistic discourse does. It invites careful monitoring of how and where this competition occurs, and the motives that speakers have.

A final issue concerns the scope of metajournalistic discourse. Journalism studies, as the name indicates, has tended to narrow its gaze to journalists at the expense of attending to how non-journalists – audiences, critics and even academics – confront and respond to the news. Any accounting of metajournalistic discourse ought to consider a wider range of voices than just journalists. From the printing press onwards, the technology of mass communication precluded all but a limited number of voices from participating in journalism. Moreover, in different places, a mix of governmental control, legal regimes and market forces proscribed many from entering into the message amplifying spaces of mass communication. These barriers to entry have been drastically reduced through the expansion of internet access and the availability of easy-to-use communication software, leading to the rise of blogs, micro-blogs and social media. Networked digital technologies have transformed access to what we may call the mediated public sphere. Although press criticism likely lags behind pictures of cats in terms of the uses of this technology, we should take into account the interconnectedness afforded by social media (see Vos, Craft and Ashley, 2012). The abundance of messages makes any one message less likely to be heard, but, by the same token, the architecture of social media allows for the amplification and extensive sharing of certain messages. Just as the expansion of mediated voices has raised new questions regarding who should participate in the creation of news (Lewis, 2012), so too should it raise questions about the expansion of metajournalistic discourse.

In summary, metajournalistic discourse directs attention to a complex array of voices that speak publicly about journalism. Journalists actively work to establish meaning about what they do, even in competition with one another. The news is also subject to scrutiny from a lone Twitter user complaining about her local newspaper, well-funded media watch organizations pressuring reporters to alter story frames (Carlson, 2015b) and even satirists making light of news coverage (see Gray, Jones and Thompson, 2009). This discursive environment makes it difficult for journalists to advocate for the position Barnhurst and Nerone (2001) dub the 'monovocality' of modern journalism – the idea that journalists are able to speak from the one correct perspective on any news story. Instead, news stories represent the world, and these representations are susceptible to challenges. Understanding the consequences of metajournalistic discourse requires further conceptualization to clarify its effect on news and efforts to rethink journalism.

Journalistic boundary work

Metajournalistic discourse not only names an area of public talk about journalism, it also indicates the means through which ideas of what journalism is are created and circulated. One way to conceptualize the consequences of metajournalistic discourse is by looking outside of journalism studies to the literature on boundary work (Carlson, 2015a). The problem of demarcation has long been at the forefront of sociological inquiry. Complex societies are criss-crossed with differences, some stringently enforced and others a matter of convention (Lamont and Molnár, 2002). Moreover, these differences are not naturally derived, but constructions arising through cultural practice. Scholarship on boundaries within science and technology studies and the sociology of the professions dovetail in their attempts to understand how systems of knowledge production are constructed. A well-developed concept elsewhere in the social sciences, boundary work is increasingly being applied to the particularities of journalism as a cultural form (see Carlson and Lewis, 2015; Lewis, 2012; Schudson and Anderson, 2008; Winch, 1997).

The fullest conceptualization of boundary work has been put forward by Thomas Gieryn (1983, 1995, 1999) in the sociology of science. His work rejects trait-based schemes by such scholars as Karl Popper in favor of boundary work as the rhetorical delimitation of science from non-science. In this anti-essentialist perspective, what constitutes science is a matter of ongoing social struggle over who may possess 'epistemic authority' to create legitimate knowledge about particular topics (1999, p. 1). Gieryn usefully foregrounds competition over knowledge production by focusing on often fierce clashes in which social actors compete to define the boundaries of proper science. These boundaries matter in establishing what Abbott (1988) calls a jurisdiction – the dominion over an area of work by a professional group – and the concomitant normative and material rewards ranging from cultural prestige to autonomy and financial security.

At first glance, Gieryn's boundary work perspective appears to be a good match for journalism. Both scientists and journalists seek epistemic authority to create and relay knowledge about the world through adherence to epistemological conventions (see Ekström, 2002; Matheson, 2004). They both exist within competitive contexts in which how the world comes to be known is forever contested. To take one example in which these two areas meet, the research on global warming draws skeptics who question both scientists' motives behind their studies and journalists' motives for conveying these studies to the public (Carvalho, 2007). However, given the diversity of journalistic activities and actors laying claim to the title of journalist, journalism is too peculiar a cultural practice to simply import boundary work wholesale from science studies. Studies of journalistic professionalism (summarized in Schudson and Anderson, 2008; Waisbord, 2013) expose the difficulty of identifying criteria to demarcate journalists from non-journalists. In many countries, no mechanisms exist to close off journalism's ranks in any consistent way. The enlargement of public voices made possible through digital media further complicates efforts to enact boundaries (see Singer, 2003). In an era when the centrifugal forces pulling journalism in different directions give rise to questions concerning the very viability of 'journalism' as a meaningful descriptor (Ryfe, 2012, pp. 140–1), the centripetal concept of boundary work is bound to be problematic. This issue is exacerbated by journalism's use of plain language rather than boundary-marking abstract knowledge associated with other professional domains (Abbott, 1988). Obfuscation makes for bad journalism. This issue of abstract expert knowledge raises further questions about what constitutes journalistic expertise (see Anderson, 2013; Reich, 2012). The red flags raised above make it clear that taking up the boundary work concept for journalism is more a matter of adaptation than adoption.

Instead of dissuasive deficiencies, boundary work opens up the analysis of how journalists negotiate the idiosyncrasies of journalism as a knowledge producing practice and seek to establish continuity across a broad swath of work. In this sense, boundary work is not merely an instrumental attempt to sort out social space, but a value-laden exercise. It acts as a conservative force in that it provides a notion of a journalistic core from which boundaries arise. This can be seen in the ways in which journalists articulate their work as particular, specialized and deserving of social recognition. The latter includes the supposition of particular privileges and legal rights – a matter of debate around the world. These jurisdictional arguments often stem from an appeal to professionalism as ensuring the worthiness of journalists (Waisbord, 2013). Even if journalism can never attain professionalism on a par with other 'classic' professions, journalists still retain what Lewis (2012) calls a 'professional logic' in how they understand their work (see also Soloski, 1989). Professionalism provides not just a shared identity, but a way of presenting oneself to the public as a legitimate actor. From this viewpoint, boundary work seems most useful when confronting definitional struggles arising over whether certain forms, practices, norms and persons are adequately journalistic. These 'credibility contests' – as Gieryn (1999, p. 1) calls them – develop around what may be appropriately labelled journalism or who may be called a journalist.

Coddington (2012) usefully draws on the boundary work perspective to examine how the *New York Times* and *The Guardian* newspapers reinforced their distance from WikiLeaks while simultaneously collaborating with the site in a series of high-profile stories based on leaked documents it had obtained. The two newspapers trumpeted the strengths of journalistic institutionality while placing the stateless, loosely organized and activist-oriented WikiLeaks outside the bounds of professional journalism as a source rather than a partner. This interpretive move allowed the newspapers to work with WikiLeaks while placing it outside acceptable practices and therefore unworthy of either emulation or inclusion within the walls of journalism.

This excursion into the concept of boundary work brings us back to the question of what metajournalistic discourse does. By engaging in talk about journalism, journalists and others work to establish culturally constructed boundaries between journalism and non-journalism. That these boundaries are not binding can be understood as indicative of ever-present interpretive struggle, a condition that encourages ongoing definition construction (Dahlgren, 1992). Boundary work provides a means for thinking about the consequences of metajournalistic criticism and a way to get beyond the lack of self-reflexivity within this discourse. It also brings in voices from outside of journalism that critique the boundaries of journalism, including those wishing to be included within the domain. What matters is not that journalists seek to establish boundaries, but how such claims shape ideas of what the news is, what role it should play culturally and democratically, and what news audiences should do. These questions require us to turn to the third concept in this chapter: journalistic authority.

Journalistic authority

The anti-essentialist foundation of boundary work implies social distinctions to always be provisional, malleable alignments sanctioning some subgroup with the right to perform certain tasks while leaving everyone else out. In many sectors of social life, we might welcome such distinctions, say, in who we see during a trip to the emergency room. We rely on institutionalized distinctions for the public good. However, in the particular case of journalism, the restrictiveness underlining boundary work might reasonably strike one as overly protective. Proponents of citizen journalism and user-generated content advocate for the dissolution, either in part or in whole, of boundaries in favor of greater participatory opportunities (see Lewis, 2012). In a larger sense, the contemporary media environment is marked by the complexity of what Graeme Turner (2009) has called 'the demotic turn' in which regular people increasingly produce, appear in and share media content – albeit often through existing media organizations. Journalists continue to argue for a public mandate on the grounds that their work sustains the functioning of democratic governance, but these other developments are democratizing on their own merits. Given these forces, journalistic boundary work aimed at closing off the ranks of who may rightfully create news could easily be dismissed as reactionary.

Ascribing the motive of protectionism alone to journalists engaged in boundary work errs by privileging self-preservation above all while tossing normative arguments into the bin of disingenuousness. A deeper understanding of the urge towards boundary making requires the enunciation of the third main concept of this chapter: journalistic authority. Public attempts to define journalism's boundaries, proclaim its social utility and identify who may be properly labelled a journalist are efforts to shape what makes journalism an authoritative means of producing knowledge about the world (see Carlson, 2016b). But beyond an intuitive sense of authority, the concept has been all too rarely fleshed out in its application to journalism.

To begin with, the general concept of 'authority' is shrouded in ambiguity and complexity as it traverses social science, political philosophy and religious studies, to name but a few domains (Lincoln, 1995, p. 1). Lessening this haziness necessitates a thumbnail conceptualization of just what authority *is*. The first point of clarification is to invoke a division between being 'in authority' – a person empowered by position to enforce action – and being 'an authority' – a person with expertise over a domain of knowledge (Friedman, 1990, p. 57). The latter can be traced back to its Latin origin of *auctoritas*, which translates as possessing 'a right to be listened to' (Höpfl, 1999, p. 219). The language here is tricky. Authority is often assumed to have the solidity of a thing possessed – an object that is transferrable or measurable. To do so reifies authority while decontextualizing it. Instead, authority is understood here as relational. Authority involves those laying claim to authoritative speech and those recognizing it as such. And since the idea of being 'an authority' eschews coercion, it relies on recognition from those positioned outside of this authority. In other words, authority cannot be claimed without assent. However, being 'an authority' is not a function of persuasion; to speak authoritatively is to appeal to such authority in making pronouncements.

The shift away from authority as a thing to be had to a characteristic of a relation between those who have it and those who assent to it points to the discursive quality of authority (White, 1995). Authority is not static, but a relationship constantly produced and reproduced through positions assumed in everyday interactions – be it in the doctor's office or in watching the evening news broadcast. Aside from its discursive character, different instantiations of authority give rise to particular enduring structures. From the courtroom to the search warrant, the discursive joins with the material. These formulations concretize authority relations through institutional forms that become a familiar backdrop to contemporary life. Yet all institutions that possess authority (as opposed to purely coercive power or the lack of authority) depend on sanctioned legitimacy – a public mandate – that should help defeat taken-for-granted views of authority.

Applying authority to the specific case of journalism begins with the question of how journalism establishes its public mandate. Authority derives from the social good, but what journalism provides is more difficult to conceptualize than government, law and medicine. Moreover, journalists cannot dictate what authoritative journalism looks like independent of the wider public or the constraints of particular media systems. It is always a socially constructed form of cultural production embedded within a specific context, and therefore prone to change. To establish its public mandate, the negotiation of authoritative journalism takes place through both news forms (Barnhurst and Nerone, 2001; Broersma, 2010) and metajournalistic discourse about the news seeking to plot its boundaries among competing forms of cultural production. The result is both the production of particular forms of knowledge considered to be legitimate (e.g. the news account) and the establishment of relational roles joining actors inside and outside of journalism (e.g. reporters, news sources and audiences).

The connection between journalistic authority and the establishment of journalism's public mandate can be seen in conventionalized forms of news (Eason, 1986). News stories are less arguments to persuade news audiences about what is real than assertions of the realness of news accounts. Journalists act as cultural authorities in their construction of knowledge (Starr, 1982). This notion is central in Zelizer's definition of journalistic authority as 'the ability of journalists to promote themselves as authoritative and credible spokespersons of "real-life" events' (1992, p. 8). The position of 'spokesperson' entitles control over knowledge in a particular domain as well as having this knowledge accepted as legitimate by those on the outside. It is important to reiterate, based on the previous two aspects, that such control over knowledge is context-bound and prone to variability as well as contestation – as the title of this book suggests.

In thinking through the range of criticisms directed at news discourse, attacks on credibility should not be conflated with attacks on journalistic authority. Credibility speaks to issues of belief – is this news story a 'true' rendering of what happened? Can this news outlet be trusted, or is it biased or incompetent? But questions of belief are not the same as questions of authority. The distinction is clear if we look at authority as more closely connected to legitimacy. To consider journalism to be legitimate is to concede its utility to communicate knowledge. By contrast, to criticize the credibility of journalism is to condemn the behaviour of journalists in conveying the news. Attacking the credibility of specific cases may even *reinforce* the general assumption that legitimate journalism is possible, just not executed well in a particular case. Often, critics of the press draw on journalism's own normative claims when accusing journalists of not meeting their own standards in a specific case (Carlson, 2009).

If we push aside credibility, we are in a better position to ask how journalistic forms and practices are being challenged on a more fundamental level than whether or not a story may be accurate. The contestation over appropriate boundaries taking place through metajournalistic discourse indicates wider skirmishes over the constitution of legitimate journalism. We may ask how journalistic authority is changing or splintering under such conditions and how this affects a slew of stakeholders – journalists, powerful social actors, new participants in the mediated public sphere and the larger news audience, to name but a few. The drama surrounding journalism is ultimately about the desirability of the forms of news we receive and the institutional arrangements that make them possible.

In many ways, arguments for journalistic authority are conservative. Journalists seek to conserve and extend set routines and normative convictions even as the media environment changes around them. Analyses need to move beyond this observation to interrogate incidents in which journalists and others negotiate the way forward for journalism through metajournalistic discourse. Such inquiry requires the careful grounding of metajournalistic discourse in the conditions of its creation, circulation and consumption. As such, a number of pressing questions need to be rounded out to better conceive of the connections between metajournalistic discourse, boundary work and journalistic authority. First, any analysis of metajournalistic discourse requires careful attention to who is speaking, to whom they speak, and who does not speak. Returning to Bourdieu's concept of interfield competition, which voices are structured so as to speak for and to larger communities? Second, the types of boundary work taking place regarding journalism need to be more carefully differentiated (see Carlson, 2014, 2015a). One distinction is between what may be termed arguments of essence – efforts to define the core of journalism – versus arguments of particularity – the recognition of journalistic diversity. Finally, studies of metajournalistic discourse must consider the interplay between the rhetorical and the material. Boundaries aren't only talked into existence; they have enduring structural aspects as well.

Conclusion: the case for reflexivity

Answering the question 'how is journalism changing?' requires careful attention to a host of economic, technological and cultural developments that have hindered legacy media and raised new questions about journalism's normative commitments, organizational structures and delivery platforms. This inquiry necessitates a parallel question, 'how does journalism change?', to account for the material and discursive mechanisms through which the transformation of journalism occurs. Shifts in news structures are accompanied by discourse about these variations and what they mean. As this chapter has argued, this is not idle chatter, but the space in which various stakeholders compete to define the shape of journalism's public mandate. This rethinking occurs out loud, in public, with specific purpose. It does something that should not be ignored.

The explorations of metajournalistic discourse, boundary work and journalistic authority above have often proceeded from an external vantage point untroubled by the position of the author. Yet this viewpoint is ultimately untenable for neglecting journalism scholars' participation in the very processes described in this chapter. In crafting an inclusive vision of metajournalistic discourse and its relationship with journalistic authority, this final section engages the thorny topic of scholarly self-reflexivity: the need for 'examining one's own personal, possibly unconscious, reactions' as a means of 'exploring the dynamics of the researcher–researched relationship' (Finlay, 2002, p. 224). Issues at the core of self-reflexivity – attunement to method, personal biases and situated knowledge – deserve acknowledgment since, as argued above, journalism researchers cannot stand outside the social world they study. Instead, our social location interacts with what we study in complex ways.

Recognizing our own place within discussions of journalism requires attention to the larger institutional context that envelops both journalism and journalism research. In a fundamental way, the institutional stability and cultural recognition of journalism bears on the institutional stability of journalism studies as a legitimate subfield. They are inexorably linked. In one sense, the proliferation of novel news forms and the decline of legacy news have benefited journalism studies by presenting new sites for inquiry. There are many pressing questions about journalism these days, as books such as this one attest. Conversely, the growing heterogenization of journalism necessarily spurs questions regarding the coherence of journalism studies as a topical subfield. In concert with changes to journalism, the domain of journalism studies is being stretched in ways that will likely spark contentious academic boundary work about what it means to study journalism. Internal scholarly divisions mirror external journalistic divisions.

Another institutional issue concerns the closeness of journalism studies with its object of study. Journalism researchers interact with journalism in a number of ways, including as educators, commentators, expert sources for news stories, consultants, and through professional and social gatherings. Significant crossover occurs as well, with journalists leaving news to become 'hackademics' (Harcup, 2011) and journalism education becoming a site for experimentation. These persistent ties raise questions regarding the possibility, or even the desirability, of distance between the researcher and what is being researched. This closeness gives rise to a parallel set of issues concerning the cognitive dimensions of journalism studies. This issue is most pronounced when normative assumptions go unexamined. A lack of critical attention to the fundamental beliefs of journalism owes much to the other-directed nature of journalism's self-image; in purporting to serve democracy, journalism offers an easily supportable set of social goals. The centrality of journalism's social role and the permanence of its public mandate are assumed starting points for inquiry. The very significance of journalism studies as a distinct subfield relates to this assertion of news as socially important. Yet the perspective proposed here pushes researchers to interrogate naturalized normative assumptions and their role in creating definitions and erecting boundaries. In short, journalism scholars need to be aware of how their embedded, institutionalized position affects how they speak about journalism.

The issue of self-reflexivity is not meant to stymie journalism research, cast suspicion on scholars' intentions or insult those who study news. To do so would hinder important work and impugn dedicated individuals. This argument is not intended to make any enemies. Instead, the purpose of invoking the need for self-reflexivity is to acknowledge the position of journalism scholars as stakeholders who are part of the process described in this chapter. At the very least, this position requires sensitivity to the roles scholars play in the mechanisms that sustain and transform journalism's public mandate. Through writing and teaching about journalism, journalism studies scholars are reliable sources of a steady stream of metajournalistic discourse, whether we reproduce or challenge existing assumptions in our work. At the other extreme, the perspective developed here suggests ample room for earnest intervention by scholars – and really the entire public. This is not an unfamiliar idea; the very existence of media and journalism studies indicates disquiet with much of contemporary journalism – dissatisfaction drives many researchers to want to take up this area of study. The power of any individual – journalist, scholar or critic – to shape the news might be miniscule, but in the aggregate the discourses about news that develop, the boundaries that are argued for and the modes of legitimacy that are supported all shape how the news is understood as a form of cultural production operating according to certain constraints and expectations.

The adaptability of journalism's public mandate inherent in the perspectives argued for in this chapter provides a space to move beyond examinations of what journalistic authority looks like to take up suggestions for what type of journalism we want. Put slightly differently, journalism requires authority if it is to be a source of public knowledge, but the basis for this authority is plastic. Without taking for granted the past, what should the future of legitimate journalism look like? Scholars already participate in answering these questions through their work, but perhaps what is needed is a clear embrace of 'rethinking journalism' as an active goal. This position is not only reserved for the academy; the public too should advocate for what it wants from journalism. After all, journalism's need for a public mandate suggests the unending negotiation of legitimate news; this is a conversation that should involve everyone – and journalism studies especially – as active participants and not as detached observers.

References

Abbott, A. (1988). *The system of professions: An essay on the division of expert labor.* Chicago: University of Chicago Press.

Anderson, C. W. (2013). What aggregators do: Towards a networked concept of journalistic expertise in the digital age. *Journalism, 14*(8), 1008–1023.

Barnhurst, K. G., & Nerone, J. C. (2001). *The form of news: A history.* New York: Guilford Press.

Berkowitz, D. (2000). Doing double duty: Paradigm repair and the Princess Diana what-a-story. *Journalism, 1*(2), 125–143.

Bourdieu, P. (1993). *The field of cultural production: Essays on art and literature.* New York: Columbia University Press.

Bourdieu, P. (2005). The political field, the social science field, and the journalistic field. In R. Benson & E. Neveu (Eds.), *Bourdieu and the journalistic field* (pp. 29–47). Cambridge: Polity Press.

Broersma, M. (2010). Journalism as performative discourse: The importance of form and style in journalism. In V. Rupar (Ed.), *Journalism and meaning-making: Reading the newspaper* (pp. 15–35). Cresskill, NJ: Hampton Press.

Carlson, M. (2006). War journalism and the 'KIA journalist': The cases of David Bloom and Michael Kelly. *Critical Studies in Media Communication, 23*(2), 91–111.

Carlson, M. (2007). Making memories matter: Journalistic authority and the memorializing discourse around Mary McGrory and David Brinkley. *Journalism, 8*(2), 165–183.

Carlson, M. (2009). Media criticism as competitive discourse: Defining reportage of the Abu Ghraib scandal. *Journal of Communication Inquiry, 33*(3), 258–277.

Carlson, M. (2012). 'Where once stood titans': Second-order paradigm repair and the vanishing US newspaper. *Journalism, 13*(3), 267–283.

Carlson, M. (2014). Gone, but not forgotten: Memories of journalistic deviance as metajournalistic discourse. *Journalism Studies, 15*(1), 33–47.

Carlson, M. (2015a). The many boundaries of journalism. In M. Carlson & S. C. Lewis (Eds.), *Boundaries of journalism* (pp. 1–18). New York: Routledge.

Carlson, M. (2015b). Keeping watch on the gates: Media criticism as advocatory pressure. In T. Vos & F. Heinderyckx (Eds.), *Gatekeeping in transition* (pp. 163–179). New York: Routledge.

Carlson, M. (2016a). Metajournalistic discourse and the meanings of journalism: Definitional control, boundary work, and legitimation. *Communication Theory.* In press.

Carlson, M. (2016b) *Journalistic authority: A relational approach.* New York: Columbia University Press. In press.

Carlson, M., & Berkowitz, D. A. (2012). Twilight of the television idols: Collective memory, network news and the death of Walter Cronkite. *Memory Studies, 5*(4), 410–424.

Carlson, M., & Lewis, S. C. (Eds.). (2015). *Boundaries of journalism.* New York: Routledge.

Carvalho, A. (2007). Ideological cultures and media discourses on scientific knowledge: Re-reading news on climate change. *Public Understanding of Science, 16*(2), 223–243.

Coddington, M. (2012). Defending a paradigm by patrolling a boundary: Two global newspapers' approach to WikiLeaks. *Journalism & Mass Communication Quarterly, 89*(3), 377–396.

Dahlgren, P. (1992). Introduction. In P. Dahlgren & C. Sparks (Eds.), *Journalism and popular culture* (pp. 1–23). London: Sage.

Eason, D. (1986). On journalistic authority: The Janet Cooke scandal. *Critical Studies in Mass Communication, 3*(4), 429–447.

Ekström, M. (2002). Epistemologies of TV journalism: A theoretical framework. *Journalism, 3*(3), 259–282.

Finlay, L. (2002). Negotiating the swamp: The opportunity and challenge of reflexivity in research practice. *Qualitative research, 2*(2), 209–230.

Friedman, R. B. (1990). On the concept of authority in political philosophy. In J. Raz (Ed.), *Authority* (pp. 56–91). New York: NYU Press.

Gieryn, T. F. (1983). Boundary-work and the demarcation of science from non-science: Strains and interests in professional ideologies of scientists. *American Sociological Review, 48*(6), 781–795.

Gieryn, T. F. (1995). Boundaries of science. In S. Jasanoff, G. E. Markle, J. C. Peterson & T. Pinch (Eds.), *Handbook of science and technology studies* (pp. 393–443). Newbury Park, CA: Sage.

Gieryn, T. F. (1999). *Cultural boundaries of science: Credibility on the line*. Chicago: University of Chicago Press.

Gray, J. A., Jones, J. P., & Thompson, E. (Eds.). (2009). *Satire TV: Politics and comedy in the post-network era*. New York: NYU Press.

Haas, T. (2006). Mainstream news media self-criticism: A proposal for future research. *Critical Studies in Media Communication, 23*(4), 350–355.

Haas, T., & Steiner, L. (2002). Fears of corporate colonization in journalism reviews' critiques of public journalism. *Journalism Studies, 3*(3), 325–341.

Harcup, T. (2011). Hackademics at the chalkface: To what extent have journalism teachers become journalism researchers? *Journalism Practice, 5*(1), 34–50.

Hindman, E. B. (2005). Jayson Blair, the *New York Times*, and paradigm repair. *Journal of Communication, 55*(2), 225–241.

Höpfl, H. M. (1999). Power, authority and legitimacy. *Human Resource Development International, 2*(3), 217–234.

Kitch, C. (2002). Anniversary journalism, collective memory, and the cultural authority to tell the story of the American past. *Journal of Popular Culture, 36*(1), 44–67.

Lamont, M., & Molnár, V. (2002). The study of boundaries in the social sciences. *Annual Review of Sociology, 28*(1), 67–95.

Lewis, S. C. (2012). The tension between professional control and open participation: Journalism and its boundaries. *Information, Communication & Society, 15*(6), 836–866.

Lincoln, B. (1995). *Authority: Construction and corrosion*. Chicago: University of Chicago Press.

Matheson, D. (2004). Weblogs and the epistemology of the news: Some trends in online journalism. *New Media & Society, 6*(4), 443–468.

Meltzer, K. (2009). The hierarchy of journalistic cultural authority: Journalists' perspectives according to news medium. *Journalism Practice, 3*(1), 59–74.

Nemeth, N. (2003). *News ombudsmen in North America: Assessing an experiment in social responsibility*. Westport, CT: Praeger.

Reese, S. D. (1990). The news paradigm and the ideology of objectivity: A socialist at the Wall Street Journal. *Critical Studies in Media Communication, 7*(4), 390–409.

Reich, Z. (2012). Journalism as bipolar interactional expertise. *Communication Theory, 22*(4), 339–358.

Ryfe, D. M. (2012). *Can journalism survive: An inside look at American newsrooms*. Cambridge: Polity Press.

Schudson, M. (1982). The politics of narrative form: The emergence of news conventions in print and television. *Daedalus, 111*(4), 97–112.

Schudson, M., & Anderson, C. W. (2008). Objectivity, professionalism, and truth seeking in journalism. In K. Wahl-Jorgensen & T. Hanitzsch (Eds.), *Handbook of journalism studies* (pp. 88–101). New York, Routledge.

Singer, J. B. (2003). Who are these guys? The online challenge to the notion of journalistic professionalism. *Journalism, 4*(2), 139–163.

Soloski, J. (1989). News reporting and professionalism: Some constraints on the reporting of the news. *Media, Culture & Society, 11*(2), 207–228.

Starr, P. (1982). *The social transformation of American medicine*. New York: Basic Books.

Turner, G. (2009). *Ordinary people and the media: The demotic turn*. London: Sage.

Usher, N. (2010). Goodbye to the news: How out-of-work journalists assess enduring news values and the new media landscape. *New Media & Society, 12*(6), 911–928.

Vos, T. P., Craft, S., & Ashley, S. (2012). New media, old criticism: Bloggers' press criticism and the journalistic field. *Journalism, 13*(7), 850–868.

Waisbord, S. (2013). *Reinventing professionalism: Journalism and news in global perspective.* Cambridge: Polity Press.

White, J. B. (1995). *Acts of hope: Creating authority in literature, law, and politics.* Chicago: University of Chicago Press.

Winch, S. P. (1997). *Mapping the cultural space of journalism: How journalists distinguish news from entertainment.* Westport, CT: Praeger.

Zelizer, B. (1992). *Covering the body: The Kennedy assassination, the media, and the shaping of collective memory.* Chicago: University of Chicago Press.

Zelizer, B. (1993). Journalists as interpretive communities. *Critical Studies in Media Communication, 10*(3), 219–237.

4

THE DISRUPTION OF JOURNALISTIC EXPERTISE

Zvi Reich and Yigal Godler

Journalism, as Lord Northcliffe has once noted, is a 'profession whose business is to explain to others what it personally does not understand'. Northcliffe's statement is probably excessively vitriolic, especially when compared to the accepted wisdom (Gans, 2003; Maier, 2005; Miller, 2009). However, it is directed at one of journalists' main weaknesses as mediators of information: limited expertise in the subject matter of coverage. In what follows we argue that the current crisis of the Western media is also a crisis of journalistic expertise in the subject matter of the news they cover. Moreover, even if journalistic expertise remained constant in a post-industrial society characterized by growing complexity, it would still leave journalists in a state of relative knowledge-inferiority. This chapter invites scholars, journalists and journalism educators to rethink journalistic expertise. Such rethinking may prove valuable because of the significance of journalistic expertise for democracy and public knowledge, and because the crisis avails an opportunity to see in a new light the past idealizations and the nostalgic reminiscences about a 'golden age' of journalistic expertise.

We posit that journalistic expertise was always a compromise between the knowledge constraints and knowledge ideals of journalism training and practice. It was always shaped by the divergent backgrounds and contradictory interests and needs of different stakeholders (e.g. employers, reporters, editors, competitors and extra-media forces such as institutions, expert sources and audiences). Under the pressures of these stakeholders' actual and perceived needs and expectations, journalistic expertise cannot function as an exclusively epistemic phenomenon, but rather reflects political, cultural, organizational, operational and image-related forces. Obviously, no expertise is free of non-epistemic factors (Fantl and McGrath, 2009); however, journalistic expertise is relatively more malleable at the hands of non-epistemic forces due to its lack of an esoteric knowledge base and journalists' dependence on news sources, who tend to lead the reporter–source tango dance (Gans, 2003).

Still, Northcliffe's characterization illuminates some of the contradictions and paradoxes which often lurk behind journalistic expertise in the subject matter of news or underlie the extent to which journalists know 'what they are talking about' (Collins and Evans, 2007, p. 2). The contradictory nature of journalistic expertise has been noticed by prominent scholars, who argue that 'journalism seems to simultaneously make a grandiose knowledge claim (that it possesses the ability to isolate, transmit, and interpret the most publicly relevant aspects of social reality) and an incredibly modest one (that really, most journalists are not experts at all but are simply question-asking generalists)' (Schudson and Anderson, 2009, p. 96).

It is important to distinguish here between journalists' expertise in the subject matter of news from their expertise in the practice of journalism. For instance, to cover a new reform in the environmental protection agency which is presented at a press conference, a journalist is required to possess some expertise in environmental issues, as well as some expertise in covering press conferences. Although the two kinds of expertise partly interact, the present chapter focuses on expertise of the first kind, as it is the expertise which eventually shapes the knowledge of journalists and news audiences in public affairs.

Expertise and journalistic change

Because the knowledge of experts in any field is not easy to formalize or verbalize, as most sociologists and researchers of expertise acknowledge (Collins and Evans, 2007; Dreyfus and Dreyfus, 2000; Eyal, 2013), the elucidation of journalistic expertise is a worthwhile scholarly endeavour. In terms of the sociology of knowledge and expertise research, journalistic knowledge may constitute a 'capacity to get a task accomplished better and faster because one is more experienced' (Eyal, 2013, p. 869), a form of tacit knowledge, a 'diagnostic accuracy' (Norman *et al.*, 2006) vis-à-vis specific social and political problems and situations, as well as a capacity to assess subject-specific information thoughtfully and efficiently. These may amount, in the context of journalism practice, to what Donsbach has dubbed 'subject competence', embodying knowledge 'sufficiently deep so that the structure of the field is understood and the main actors are known', as well as 'knowledge-based reporting' and the habit of providing 'evidence that is always tested against alternative explanations' (2014, p. 668). Moreover, journalistic expertise at its best may be conceptualized through the help of the Aristotelian notion of *phronesis*, which, according to Flyvbjerg, 'involves judgments and decisions made in the manner of a virtuoso social and political actor' (2001, p. 2). We adopt here the proposal of sociologists of science Harry Collins and Robert Evans (2007), who originally sought to describe what sociologists of science know about science. In the journalistic context, we are referring to the journalists' mastery of the discourse and judgements of experts in fields which they have covered for years, while constantly interacting with expert sources.

Take health reporting as an example – a news beat characterized by some of the most intricate scientific knowledge. With a few exceptions, such as the *New York*

Times and CNN, journalists covering health are rarely trained physicians. Clearly, the health reporter's expertise in medicine falls short of the expertise possessed by a medical unit director in a hospital and yet it is obvious that after years of sustained journalistic work, this health reporter knows 'something' about the subject, surpassing the knowledge of most of his or her news audiences. The central questions tackled in this chapter are precisely what is this 'something'? What has happened to this 'something' in recent years given far-reaching societal, technological and economic changes? And what does the future hold for journalistic expertise in the subject matter?

Below we offer several interrelated arguments. First, according to a mapping that will be offered at the core of this chapter, the forces shaping journalistic expertise can be seen across five continua, each of which embodies a dialectic battle between the forces of greater and lesser expertise. Second, in recent years, following economic, technological and organizational changes, there has been an overall shift across all five continua towards lesser expertise and a greater emphasis on its image-related aspects. Third, in the future, the conflicting elements of journalistic specialization and non-specialization are likely to persist. Thus, it is more urgent to develop novel ways to optimize and cope with non-specialization rather than to lament its arrival. Finally, the research agenda for the coming years should give more focus to journalistic expertise that, according to our mapping, may reflect not only on what journalists know, and the extent to which their accounts are susceptible to manipulations, pseudo-expertise, errors and misinformation, but also on their levels of adversariality and the extent to which audiences trust public institutions (Pew Research Center, 2013). Without further empirical studies, it would be very difficult to determine if the crisis of journalistic expertise that has taken place in recent years had been the cause of the crisis plaguing journalism in this period (Anderson, Bell and Shirky, 2012; Downie and Schudson, 2009), its consequence or some combination of both.

The consequence of the crisis is that journalistic expertise vis-à-vis the subject matter of news is eroding. Despite heavy cutbacks,[1] which exacted a major toll on the labour-intensive system of news beats (Nikunen, 2014; Skovsgaard and van Dalen, 2013), existing scholarly evidence regarding opening holes in the news net of expertise are mostly anecdotal (Lublinski, 2011; Nikunen, 2014; Skovsgaard and van Dalen, 2013). Yet, we know that many beats were unified, closed down and replaced by the establishment of 'team-based systems and general reporting without specific areas of expertise' (Nikunen, 2014, p. 875). Specific areas, such as science reporting, investigative reporting, business, arts, lifestyle and statehouse reporting in the US media, have shrunk notably (Houston, 2010; Lublinski, 2011; Nolan and Setrakian, 2013; Pew Research Center, 2008), significantly shortening the employment duration of relatively informed reporters (Nikunen, 2014; Nolan and Setrakian, 2013). If a single beat has not been a guarantee of expertise, assigning one reporter to three different beats, as is often done today, is surely a guarantee that expertise will be lacking. Efforts to fill the void created by the declining beats include single-subject news organizations (Nolan and Setrakian, 2013) and academic forces such as The Conversation,[2] a collaborative online project of journalists and academics providing informed, evidence-based news analysis. News organizations such as the *New York Times* (NYT, 2014) and the *Financial Times* (Lamont, 2014) point to a redeployment around newly opened journalistic positions which are not necessarily anchored in subject matter, but in various technological platforms. Against this backdrop, both journalists and scholars lament the decline – sometimes even 'the death' – of the news beat (Brumfiel, 2009; Dick, 2012; Nikunen, 2014). Furthermore, under accelerating news cycles, mounting competition and work pressures, the remaining journalists are undergoing a process of deskilling (Nygren, 2008; Örnebring, 2010; Ursell, 2004), and can decreasingly resist second-hand materials produced by third parties with vested interests, such as the PR industry and NGOs (Lewis, Williams and Franklin, 2008).

But journalistic expertise could also be one of the causes behind journalism's present predicament, as it has always been a crisis waiting to happen. In other words, journalism has never been in a position to achieve mastery of complex subject matter (Gans, 1979; Hess, 1981; Tuchman, 1978), and its range and efforts had always fallen short of the index of potential topics in the world (Bennett, 2003). Over time, as modern society grows in specialization and complexity (Urry, 2005), the limitations of journalistic expertise may lead to a value drop in the eyes of crucial stakeholders (Anderson, Bell and Shirky, 2012; Downie and Schudson, 2009), such as the broad public and specifically news consumers.

The proposed model of journalistic expertise presented in Figure 4.1 was collated and integrated from disparate literatures in journalism studies and the sociology of knowledge. The model encompasses dialectical continua over which journalistic expertise has oscillated throughout the years and continues to oscillate today, further summarizing two dynamics which shape contemporary journalistic expertise. The 'shaping forces' of journalistic expertise indicate how it is moulded through five specific oscillations: between intra-organizational and external expertise; between specialization and general reporting; between interactions with sources' conceptual schemes and those of the audiences; between journalists' specialization and their responsibility vis-à-vis assigned news beats; and between the substance of expertise and its public image or attribution. These continua reflect forces and pressures mediated by organizational coping mechanisms in the face of contradictory demands. The crisis of recent years, denoted by the larger arrow in Figure 4.1, marks an overall rightward shift across all five continua, a movement that epitomizes: greater reliance on external expertise of sources, more general reporting, more emphasis on audience interaction and on the news beat as a domain of responsibility, as well as greater importance of attributed expertise. Unpacking these shifts constitutes the analytic core of this chapter.

Between reliance on intra-organizational and external resources of expertise

News coverage has been shaped through a dialectic of internal and external expertise for quite some time. In other words, the level of expertise expressed in news

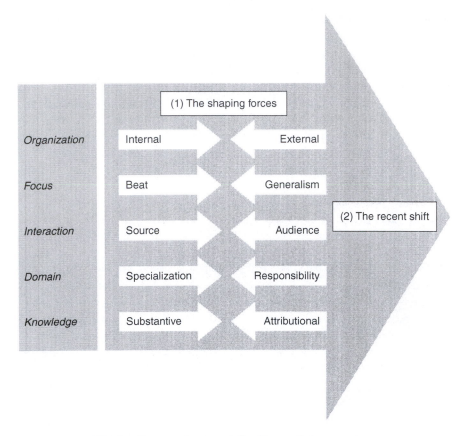

FIGURE 4.1 Shaping forces and recent shift of journalistic expertise

Note: the shaping forces (1) represent five contradictory powers, whose interplay has always moulded journalistic expertise. The recent shift (2) marks the movement of the entire system to the right, following the transformation of the news environment

products constituted a fusion between journalistic understanding vis-à-vis the subject matter with which the news item dealt and the expertise of the sources which were interviewed or consulted to produce the news item. What is taking place now, with the decline in the number of beat reporters and in their professional experience, is a pendulum movement towards greater dependence on external expertise. Greater reliance on external experts is not a result of abandoning the notion of expert reporting as journalism's core business. Instead, it is opted for because it became too costly; news organizations experienced a growing disillusionment regarding their capacity to cover the flow of traditional and emerging topics using a network of dedicated reporters with real expertise in their fields in the face of a progressively shrinking journalistic workforce (Pew Research Center, 2008).

Journalism is an unusual factory because it is capable not only of obtaining raw materials free of charge (Gans, 1979), but also of tapping gratis extra-organizational expertise. While other commercial and public institutions surely use external experts, they do so under different circumstances. Their experts normally expect financial rewards, do not lend their expertise with the same intensity and frequency (Barthelemy, 2003; Connelly and Gallagher, 2004; Oshri, Kotlarsky and Willcocks, 2007), do not respond as quickly and do not receive broad public exposure (Caulfield, 2004; Lewison, Tootell, Roe and Sullivan, 2008; Miller, 2009). Journalism, conversely, rewards its expert sources with fame and status.

News organizations cannot rely exclusively on the expertise of their specialist reporters, however informed they are. Hence, they learned to draw on a two-tier system of expertise: a paid-for network of reporters, who had developed some expertise in the field to which they were assigned, and a network of external experts, who were relied upon when needed, free of charge.

Under mounting commercial and organizational pressures, which shrink the intra-organizational resources of expertise, external expertise is likely to play a growing role both in the news and behind the scenes in production. The harbingers of this process can already be seen in the rise of single-subject news organizations, which strive to close the holes resulting from specific declining news beats (Nolan and Setrakian, 2013). Likewise, disappearing investigative reporting (Houston, 2010) and calls to media organizations to increase cooperation with external providers of content and with public authorities so as to increase direct communication with the public (Anderson, Bell and Shirky, 2012, p. 19) reflect the burgeoning of external expertise. In addition, the rising cooperation with NGOs (Powers, 2015) as well as investigative initiatives such as ProPublica, which are willing to contribute their work to other news organizations, indicate this growing dependence.

The balance of power between external and internal expertise may shift in the coming years, especially in news beats that have been merged or abolished. Of special interest here are the patterns of initiative-taking. As long as journalists took the initiative and contacted the vast majority of the expert sources interviewed (Albæk, 2011; Esser and Umbricht, 2014), they could control the identity of the experts, maintain editorial supervision and some critical distance. On the other hand, expert-initiated contacts may favour pseudo-experts, self-appointed experts, experts with an axe to grind and specialists who work in organizations with strong public relations apparatuses. In a world of rising expertise, news organizations need external expert sources more than ever. However, in order to provide quality information, news organizations and journalists are not exempt from fostering internal expertise. This would allow them not only to choose wisely between available experts and pseudo-experts, and better traverse disputed territory, but crucially would enable them to avoid uncritical and indiscriminate reliance on their versions and studies.

Between expertise and generalism

Journalistic expertise has long been a dialectic interplay between specialization and generalism. Its generalism did not reside merely in the obvious spaces occupied by general reporters, those 'who cover everything … and therefore appear on many different turfs' (Gans, 2003, p. 131), but also in a largely generalistic editorial oversight. Even among specialist reporters, which were assigned news beats that necessitated expertise, generalism had a rather strong foothold, since the boundaries of any predefined beat was challenged by the endless flow of variegated, miscellaneous, hybrid and multidisciplinary events and topics. However, in recent years, the pendulum has leaned more towards generalism.

Gaye Tuchman's pioneering insight that in journalism 'each specialist must be a generalist' (1978, p. 67) has been adopted by other prominent scholars such as Gans (1979) and Hess (1981), who have acknowledged this during the heyday of the news beat. Thus, White House reporters, to use Gans' (1979) example, may be specialists in White House politics, but they constantly find themselves in a position of being generalists vis-à-vis a variety of specific issues and policies the president deals with from day to day. As Tuchman put it, 'newsmen, in general, see themselves as "specialists in knowing, gathering and processing general knowledge"' (1978, p. 25, citing Kimball, 1967). According to Patterson, today's journalists 'cannot be expected to become experts' (2013, p. 77). It is worth noting the complex and misleading role of news beats – the dominant methodology of Western news media since the late nineteenth century (Anderson, 2012) in assigning permanent reporters to thematic beats (such as police, science, politics, the environment and business) or regional ones (Washington, Moscow or Baghdad). This specialization dovetailed a specialization in the wider society, including the specialization of medicine which occurred around the same time (Weisz, 2003).[3] Beat reporting is neither synonymous with nor a guarantee of expertise. A journalist may suffer from ignorance even while covering a permanent news beat and develop expertise without any permanent beat whatsoever. However, despite their serious shortcomings of encouraging conformity, co-optation and political status quo (Fishman, 1981; Gans, 1979; Reich, 2012; Sigal, 1973), news beats served as a facilitator and common carrier of familiar and desirable standards of journalistic expertise.

Contrary to a superficial first impression, it is not that news organizations couldn't employ higher levels of expertise. They had no such desire. In order to achieve a series of organizational interests, they preserved the generalistic element even among their best expert reporters. The main interests included coping with a torrent of changing subject matter even within relatively well-defined fields. Another goal was to maintain a versatile and affordable journalistic workforce, which could be employed at acceptable salaries (Hess, 1981). Such a workforce would lend itself more easily to rotation from one assignment to another and from one beat to another (Nikunen, 2014). It would also be capable of accommodating changes in 'governmentality' (Foucault, 1980; Manning, 2001), that is, administrative and structural changes in the society which led to changes in the focus of news. Not least, news organizations would guarantee greater relevance to wider segments of the population while avoiding excessively esoteric, 'insider' reporting (Gans, 2003). They would also be better positioned to close the gap between the complexity of the world and the ever-limited workforce (Bennett, 2003; Hess, 1981; Urry, 2005).

Even in journalism, whose professional status remains questionable (Örnebring, 2010; Schudson and Anderson, 2009; Zelizer, 2004), no one really becomes an expert overnight. To determine how long it would take, studies of expertise suggest 'magic numbers' – roughly 10,000 hours of sustained practice before the age of 18 in cases of professional athletes, chess players and virtuoso musicians (Ericsson, Krampe and Tesch-Römer, 1993; Gladwell, 2008; Howe, 2001; Levitin, 2011), 17 years in the case of pianists and 15 years in the case of Olympic swimmers (Sosniak, 1990). No systematic data is available for journalism. However, according to Reich (2012), journalistic expertise is not only a matter of time. Its development necessitates a neatly circumscribed field which is not a federation of too many subfields, as well as meticulous news-gathering strategies which aren't hand-to-mouth journalism, but systematically aspire to wider margins of information-gathering beyond the minimum necessary for the nearest news item in order to attain breadth and depth of knowledge in the field.

What, then, is the meaning of a rising generalism in terms of information quality? Obviously, beats without fixed reporters are expected to receive lesser and shallower coverage, contain more errors and emphasize trivial details at the expense of in-depth reporting. A less obvious epistemic cost, according to Gans (1979), is the tendency of general assignment reporters to consult fewer knowledgeable sources in cases of controversies, since they are not only less aware of all contesting parties (or that there are contesting parties at all), but are also afraid of collapsing in the face of contradictions stemming from excessive information-gathering. In addition, one of the most interesting questions to explore in the coming years is whether the shrinking expertise results in a more conformist or in a more adversarial tone of reporting, and if this adversariality would be grounded in specific knowledge or in blanket cynicism (Patterson, 2013). The challenge of employment models which are being developed inside and outside of mainstream news organizations is therefore to find new syntheses between the flexibility and critical mindset of general reporters, on the one hand, and the informed coverage of beat reporters, on the other.

Between expert-centred and audience-centred 'interactional expertise'

Journalism has always been pressed between the need to communicate with expert sources and the need to communicate with the news audience. These distinct interlocutors, possessing different sets of knowledge, can be viewed as two poles of expertise: one pole which fed on expert sources' professional knowledge, such as natural sciences, politics or economics, and another pole which represented the needs and preferences of news-consuming audiences, which were mostly laymen, requiring an accessible and lucid presentation of information. Lately, however, the push of the audience pole of interactionism has received a boost from a composite of new economic and marketing trends, which are discussed throughout the chapter.

According to sociologists of scientific knowledge, it is possible to compare the relationship between journalists and expert sources to the relationships between sociologists of science and the scientists with whom they interact as part of their observations. Both the journalists and the sociologists can be viewed, under particular circumstances, as 'interactional experts' (Collins and Evans, 2007, p. 35), as opposed to the scientists, who are regarded as 'contributory experts' (2007, p. 60), that is, people who are capable of using methods and making discoveries by virtue of their specialized knowledge, competences and skills. In this sense, the interactions (of sociologists with scientists and journalists with their sources) are not merely a learning channel, but also a form of knowledge. To test whether a practitioner had indeed gained full interactional expertise, Collins and Evans propose a Turing-like test, in which a panel of contributory experts (i.e. scientists) send identical subject-specific questions (in writing) to pairs of sociologists and scientists seated in different rooms. If the panel cannot determine on the basis of the jargon and professional judgments exhibited by both respondents who is the scientist and who is the sociologist, then the sociologist may be regarded as an interactional expert.

Adapting their model to the journalistic context, Reich (2012) argues that unlike scientists, journalists are characterized by a 'bipolar' interaction – on the one hand, with expert sources, and on the other, with audiences. Unlike other professions, which also need to communicate with audiences, news consumers are not only permanently present in journalists' daily activity and in every unit of their professional input and output, but the overwhelming majority of them are outsiders to most news' subject matter, lacking education and the relevant background. Thus, news reporting necessitates a dramatic mediation effort vis-à-vis both poles – that is, a mediation between expert sources and audiences that shapes the scope, the limits and the language of reporting.

The growing emphasis on audience interaction draws on a series of technological, commercial, cultural and social developments taking hold more or less in the same period: a growing financial pressure to woo the fragmenting audiences, an impulse to expand the reach of the medium and foster more dialogic relationships between news producers and 'the people formerly known as the audience' (Rosen, 2006); the emergence of audience metrics that gave rise to a new regime of media 'click-o-nomics' (Karlsson and Clerwall, 2013, p. 69, see also Anderson, 2011); and new forms of digital storytelling and data presentation that were marked by harbingers such as the *New York Times* 'Snow Fall' story (2012) and *The Guardian* data blog (see also Barnhurst, 2003; Finke and Schudson, 2014). In addition, a novel set of journalistic competences prioritizes technological skills and puts emphasis on journalists' connectivity, distribution capacities, audience construction, optimization of news stories, virality enhancement and new ways of self-branding (Albeanu, 2014), as detailed hereafter in the substantive-attributional continuum.

In the future, it would be interesting to examine in greater detail how the journalistic skill-set incorporates audience interaction and source interaction competences, as these are expressed in the formats and contents of news, as well as in the priorities of different newsrooms and their policies of hiring, evaluating, promoting and firing editorial workers and in their day-to-day conduct. Simultaneously, journalists may want to explore new ways of balancing the two skill-sets by finding more audience-friendly sources without necessarily compromising on their quality and technical knowledge.

Between the news as a domain of expertise and as a domain of responsibility

Assigning a journalist to cover a new beat, often performed 'by a stroke of the Editor's pen' (Tunstall, 1971, p. 116), has always been an ambivalent act. On the one hand, it reflected an ambitious epistemic aspiration that the journalist would become an expert in his or her domain. On the other hand, it reflected a modest administrative and logistic expectation that this will be no more than his or her domain of responsibility, i.e. an area in which the journalist is expected to serve as a personally identifiable address for source materials, minimizing defeats vis-à-vis competitors and maximizing exclusive stories. What happened in recent years has been an increasing emphasis on the beat as a domain of responsibility.

Since journalism is a pragmatic achievement (Kovach and Rosenstiel, 2007; Ward, 2005, 2009), the creative ambivalence of whether to expect real expertise or sheer responsibility enabled media organizations to evade the need to develop coherent epistemic standards for journalistic expertise, which are not only elusive but also change from one field to another and under different circumstances. The expertise–responsibility continuum explains why even when news organizations have to merge different news beats, many of them still adhere to the beat doctrine – an occupational lens thorough which the world is seen as an abstract index of beats (Fishman, 1981; Galbraith, 2010; Scanlan, 2014). However, beyond any epistemic role, news beat expertise is also a logistical-economic matter for news organizations (Anderson, 2012). It is designed to create an effective flow of information between social networks of individual sources, institutions and journalistic addressees that cover their words and deeds on a regular basis. The habitual and repetitive coupling between both networks renders daily coordination between reporters, sources and topics of coverage unnecessary, enabling journalistic self-management without newsroom intervention, shortening learning curves and enabling a gradual accumulation of contacts and knowledge in the subject matter.

In the coming years it would be interesting to examine the impact of the changing mix of expertise and responsibility on the division of labour within news organizations. This may include the analysis of the expectations towards specialist and non-specialist reporters versus their performance, the mix of single beat reporters versus multi-beat reporters, as well as the professional and ethical aspects of covering beats without regular reporters.

Between substantive and attributional expertise

Journalists have often moved between a reasonable level of understanding vis-à-vis the substance of news coverage and the tendency to present themselves to the public as authoritative and qualified knowers even when their understanding fell short. In recent years, news organizations and individual journalists have made use of a series of attri-butional and image-making means to promote their perceived authority among their audiences and have engaged in performances of knowledgeability, as discussed below.

Though we oppose the dominant tendency in the scholarly literature to focus on the attributional and social constructionist aspects of journalistic expertise (Collins and Evans, 2007; Ericson, 1998; Schudson and Anderson, 2009; Tuchman, 1978) because it avoids addressing the slippery parts of substantive expertise, we do not ignore the pervasiveness of image-making vis-à-vis journalistic expertise. Virtually all professions must invest not only in expert knowledge but also in boosting their public legiti-macy (Abbott, 1988; Eyal, 2013; Weber, 2009). However, image maintenance seems especially prominent in journalism: first, since most journalists lack formal education in their domain of coverage, as well as credentials and certificates that are used by potential clients to assess the expertise of professionals (Collins and Evans, 2007); and, second, since most news audiences are not in a position to evaluate the quality of most news even after consuming them (McManus, 1992). Hence, both news organizations and their employees enjoy broader leeway in constructing journalists' image as experts – among other things – through a series of branding attributes.

The ways in which journalistic expertise is established are especially illustrative in television news, where they are expressed in a series of rhetorical and format-ori-ented practices, such as the positioning of specialist reporters in newscasts, introduc-ing them as knowledgeable investigators of reality, interviewing them and engaging them in seemingly professional and technical discussions (Clayman, 2001; Clayman and Heritage, 2002; Ekström and Lundell, 2011; Roth, 2002). Other media use not only bylines (Reich, 2010; Reich and Boudana, 2014), but also super bylines, cap-tions, titles and sub-headlines. These may include: 'headlines in print and promotions for upcoming stories … the association of the delivery of the news with a particular anchor or reporter…to signal what the news product will contain' (Hamilton, 2011, p. 215). More recently, reporters themselves started launching self-branding cam-paigns, mainly by communicating with their audiences on social media and telling behind-the-scenes stories, trying to establish themselves as experts (Lawrence et al., 2014; Molyneux and Holton, 2014; Revers, 2014).

In the future, it would be interesting to examine how lay audiences gauge jour-nalistic expertise, which image-related and substantive signs are relied upon in these assessments, and whether audience assessments of expertise are at all comparable to how specialist reporters and expert sources evaluate the expertise of journalists in their domains of coverage. Meanwhile, journalists ought to carefully consider which communication practices can promote greater transparency vis-à-vis news audiences, as avoiding the temptation to convey knowledgeability when projecting one's actual expertise can be equally illuminating.

Conclusion

The crisis that journalism has undergone in recent years also marks a crisis of exper-tise in the domains of coverage. Paradoxically, as most of society continues to grow in complexity (Urry, 2005) and specialization (Hardwig, 1991; Posner and Posner, 2009; Sokal, 2008), journalism is undergoing a trend of de-specialization. This growing discrepancy may diminish the relevance of media in post-industrial societies, where citizens need more expert knowledge to effectively address the growing complexities in numerous aspects of their lives.

To flesh out the forces and pressures implicated in shaping journalistic expertise, the processes it undergoes during the crisis and the likely consequences for the future, this chapter has proposed conceptualizing journalistic expertise as a dialectic interplay across five continua, noting shifts that may have implications for journalistic epistemology, organizational theory and journalism history. With respect to epistemology and truth-seeking, it appears that the shift away from specialization undercuts further journalism's already troubled ethical commitment of being a 'discipline of verification' (Kovach and Rosenstiel, 2007, p. 71), as fact-finding becomes subservient to increasingly more practical and logistical goals which direct journalistic resources away from reality depiction and towards commercial and audience considerations. This does not mean that truth-seeking ceased to be the centrepiece of journalism. In the coming years journalists may draw more consciously on pragmatic conceptions of truth, which regard truth not as a finite point of professional achievement, but rather as a never-ending process, requiring greater flexibility and openness vis-à-vis partial, scattered and contradictory information (Ward, 2005, 2009).

Organizationally, it appears as though considerations of management – which become more acute at times of crisis (Giddens, 2009; Green, 2006) – produce de-specialization across different branches of industrial production. Indeed, the decline in journalistic specialization is mirrored in other models of organizational management, as has been the case in Japanese manufacturing corporations such as Nissan and Panasonic (White and Trevor, 1983), that implemented policies of rotation between positions in order to foster a more well-rounded and adaptive workforce. The *Financial Times* maintains a similar policy vis-à-vis its reporters (Lamont, 2014).

Historically, it appears as though journalism has gone from little or no specialization late in the nineteenth century to a significant level of specialization as mandated by the Modernist ideal of expertise in the second half of the twentieth century, and since then began to gradually de-specialize, reaching what could be described as a 're-generalization' since the start of the new millennium. This reflects on the nature of journalism as many news beats are unique embodiments of specific 'microcultures', 'social spaces', 'subspaces' or 'subuniverses' (Marchetti, 2005, p. 65), which entail constant accumulation of specific knowledge in particular fields.

Neither specialized nor non-specialized reporting is likely to disappear from the journalistic scene. The tug of war between them is likely to persist. Hence, instead of lamenting the demise of journalistic expertise, combined teams of practitioners, educators and scholars should work out new ways to attract, train, hire, employ and promote not only the traditional expert reporters, but also a new species of 'enlightened generalists' who will be purposefully trained to rotate between several beats, to demonstrate steeper learning curves and to use shortcuts, digesting new topics quicker, yet well-enough to cover them intelligently and with minimal errors, in a fashion reminiscent of the aforementioned Japanese industrial model. In the widely debated phrase of US Secretary of Defense Donald Rumsfeld, these 'enlightened generalists' will be trained to cover not only the 'known knowns' and 'known unknowns', but also the 'unknown unknowns', and develop sensitivities towards complexities and nuance even in fields in which they have no in-depth and technical understanding.

To fine-tune the observations of this chapter and to pursue its recommendations for future exploration, studies should devote themselves to an extensive mapping of journalistic expertise across time, media and news cultures. News organizations, which have a vested interest in concealing the growing holes in their 'news nets' (Tuchman, 1978), aren't expected to go out of their way to cooperate with these studies. Yet they are essential to expose the strengths and weaknesses of current journalistic expertise and the distribution of its shrinking resources; to identify emerging and dying beats, and map the common distribution of single-beat versus multi-beat reporting areas, the considerations for merging beats or leaving them as standalones and the ways in which reporters in different fields are evaluated today as compared to the past.

Future studies may inform decisions of training, hiring, appointing and promoting, and explore comparatively patterns of expertise among science-laden beats, such as health, the environment and high-tech, and more 'commonsensical' beats, such as police or regional reporting. They should also record and typify the methods which news organizations develop to cover areas in which they have no regular reporters, using aggregation, cooperations and third-party materials. Their findings may inspire mutual consultations between all relevant parties – publishers, editors, journalism educators, heads of news agencies, representatives of single-issue websites, etc. – in order to find the optimal division of labour and outsource less necessary or cancelled domains of coverage, at least until the pendulum swings back to more favourable conditions for journalistic expertise.

Notes

1   Between 2000 and 2012, the journalistic workforce in the USA shrank by 18,400. In the UK, about 27–33 per cent of the journalistic workforce or roughly 15,000–20,000 had been laid off between 2001 and 2010. http://www.journalism.org/media-indicators/newsroom-workforce.
2   https://theconversation.com/au.
3   According to Weisz (2003), specialization in medicine had matured c. 1880 with the number of specialized departments in London's hospitals having more than doubled in the preceding decades – around the time when the first harbingers of the news beat in the USA and the UK had made their appearance.

References

Abbott, A. (1988). *The system of professions: An essay on the division of expert labor*. Chicago: University of Chicago Press.

Albeanu, C. (2014). *A collection of tools and resources for journalists for 2014.* Retrieved from https://www.journalism.co.uk/news/a-collection-of-tools-and-resources-for-journalists-from-2014/s2/a563429/.

Albæk, E. (2011). The interaction between experts and journalists in news journalism. *Journalism, 12*(3), 335–348.

Anderson, C. W. (2011). Deliberative, agonistic, and algorithmic audiences: Journalism's vision of its public in an age of audience transparency. *International Journal of Communication, 5,* 529–547.

Anderson, C. W. (2012). What happens when news organizations move from 'beats' to 'obsessions'?. *Nieman Lab.* Retrieved from http://www.niemanlab.org/2012/09/what-happens-when-news-organizations-move-from-beats-to-obsessions/.

Anderson, C. W., Bell, E., & Shirky, C. (2012). *Post-industrial journalism: Adapting to the present.* New York: *Columbia Journalism School.*

Barnhurst, K. G. (2003). The makers of meaning: National Public Radio and the new long journalism, 1980–2000. *Political Communication, 20*(1), 1–22.

Barthelemy, J. (2003). The seven deadly sins of outsourcing. *Academy of Management Executive, 17*(2), 87–98.

Bennett, W. L. (2003). *News: The politics of illusion.* New York: Longman.

Brumfiel, G. (2009). Science journalism: Supplanting the old media. *Nature, 458,* 274–277.

Caulfield, T. (2004). Biotechnology and the popular press: Hype and the selling of science. *TRENDS in Biotechnology, 22*(7), 337–339.

Clayman, S. E. (2001). Answers and evasions. *Language in Society, 30*(3), 403–442.

Clayman, S. E., & Heritage, J. (2002). Questioning presidents: Journalistic deference and adversarialness in the press conferences of US Presidents Eisenhower and Reagan. *Journal of Communication, 52*(4), 749–775.

Collins, H., & Evans, R. (2007). *Rethinking expertise.* Chicago: University of Chicago Press.

Connelly, C. E., & Gallagher D. G. (2004). Emerging trends in contingent work research. *Journal of Management, 30*(6), 959–983.

Dick, M. (2012). The re-birth of the 'beat': A hyperlocal online newsgathering model. *Journalism Practice, 6*(5–6), 754–765.

Donsbach, W. (2014). Journalism as the new knowledge profession and consequences for journalism education. *Journalism, 15*(6), 661–677.

Downie, L., & Schudson, M. (2009). The reconstruction of American journalism. *Columbia Journalism Review, 19.* Retrieved from http://www.cjr.org/reconstruction/the_recon-struction_of_american.php.

Dreyfus, H., & Dreyfus, S. E. (2000). *Mind over machine.* New York: Simon & Schuster.

Ekström, M., & Lundell, Å. K. (2011). The joint construction of a journalistic expert identity in studio interactions between journalists on TV news. *Text & Talk: An Interdisciplinary Journal of Language, Discourse & Communication Studies, 31*(6), 661–681.

Ericson, R. V. (1998). How journalists visualize fact. *Annals of the American Academy of Political and Social Science, 560,* 83–95.

Ericsson, K. A., Krampe, R. T., & Tesch-Römer, C. (1993). The role of deliberate practice in the acquisition of expert performance. *Psychological Review, 100*(3), 363–406.

Esser, F., & Umbricht, A. (2014). The evolution of objective and interpretative journalism in the Western press comparing six news systems since the 1960s. *Journalism & Mass Communication Quarterly, 91*(2), 229–249.

Eyal, G. (2013). For a sociology of expertise: The social origins of the autism epidemic. *American Journal of Sociology, 118*(4), 863–907.

Fantl, J., & McGrath, M. (2009). Pragmatic encroachment. In S. Bernecker & D. H. Pritchard (Eds.), *Routledge companion to epistemology* (pp. 558–568). London: Routledge.

Finke, K., & Schudson, M. (2014). The rise of contextual journalism, 1950s–2000s. *Journalism*, *15*(1), 3–20.

Fishman, M. S. (1981). *Manufacturing the news: The social organization of media news production*. University Microfilms.

Flyvbjerg, B. (2001). *Making social science matter: Why social inquiry fails and how it can succeed again*. Cambridge: Cambridge University Press.

Foucault, M. (1980). *Power/Knowledge: Selected interviews and other writings by Michel Foucault, 1972–77*. New York: Pantheon.

Galbraith, K. (2010). The capriciousness of beat. *Nieman Reports*. Retrieved from http://niemanreports.org/articles/the-capriciousness-of-beats/.

Gans, H. J. (1979). *Deciding what's news: A study of CBS Evening News, NBC Nightly News, Newsweek, and Time*. Evanston, IL: Northwestern University Press.

Gans, H. J. (2003). *Democracy and the news*. Oxford, UK: Oxford University Press.

Gans, H. J. (2009). Can popularization help the news media. In B. Zelizer (Ed.), *The changing faces of journalism. Tabloidization, technology, and truthiness* (pp. 17–28). London & New York: Routledge.

Giddens, A. (2009). *Sociology* (6th ed.). Raanana, Israel: Open University of Israel (Hebrew).

Gladwell, M. (2008). *Outliers: The story of success*. London: Hachette UK.

Green, F. (2006). *Demanding work: The paradox of job quality in the affluent economy*. Princeton: Princeton University Press.

Hamilton, J. T. (2011). *All the news that's fit to sell: How the market transforms information into news*. Princeton: Princeton University Press.

Hardwig, J. (1991). The role of trust in knowledge. *Journal of Philosophy*, *88*(12), 693–708.

Hess, S. (1981). Washington reporters. *Society*, *18*(4), 55–66.

Houston, B. (2010). The future of investigative journalism. *Daedalus*, *139*(2), 45–56.

Howe, M. J. (2001). *Genius explained*. Cambridge: Cambridge University Press.

Karlsson, M., & Clerwall, C. (2013). Negotiating professional news judgment and 'clicks'. *Nordicom Review*, *34*(2), 65–76.

Kimball, P. (1967). Journalism: Art, craft or profession? In K. Lynn *et al.* (Eds.), *The professions in America*. Boston: Beacon Press, 242–260.

Kovach, B., & Rosenstiel, T. (2007). *The elements of journalism: What newspeople should know and the public should expect*. New York: Three Rivers Press.

Lamont, J. (2014). *The FT's digital strategy*. A Reuters Institute for the Study of Journalism audio lecture, March 17. Retrieved from: http://podcasts.ox.ac.uk/ft-s-digital-strategy.

Lawrence, R. G., Molyneux, L., Coddington, M., & Holton, A. (2014). Tweeting conventions: Political journalists' use of Twitter to cover the 2012 presidential campaign. *Journalism Studies*, *15*(6), 789–806.

Levitin, D. J. (2011). *This is your brain on music: Understanding a human obsession*. London: Atlantic Books Ltd.

Lewis, J., Williams, A., & Franklin, B. (2008). A compromised fourth estate? UK news journalism, public relations and news sources. *Journalism Studies*, *9*(1), 1–20.

Lewison, G., Tootell, S., Roe, P., & Sullivan, R. (2008). How do the media report cancer research? A study of the UK's BBC website. *British Journal of Cancer*, *99*(4), 569–576.

Lublinski, J. (2011). Structuring the science beat: Options for quality journalism in changing newsrooms. *Journalism Practice*, *5*(3), 303–318.

Maier, S. R. (2005). Accuracy matters: A cross-market assessment of newspaper error and credibility. *Journalism & Mass Communication Quarterly*, *82*(3), 533–551.

Manning, P. (2001). *News and news sources*. London: Sage.

Marchetti, D. (2005). Subfields of specialized journalism. In R. Benson & E. Neveu (Eds.), *Bourdieu and the journalistic field* (pp. 64–82). Cambridge: Polity Press.

McManus, J. H. (1992). What kind of commodity is news. *Communication Research*, *19*(6), 787–805.

Miller, B. (2009). What does it mean that PRIMES is in P? Popularization and distortion revisited. *Social Studies of Science*, *39*(2), 257–288.

Molyneux, L., & Holton, A. (2014). Branding (health) journalism: Perceptions, practices, and emerging norms. *Digital Journalism*, *3*(2), 225–242.

Nikunen, K. (2014). Losing my profession: Age, experience and expertise in the changing newsrooms. *Journalism*, *15*(7), 868–888.

Nolan, K., & Setrakian, L. (2013). *Seeking the single-subject news model. Tow Center for Digital Journalism*. New York: Columbia Journalism School.

Norman, G., Eva, K., Brooks, L., & Hamstra, S. (2006). Expertise in medicine and surgery. *Cambridge Handbook of Expertise and Expert Performance*, 339–353.

Nygren, G. (2008). *Is there a de-professionalization of journalism?* Paper for the conference: Nordic Media in Theory and Practice.

NYT. (2014, March 14). *Innovation report*. Retrieved from http://www.scribd.com/doc/224608514/The-Full-New-York-Times-Innovation-Report#scribd.

Örnebring, H. (2010). Reassessing journalism as a profession. In S. Allan (Ed.), *The Routledge companion to news and journalism* (pp. 568–575). New York: Routledge.

Oshri, I., Kotlarsky, J., & Willcocks, L. P. (2007). Managing dispersed expertise in IT offshore outsourcing, lessons from Tata consultancy services. *MIS Quarterly Executive*, *6*(2), 53–65.

Patterson, T. E. (2013). *Informing the news*. New York: Vintage.

Pew Research Center. (2008). *Changing content*. Journalism Project. Retrieved from http://www.journalism.org/2008/07/21/changing-content/.

Pew Research Center. (2013). *Public trust in government: 1958–2013*. Retrieved from http://www.people-press.org/2013/10/18/trust-in-government-interactive/.

Posner, R. A., & Posner, R. A. (2009). *Public intellectuals: A study of decline*. Cambridge, MA: Harvard University Press.

Powers, M. (2015). The new boots on the ground: NGOs in the changing landscape of international news. *Journalism*. doi:1464884914568077.

Reich, Z. (2010). Constrained authors: Bylines and authorship in news reporting. *Journalism*, *11*(6), 707–725.

Reich, Z. (2012). Journalism as bipolar interactional expertise. *Communication Theory*, *22*(4), 339–358.

Reich, Z., & Boudana, S. (2014). The fickle forerunner: The rise of bylines and authorship in the French press. *Journalism*, *15*(4), 407–426.

Revers, M. (2014). The augmented newsbeat: Spatial structuring in a Twitterized news ecosystem. *Media, Culture & Society*, *37*(1), 3–18.

Rosen, J. (2006). The people formerly known as the audience. *PressThink*, 27 June. Retrieved from http://journalism.nyu.edu/pubzone/weblogs/pressthink/2006/06/27/ppl_frmr.html.

Roth, A. L. (2002). Social epistemology in broadcast news interviews. *Language in Society*, *31*, 355–381.

Scanlan, C. (2014). Beat reporting: What does it take to be the best? *Poytner*. Retrieved from http://www.poynter.org/news/media-innovation/5229/beat-reporting-what-does-it-take-to-be-the-best/.

Schudson, M., & Anderson, C. (2009). Objectivity, professionalism, and truth seeking in journalism. *Handbook of Journalism Studies*, 88–101.

Sigal, L. V. (1973). *Journalists and officials*. Lexington: DC Heath And Company.

Skovsgaard, M., & van Dalen, A. (2013). The fading public voice: The polarizing effect of commercialization on political and other beats and its democratic consequences. *Journalism Studies*, *14*(3), 371–386.

Sokal, A. (2008). *Beyond the hoax: Science, philosophy and culture.* Oxford: Oxford University Press.

Sosniak, L. A. (1990). From tyro to virtuoso: A long-term commitment to learning. *Proceedings of the 1987 Denver Conference: Music and child development.*

Tuchman, G. (1978). *Making news.* New York: Free Press.

Tunstall, J. (1971). *Journalists at work.* London: Constable.

Urry, J. (2005). The complexity turn. *Theory Culture and Society,* 22(5), 1–14.

Ursell, G. (2004). Changing times, changing identities: A case study of British journalists. In T. E. Jensen & A. Westenholz (Eds.), *Identity in the age of the new economy* (pp. 34–55). Northampton, MA: Edward Elgar.

Ward, S. J. (2005). *Invention of journalism ethics: The path to objectivity and beyond.* Quebec: McGill-Queen's Press-MQUP.

Ward, S. J. (2009). Truth and objectivity. *Handbook of Mass Media Ethics,* 71–83.

Weber, M. (2009). *From Max Weber: Essays in sociology.* New York: Routledge.

Weisz, G. (2003). The emergence of medical specialization in the nineteenth century. *Bulletin of the History of Medicine,* 77(3), 536–574.

White, M. R. M., & Trevor, M. (1983). *Under Japanese management: The experience of British workers.* London: Heinemann Educational Publishers.

Zelizer, B. (2004). *Taking journalism seriously: News and the academy.* Thousand Oaks, CA: Sage.

5

NEWS MEDIA, SEARCH ENGINES AND SOCIAL NETWORKING SITES AS VARIETIES OF ONLINE GATEKEEPERS

Rasmus Kleis Nielsen

In recent years, we have seen headlines like '4 Changes Google is Making and How They Affect Content Creation', 'Facebook Says Publishers Shouldn't Fret about News Feed Changes' and 'Twitter "Related Headlines" Deliver News'. They illustrate how search engines and social networking sites are becoming more and more integral to how people find information online and, in the process, change the conditions for content production. News is amongst what people find when they search and is one of the things they encounter, share and discuss on social media. All over the world, search engines and social media are increasingly important ways of finding and accessing news online, and off-platform publishing directly to these intermediaries is a growing phenomenon. The complex relationships between these different sites and the paths that people carve between them are important examples of how 'old' and 'new' media are intertwined in today's media systems (Chadwick, 2013). It is crucial to understand these relationships to understand journalism today, its place in a changing media environment, how people get the news produced by journalists and how that content is filtered.

The purpose of this chapter is to outline a general approach to think about the role of search engines and social networking sites amongst the varieties of online gatekeeping found in an increasingly digital and networked media environment, identifying some of the key questions this raises for journalism studies in particular. Linear, scheduled television remains the most widely used and most important source of news for most people in most countries today and print is still an important part of some people's cross-media repertoires (Newman *et al.*, 2015). But digital media have overtaken print in many places, rival television in some groups, and continue to grow in importance. News media organizations are still central in the digital environment as *producers* of news, as disseminators of news across platforms, and as brands with privileged access to the socially and symbolically significant category 'news' (as distinct from the broader terms 'content' or 'information'). But people increasingly *access* and *find* their digital content not only directly via news media organizations' own websites and apps, but also via a variety of other gateways, including search engines and social networking sites. As Emily Bell (2014) has underlined, this means news organizations no longer enjoy the kind of control over their relationship with users that broadcasters and print publishers formerly had. This is a major challenge for journalists and for news media organizations, who have to assess and act on both threats (loss of control over editorial content, data and revenue) and opportunities (to reach wider and different audiences and to increase their visibility). It is also a challenge for journalism studies scholars, who have often privileged these two types of actors (journalists and news media) as objects of analysis while paying less attention to other parts of the information cycle and the role played by other actors in the dissemination and filtering of news.

How do we best understand this new, mixed media environment? The information scientist Karine Nahon has argued that understanding how information flows today requires, amongst other things, a much broader notion of what she calls 'network gatekeeping' and has called for collaboration across media and communication studies, information management systems research, legal studies and more to examine a wide range of gates, gatekeeping processes, gated (those subject to gatekeeping), gatekeeping mechanisms and network gatekeepers (Barzilai-Nahon, 2008, 2009). But the complexity and vastness of the general topic means it is worth carving out a set of more specific questions concerning varieties of online gatekeeping that are particularly pressing for journalism studies. Doing that is my aim here.

News and gatekeepers in a digital era

I start from the premise that we know that most people still rely primarily on news produced by established news media organizations when following current affairs, but also that, in the online environment, they increasingly arrive at news via, for example, search engines and social networking sites (Newman *et al.*, 2015; Nielsen and Schrøder, 2015). What does this new variety and these new combinations mean for how we understand the flow of news online? I will suggest as a starting point that we conceptualize news media organizations as *primary gatekeepers* and expand the notion of *secondary gatekeepers* (Shoemaker and Vos, 2009; Singer, 2014) to encompass the growing variety of ways in which people find news published by news media organizations.

Primary gatekeepers are in this context gatekeepers who *by filtering information and publishing* decide what is specifically what we commonly understand as 'news'. This is an important and distinct form of gatekeeping because most people clearly still distinguish between information more broadly and news specifically, in large part on the basis of its origins with organizations with privileged access to the cultural category of 'news' (Newman *et al.*, 2015). Secondary gatekeepers are those that filter *already available* news content. The distinction relies on a socially significant difference between broad categories like 'content' or 'information' (including lay categories of 'interesting stuff', 'things I did not know') and the narrower category 'news'. The difference is not absolute, it is not clear-cut and it will mean different things for different people. Not everyone will accept everything published by journalists working for news media as news (crosswords, lifestyle sections, opinion columns, etc.). Some will consider some content published by other actors as news (whether friends, professional colleagues or politicians, etc. that they follow online). The ambiguity surrounding the issue is recognized in, for example, the *Oxford English Dictionary*, which under 'news' notes the broad use of 'news to me' (novelties, accounts of events and occurrences, tidings), but also highlights how the term has, especially in the twentieth century, increasingly come to mean 'news' in the narrower sense of information published or broadcast by news media.

The social significance of 'news', what is news to whom and why, especially in a changing media environment, clearly calls for more analysis, but indirectly, survey data suggests that the category may be more stable and in a way conventionally understood by many more people than one might think. If we assume that everyone regularly gets news in the broad sense of 'news to me' from personal conversation and contacts, whether online or offline, it is striking how few respondents identify anything but news media organizations – primary gatekeepers – as frequently used and important sources of news when asked, even though they will often identify many other channels – secondary gatekeepers – as important ways of accessing and finding news (see e.g. Newman *et al.*, 2015). As people increasingly get news via various new digital intermediaries – Google, Facebook, Twitter, etc. – but the news that they get (and consider as specifically 'news') is still predominantly produced by news media organizations – newspapers, broadcasters, online-only news providers – we need to understand how these different varieties of online gatekeeping interact in our digital and networked information environment.

The advantages of looking at varieties of online gatekeeping in terms of combinations of different kinds of primary (editorial) and secondary (for example, what I below term link-based, affinity-based or community-based) gatekeeping can be mapped onto three key questions that have been central to gatekeeping research for more than half a century: (1) what are the gates?; (2) how are they kept?; (3) how many people rely on which gates?

First, in terms of what the gates are, a focus on combinations of and interactions between primary and secondary gatekeepers incorporates new digital intermediaries into our understanding of the flow of information without losing sight of the continued importance of conventional gatekeepers. This is a key point. That Google, Facebook, Twitter and the like have become *more* important does not necessarily mean that broadcasters, newspapers and other news media have become *less* important in absolute terms. They still produce the bulk of what people consider to be and consume as news. The roles and relationships change, but it is not a zero-sum game.

Second, in terms of how the gates are kept, by expanding the notion of secondary gatekeeping beyond the idea of 'audience gatekeeping' developed by Shoemaker and Vos (2009) and others to capture the role of ordinary people in information dissemination to also include a variety of link-based and affinity-based ways in which new digital intermediaries filter information online, the approach highlights how different gatekeeping processes are *combined* in a new media environment. This does not entail the 'collapse of gatekeeping' that some predicted the rise of digital would entail (e.g. Williams and Carpini, 2004). Instead, what we see is an increasing variety of online gatekeepers, some of whom occupy particularly powerful positions.

Third, in terms of how many rely on which gates, the broad approach outlined here opens up the possibility to empirically examine the relative importance of different particular (primary and secondary) gatekeepers and different combinations of gatekeepers in particular cases and countries. In contrast to a political communication literature that has been particularly interested in how the growth of digital information and communication technologies facilitates disintermediation and allows for direct communication (e.g. Bennett and Manheim, 2006), the approach proposed here highlights the parallel growth of new, digital intermediaries. In contrast to a journalism studies literature that is (understandably) particularly focused on the role of journalists specifically, including studies of how they have appropriated and 'normalized' digital technologies (e.g. Mitchelstein and Boczkowski, 2009), the approach proposed here emphasizes how the continued importance of editorially based forms of primary gatekeeping goes hand-in-hand with the increasing importance of a variety of new ways of secondary gatekeeping that involves no journalistic judgements, even as they increasingly influence how we get our news.

Gatekeeping theory meets the digital media environment

The notion of 'gatekeeping' is premised on a transmission model of communication where information is seen as flowing from one point to another via various channels and where at particular points along the way, some information is passed on and some is not. These points are the gates. Gatekeeping research is focused on the selection of information for dissemination – what is privileged and passed on, what is relegated and less likely to be transmitted, and what is blocked altogether? Gatekeeping in this sense is enabling because, on the one hand, it is necessary to distinguish the signal from the noise in a world of information overload, yet, on the other hand, it is constraining – one person's selection is another's censorship. Analytically, the main questions raised by gatekeeping research are three. First, what are the gates? Second, how are the gates kept? Third, how many people rely on which gates?

The idea of gatekeeping comes from the social psychologist Kurt Lewin, who developed a holistic approach to the question of how information flows from senders to receivers through a variety of different gates positioned within a wider field and subject to a variety of different forces. It has been used in information science for a long time to study all sorts of gatekeepers in informal social settings, in formal organizations and beyond, but traditionally journalism studies scholars have been interested specifically in *editorial* gatekeeping – in how combinations of professional news considerations, organizational norms and other factors shape what is published as news. The pioneering study was David Manning White's (1950) research on how

'Mr. Gates' – the wire editor in a small-town newspaper – on the basis of personal preferences, space constraints or a perception that an issue had already been dealt with decided which of the many items provided by the wire services to use, and which not, in each day's edition.

The notion of news media as gatekeepers, every day making hundreds of decisions about which stories to publish and which to kill, came to be one of the central theoretical concepts of the nascent field of journalism studies and has since been developed into a multilayered approach, especially by Pamela Shoemaker with various collaborators (e.g. Shoemaker and Vos, 2009). A popular model today is her 'levels of analysis' approach to gatekeeping, focusing on individual, routine, organization, institution and system levels (depending on the object of analysis). The focus in the extensive literature on journalistic gatekeeping has typically been on particularly important news organizations, especially those that are not only gates, but also strategically placed gates, i.e. local monopoly newspapers, wire agencies that influence a wide range of other media, papers of record that set an agenda for other media and an elite audience, and widely watched television news bulletins.

In recent years, the rise of new forms of digital interpersonal communication and easy sharing, especially via so-called 'Web 2.0' or social media, has led journalism studies scholars to look beyond primary gatekeepers in the newsroom to examine secondary forms of gatekeeping by ordinary people making decisions in their own life to pass on some types of information (but not others). The emphasis has been on various new forms of 'audience gatekeeping' that go beyond earlier forms of word-of-mouth rumour and everyday conversation, which scholars have long recognized as key to the flow of communication (e.g. Katz and Lazarsfeld, 1955). We have seen studies of how influential individual users on social networking sites like Twitter can play a key role in disseminating information (e.g. Jürgens et al., 2011), how 'crowds' of ordinary users can elevate content to prominence (e.g. Meraz and Papacharissi, 2013) and of how media organizations have in turn responded and tried to develop strategies and tools to retain a central position in a digital and networked media environment (e.g. Coddington and Holton, 2014).

Most of these studies of secondary gatekeepers have been resolutely focused on the role played by ordinary media users – 'the people formerly known as the audience', in Jay Rosen's elegant phrase – whether conceptualized as 'brokers', 'crowds' or 'communities'. This is in line with an intellectual tradition emphasizing the decentralizing, democratizing and participatory potential of digital technologies over the parallel development of new forms of centralization, intermediation and near-monopoly (e.g. Benkler, 2006). A few researchers have, however, outlined a broader agenda and suggested the need to consider other kinds of secondary gatekeepers. Nikos Smyrnaios (2012) has highlighted the role of 'infomediaries' in the French media system and has called attention to how publishers actively seek to use sites like Google and Facebook to reach potential users, while simultaneously accepting this involves the intermediaries effectively filtering, aggregating and to some extent controlling the dissemination of the content. Kjerstin Thorson and Christopher Wells (2015) have suggested a research agenda for examining five different kinds of 'curation processes' that compete, intersect and overlap to shape the media experiences of networked individuals, namely journalists, strategic communicators, individual media consumers, social contacts (online and offline) and automated computer systems. Karin Barzilai-Nahon (2008, 2009) has developed a broader theory of 'networked gatekeeping', as mentioned above.

Theories of infomediation, curation and network gatekeeping all open up a wider research agenda where no actors can, in principle, be privileged in advance. This marks a return to Lewin's original holistic, distributed and multilayered conception of gatekeeping that did not presuppose mass media, near-monopolies on mediation or homogeneity across a class of gatekeepers (like a news institution), but simply focused on the filtering of information flows in networks. However, when it comes to the question of how specifically *news* flows, we are still at a stage where we can focus our investigation around the question of how people access content produced by news media organizations. It is true that people pick up information about public issues from many different sources well beyond professionally produced journalistic content. But when asked in surveys where they get 'information about current affairs', people – the same ones who also use social media and the like for many other purposes – still overwhelmingly point to the output of conventional news media organizations (see Newman *et al.*, 2015). This is why it is important to retain the idea of gatekeeping – information is being filtered in consequential ways, in part by primary gatekeepers that define some information as news and in part by a range of secondary gatekeepers that filter who gets what, when and where. This brings us to three of the key questions varieties of online gatekeeping presents for journalism studies.

What are the gates?

A first question is: what are the gates? Through which gates and combinations of gates do people access news in the digital and networked information environment? Things are developing so quickly, and so differently for different groups and in different contexts, that an almost ethnographic approach seems necessary.

The simplest scenario is a digitized version of the pre-digital environment, where someone reads an article on the website of a news organization or watches a television news bulletin over a Smart TV or IPTV/streaming app. In these cases, the gatekeeping process is one journalism studies understands well. Journalists and editors work to filter the flow of information coming in, they make decisions about what makes it into the news, and make this available to users via various platforms. It is worth highlighting that this kind of transmission, via one or more primary gatekeepers but with a clear distinction between a sender and a number of receivers, is very much still with us. This is in part due to the continuing centrality of television news, even in an increasingly digital media environment, and in part because a significant subset of online news use consists of people going directly to their preferred providers. The combination of brand loyalty, news routines and newsrooms promoting what they consider news means that this kind of editorially 'gatekept' flow of information is still very important, especially when it comes to areas most people do not actively seek out or share information about. (This is, for example, how Western audiences primarily encounter various jihadists, while individuals with sympathy for the cause can seek out information in other ways and circumvent editorial gatekeepers in the West; see Hoskin and O'Loughlin, 2011). Much has been made in the 1990s and the early 2000s about the interactive and participatory potential of digital technologies, but it seems clear that a growing proportion of internet use today is recognizable lean-back use where people seek out content they like, consume it and leave it at that – with little in terms of commenting, sharing or creating. Watching *BBC Newsnight* via the iPlayer is different from watching it on linear scheduled television, but not necessarily more participatory.

But a growing range of more complex scenarios are increasingly integral to many people's news media use. Online gatekeeping is not only varied, but also increasingly takes the form of combinations of different forms of primary and secondary gatekeeping. Various examples include: (1) accessing news published on one site and then aggregated or curated by another; (2) finding news published by one site via a search engine like Google or perhaps Microsoft's Bing (which also provides search results for Yahoo!); (3) accessing news published by one site via a social networking site like Facebook or Twitter; (4) getting news published by one site via other people, forwarded by email, direct message or posted on social networking site profiles, via a messaging application like Snapchat, WhatsApp, etc. More examples could be given and we will surely see new forms in the future with wearable technology and the internet-of-things developing.

All of the above scenarios, and more contemporary and future ones beyond them, can be combined in any number of ways: news story published, seen on an aggregator, sent to a friend; news story published, sent by a friend, then posted to social networking site; news story published, found via search engine, then posted, etc. Clearly, they can all go offline and travel via other channels too – a friend tells you about a story, you go home, search for it (or search on your mobile device) and find an article about it published somewhere. You see something on television, post about it on Facebook, someone responds and draws your attention to a news story, etc. Each one of this multitude of different journeys represents an empirical challenge for journalism studies researchers (how does news travel, through which gates and combinations of gates). Simply inventorying the most important combinations for different groups for different purposes in different contexts in different countries is a pressing empirical concern if we want to understand the ways in which news is disseminated and identify the gates it passes through on the way.

The classic model of such more varied understandings of the flow of communication is Elihu Katz and Paul F. Lazarsfeld's idea of the 'two-step flow', a scenario where some people pay close attention to media on certain issues and in turn disseminate this information person-to-person in their primary groups (Katz and Lazarsfeld, 1955). An important contemporary complement to this model is W. Lance Bennett and Jarol Manheim's notion of a 'one-step flow', a scenario where a combination of increased self-selection, more individualized media use, and more instrumentally effective personalization of content and targeting of communication means that more information flows from sender to receiver without the mediating influence of informal 'opinion leaders' and primary groups or other communities (Bennett and Manheim, 2006). Both of these models identify important forms of gatekeeping. In the two-step flow, there are (primary) editorial gatekeepers – well understood by journalism studies – and informal opinion leaders on various topics working as (secondary) 'audience gatekeepers' passing on some, but not all, information to other people in their primary groups. (This phenomenon is increasingly studied on social networking sites like Twitter too.) In the one-step flow, there are editorial gatekeepers (and other senders of information), but also an explicit recognition of the increasing importance of various forms of databases in tailoring and targeting information – and thereby filtering it – to individual receivers. In the current environment, these important forms of gatekeeping are increasingly supplemented by new digital intermediaries like the search engines and social networking sites that rose to prominence after the one-step and two-step models were developed and now occupy central positions in multi-step flows. The examples briefly outlined above suggest the many more steps some news now flows through and the importance of considering the wider variety of forms of online gatekeeping that have emerged.

How are the gates kept?

Given that news increasingly travels through a wider variety and various combinations of gates, a second question for journalism studies is: how are the gates kept? What is filtered out and what is let through? What is privileged and what is relegated? As noted from the outset, all forms of gatekeeping are enabling and constraining at the same time. News media cannot publish everything; they have to filter, to decide what is news. Search engines cannot give you everything; they have to filter, to decide what might be most relevant for you. Social media cannot show you everything; they have to filter, to decide what appears on your screen. Your offline and online peers cannot send you everything; they have to filter, to decide to forward some things, not others. There are no neutral display decisions.

To begin to understand the main varieties of online gatekeeping in our current digital and networked media environment, I will suggest a typology based on different ways of filtering content, in turn associated with different organizational forms, with different aims and interests, and with different histories. All of them are to some extent black boxes, where the actual social and technical filtering processes are hard to access for researchers and can sometimes only be estimated on the basis of a combination of outcomes and indirect evidence. The typology is not exhaustive and the realities of online gatekeeping will no doubt evolve in the future, but it provides a way of thinking of difference and similarities in terms of how different gates are kept and links together some of the important work that has been done historically as well as more recently by journalism studies scholars interested in various forms of gatekeeping. The four types are *editorial gatekeeping, link-based gatekeeping, affinity-based gatekeeping* and *audience gatekeeping*. Especially the first and increasingly the last type have been researched in journalism studies, but this is less so with the two others, though they are increasingly important.

Editorial gatekeeping is gatekeeping as we know it from an extensive literature in journalism studies – it is gatekeeping done by journalists and editors who, on the basis of largely shared professional values and operating with particular organizational structures and everyday work routines, make decisions about what is and what isn't news for their particular news medium. Most studies suggest a core of commonality in cross-organizational news media institutions, professional communities and national journalistic cultures, but of course also recognize that there is variation both at the individual level (journalists and editors differ), at the organizational level (media outlets differ) and at the system level (kinds of media differ). Editorial gatekeeping is associated with news media as organizational forms (both private and public) as well as professional interests developed around the concept of 'news', and has its historical origins in the news industry and journalism as a vocation.

Link-based gatekeeping is the filtering of information primarily on the basis of the number and quality of links to a page. The approach was pioneered by Larry Page and Sergey Brin as they developed what became Google Search's PageRank algorithm, operating on the assumption that the number and quality of inbound links to a website gave an indication of its importance. Similar types of link-analysis are central to Robin Li's RankDex algorithm behind what became the Chinese search engine Baidu, to Microsoft's search engine Bing as well as the TrustRank algorithm developed by Yahoo! (All of these search engines use multiple methods to rank order results, including, for example, semantic analysis of keywords and tags, personalization on the basis of search histories and other personal information, as well as data about location, etc.) Link-based gatekeeping is associated more than anything with Google as the world's most important search engine service provider, with professional roots in computer science and engineering where 'news' is simply a form of information, and has its historical origins in a technology industry that has grown up and emerged apart from legacy media companies and the journalistic profession.

Affinity-based gatekeeping is the filtering of content based in large part on user affinity with other users, a factor central to the EdgeRank algorithm used by Facebook in evolving forms to filter content for users' news feeds till 2011. (The name has since been abandoned. The algorithm lives on.) Affinity in this context means the amount a user has interacted with another user in the past by clicking on their links, liking or commenting their posts etc., as well as the number of mutual Facebook friends. The higher the affinity, the more the algorithm prioritizes the material of one user in another user's news feed. (As with many things in life, this relationship can be unequal – the score is one-way, so my affinity score for you will not be the same as your affinity score for me.) Affinity-based gatekeeping is associated especially with Facebook as the currently dominant social networking site in most countries, is again professionally rooted in computer science and engineering, and again has historical roots in the technology sector rather than in media or journalism.

Audience-based gatekeeping is a broad category centred on how media users can filter content in concert, whether through conscious collaboration or as a result of their combined individual actions. This is what Jane Singer (2014) has called 'user-generated visibility' – not so much people's ability to create content as their ability to selectively pass content on. This phenomenon obviously pre-dates digital technologies with the long-acknowledged centrality of informal opinion leaders and social communication in the flow of information. But it is an increasingly important and diverse phenomenon in the online world where people (selectively) share news via emails, listservs, bulletin boards, blogs and various forms of social networking sites. Audience-based gatekeeping is associated with many kinds of user-led or bottom-up activities, is generally seen as located outside specific organizational forms or professional communities and has no clear shared historical origin (even though individual examples of user-generated visibility may and some of the technologies used are the same).

It is important to underline that all of these types of online gatekeeping are what scholars of science and technology like Bruno Latour (2005) call 'socio-technical' practices, and that distinctions between, say, social and algorithmic forms of gatekeeping are likely to lead us astray. As Bozdag (2013, p. 209) notes, 'humans not only affect the design of the algorithms, but they also can manually influence the filtering process even when the algorithm is operational'. At any given point in time, the balance between the social, human factor and the algorithmic, technological factors will vary from very labour-intensive, manual gatekeeping to more automated processes. Almost every kind of gatekeeping imaginable involves both social and technical elements. (White's original study of 'Mr. Gates' and his small-town newspaper in part had to do with handling the technological constraints of space that came with publishing in print.) Editorial forms of gatekeeping increasingly integrate and rely upon algorithms for highlighting some forms of content over others, both in editorially led processes relying on various forms of audience measurements (Anderson, 2011) and by using recommendation engines akin to those pioneered by Amazon, Netflix and Apple's iTunes ('If you like this, you might also like…') (Thurman, 2011). Link-based forms of gatekeeping and affinity-based forms of gatekeeping are most clearly technical, but routinely involve human interventions, such as when people at Google or Facebook, in response to particular events, their own international calculations or various forms of external pressure, intervene to alter the results of otherwise automated processes (Bell, 2014). Audience gatekeeping is clearly social, driven by individuals and based on communities, but also, of course, increasingly technologically enabled when practised online.

These varieties of online gatekeeping are also historical, evolving phenomena. Just as journalism studies has long documented how editorial forms of gatekeeping have changed over time, we should expect to see link-based, affinity-based and audience gatekeeping to develop and change. New players will emerge, old ones will fade away (like AltaVista and MySpace) and existing ones will evolve. Google, for example, makes several hundreds of changes to its search algorithm every year and by now relies on more than 200 signals when ranking search results. Most of the changes are minor, but there are also major, often named, changes, like 'Google Panda' (2011–, designed to return higher-quality sites to the top of search results), 'Google Penguin' (2012–, designed to punish so-called 'black hat' search optimization schemes) and 'Google Pigeon' (2014–, designed to increase the ranking of local listings in a search). The Google Panda update is particularly important for news media, as one of the criteria used to determine whether a site is 'high quality' is whether it provides 'original content or information, original reporting, original research, or original analysis'.[1] This change greatly reduced traffic to content farms like Demand Media while placing many established news media brands in more privileged positions. Similarly, Facebook's News Feed, initially generated by the EdgeRank algorithm on the basis of three factors (user-based affinity, a variable for weighting content and a time-based decay parameter), has continually evolved and now reportedly takes more than 100,000 factors into account. Like Google, Facebook has changed its algorithm in ways that help some news media, for example, by privileging content originating with sites deemed particularly timely, relevant and trustworthy in an explicit attempt to ensure users see more high-quality articles and fewer viral memes in their News Feed.[2]

It is worth noting here that both Google and Facebook, as they have moved into more systematically considering news as part of their overall operations, have implicitly operated with a distinction between news organizations (new and old) as primary gatekeepers that by filtering and publishing information decide what is news, and themselves as secondary gatekeepers that operate to make news available to their users in ways that are accessible, relevant, timely, useful, etc. The stated goal of Google's aggregator Google News, for example, is 'to organize all the world's news and make it accessible to its users, while providing the best possible experience for those seeking useful and timely news information'.[3] Mark Zuckerberg's stated goal for Facebook's News Feed is, in his own words, 'to build the perfect personalized newspaper for every person in the world'.[4] Here both Google and Facebook talk about news, and prioritize journalistic content to provide this (increasingly displaying snippets, including headlines, short summaries, images, etc.). Both operate specifically as secondary online gatekeepers, filtering news originally produced by other, primary gatekeepers (as well as by users, strategic communicators like corporations, governments, NGOs, politicians, etc.). Neither of them produce news themselves.

Who relies on what gates?

Given the variety of forms and combinations of online gatekeeping, and how each of them operate, a third question for journalism studies is: who relies on what gates? This is an often rapidly evolving area (Google and Facebook have grown to occupy incredibly central positions in relatively few years; both now report more than one billion active users globally) and one where systematic data is often hard to come by. The Reuters Institute Digital News Report, an annual survey of online news users across a range of countries, provides one overview. Table 5.1 below gives

TABLE 5.1 Top ways of finding news online by country (2015)

	Denmark	France	Germany	Italy	Japan	UK	USA
Directly via brand	54%	27%	26%	20%	15%	52%	36%
Search engine	29%	40%	45%	66%	54%	32%	40%
Social media	38%	21%	20%	33%	14%	28%	35%

the 2015 figures for how many online news users in a subset of high-income, high internet-use countries (representing a range of different media systems) report having used news media websites, search engines and social networking sites as ways of accessing and finding news within the last week.

The numbers document the continued centrality of branded news media websites in many of these countries, but also the importance of especially search engines (given the market share in these countries, that effectively means Google, though the situation in, for example, China and South Korea is different). Social media are also a gateway to news for a significant minority, but are not as widely used in this way as news websites and search engines. Most respondents report finding news online in more than one way. The cross-national differences documented here are pronounced, and this is an area that clearly calls for more systematic analysis in terms of the interplay between different kinds of media systems, how much people trust conventional news media brands, etc. (Nielsen and Schrøder, 2015).

Separate questions in the Reuters Institute Digital News Report survey ask about various specific social media used 'for any purpose', with a follow-up question about use 'for reading, watching, sharing or discussing news in the last week?' These two questions document the centrality of Facebook in particular across most of the countries covered compared to other social networking sites, including Twitter and YouTube. They also show that use is far more widespread than use for news, again at least implicitly suggesting – as noted above – that many respondents continue to maintain a distinction between news as 'news to me' (much of what is in, for example, people's Facebook News Feed) and 'news' more narrowly as we know it from journalism (some of what is sometimes in some people's Facebook News Feed). On average, about half the users of social networking sites like Facebook and Twitter also say they get news through these platforms (Newman *et al.*, 2015). (There are, of course, generational and socio-economic differences.)

While branded news media websites continue to be a widely used and important way of accessing news online, and are on the whole more important than search engines in several countries (and more important than social media in almost all the countries covered by the Reuters Institute Digital News Report in 2015), it is important to note that the dynamics look somewhat different when seen from the point of view of individual news media organizations. The news media as a whole – as a cross-organizational institutional phenomenon with symbolic capital, user loyalty and the resources to produce quality content – still command an absolute central place in how people find news. In some ways this is a more important place than search engines and social media, and we should not lose sight of this. But no individual news media organization has the kind of online reach that Google or Facebook has, and even the most highly visible and successful news organizations increasingly rely on referrals from other online gatekeepers (and especially these two) for traffic to their website. Most news media by now invest serious resources in reaching users via search and social (in many cases including paying for exposure on, for example, Facebook). Great increases in traffic are sometimes attributed to new search or social strategies (and careers in turn are built on developing and implementing these). But the depth and degree of their dependency is hard to gauge.[5]

Conclusion

It is clear that how people find, use and share news is changing, and that the ways in which they do so are growing more complex and less centred on the activities of journalists and news media organizations than they have been in the recent past. The purpose of this chapter has been to identify key questions raised for journalism studies by the evolving varieties of online gatekeeping involved in our current digital and networked media environment, and to outline ways of asking them and some of the stakes involved. I have argued that the distinction between primary and secondary gatekeepers – between, first, gatekeepers that, by filtering information and publishing it, constitute it as specifically 'news' and, second, gatekeepers that filter already existing content (Shoemaker and Vos, 2009; Singer, 2014) – can be usefully expanded to consider the growing number of different kinds of online gatekeepers. I have offered four types that are clearly important today, including editorial (primary) gatekeepers as well as link-based gatekeepers, affinity-based gatekeepers and a variety of audience gatekeepers that all function as secondary gatekeepers. (There are – and will be – others.) I have suggested that all of them are socio-technical processes and have underlined that they increasingly operate in combination, not as separate and parallel gates, and that the key questions they raise are familiar from a long tradition of journalism studies research – what are the gates, how are they kept and who relies on them, even as the objects of analysis are constantly changing.

The first implication of this is that we should not think of the importance of different kinds of online gatekeepers for the circulation of news as a zero-sum game. News media, in particular the news institution as a cross-organizational field, remain of central importance when it comes to the production and dissemination of news. But they are not alone. Increasingly, these primary gatekeepers, who by filtering and publishing information still seem to have privileged access to the socially significant category of 'news' (in a narrower sense than the broader 'news to me'), operate in conjunction with a variety of secondary gatekeepers that include audiences sharing material selectively, but also link-based gatekeepers like Google's search engine and affinity-based gatekeepers like Facebook's News Feed.

For some, the parallel growth in how media organizations increasingly use audience data and recommendation engines to tailor and target content to specific users, and the growth in personalization of search results and social media feeds, especially those of users with very homogeneous groups of social media connections, raise the prospects of what has been called, variously, the 'Daily Me' (Sunstein, 2009), 'filter bubbles' (Pariser, 2011), or the 'Daily You' (Turow, 2012), foregrounding different parts of the driving forces behind this, including self-selection ('me'), automated algorithms ('filters') for personalization ('bubbles') and various forms of advertiser interest in particular target individuals ('you'). The shared concern is for a situation in which we are systematically confronted with less diverse news and have less news in common. This is a potentially troubling scenario, but the approach to varieties of online gatekeeping outlined in this chapter as well as the preliminary empirical evidence reviewed suggests a less dystopian interpretation of the current situation by highlighting both the underlying and ongoing importance of relatively conventional forms of news production (with their democratic strengths and weaknesses) *and* a diversity of different forms of online gatekeeping (that in turn represent new challenges analytically, normatively and in terms of media policy; see e.g. Napoli, 2015). If we relied *only* on, say, link-based or affinity-based gateways to news online, that might be a quite troubling situation – but, in fact, most people seem to rely on a variety of different gates to news online, gates that privilege different kinds of information (Newman *et al.*, 2015).

The varieties of online gatekeeping, the diverse range of gates most people rely on and the different combinations they use in one sense suggest a quite pluralistic, perhaps even fragmented, digital and networked media environment. But at the same time, this environment, where people can pick and choose from many different news providers across many different platforms and from an increasing number of ways in which to use and engage with news, is also characterized by the rise of a very few, very large, globally important and uniquely placed digital intermediaries that increasingly have a structuring influence on the entire media environment. Google and Facebook in particular loom large today, with very popular services, wide reach and an increasingly central role in many parts of many people's everyday life. Most basically, this position has made these US-based companies *profitable*. It has also clearly made them *powerful*, both in the narrow sense that they have power over other online entities, but also in the broader sense of power as constitutive of agents and actions (we 'search' differently now, we 'friend' people differently, we 'share' things differently, etc.) and power as something that is not simply possessed by individuals and exercised over others, but suffuse society as parts of discursive and material regimes (Foucault, 1979). Finally, it is increasingly making them *political*, both in the simple sense of these companies being political actors lobbying for their interests all over the world, but also in the sense of being objects of political interest and subject to political pressures, both from democratic and non-democratic states – as seen in the long-running struggles in the US over digital rights management, recent cases like the Court of Justice of the European Union and its 'right to be forgotten' ruling, the European Commission's anti-trust proceedings against Google, as well as numerous instances of government-imposed and -encouraged outright censorship and more.

Journalism studies needs to take seriously the evolving forms of editorial gatekeeping that we know so much about, and new forms of audience gatekeeping enabled by digital technologies, but also the increasingly important role of new digital intermediaries and the various forms of link-based and affinity-based gatekeeping that they represent. As our digital and networked media environment develops, it seems increasingly clear that what we face is not the collapse of gatekeeping hypothesized by some, but a combination of evolving old and new forms of online gatekeeping, some of them with unprecedented global reach.

Notes

1 http://googlewebmastercentral.blogspot.co.uk/2011/05/more-guidance-on-building-high-quality.html.
2 https://www.facebook.com/business/news/News-Feed-FYI-Showing-More-High-Quality-Content.
3 https://support.google.com/news/publisher/answer/40787?hl=en.
4 http://uk.businessinsider.com/mark-zuckerberg-wants-to-build-a-perfect-personalized-newspaper-2014-11#ixzz3RcfWVgMr.
5 During a brief Facebook outage on 1 August 2014, traffic to news websites in the UK dropped by three per cent – less than some would have expected, given the large share of referrals Facebook accounts for. See http://blog.chartbeat.com/2014/08/04/facebook-traffic.

References

Anderson, C. (2011). Between creative and quantified audiences. *Journalism*, *12*(5), 550–566. http://doi.org/10.1177/1464884911402451.
Barzilai-Nahon, K. (2008). Toward a theory of network gatekeeping. *Journal of the American Society for Information Science and Technology*, *59*(9), 1493–1512. http://doi.org/10.1002/asi.20857.
Barzilai-Nahon, K. (2009). Gatekeeping: A critical review. *Annual Review of Information Science and Technology*, *43*(1), 1–79. http://doi.org/10.1002/aris.2009.1440430117.
Bell, E. (2014). *Silicon Valley and journalism*. Presented at the Reuters Memorial Lecture 2015, Reuters Institute for the Study of Journalism. Retrieved from http://reutersinstitute.politics.ox.ac.uk/events/silicon-valley-and-journalism-make-or-break.
Benkler, Y. (2006). *The wealth of networks*. New Haven, CT: Yale University Press.
Bennett, W. L., & Manheim, J. B. (2006). The one-step flow of communication. *The ANNALS of the American Academy of Political and Social Science*, *608*(1), 213–232 http://doi.org/10.1177/0002716206292266.
Bozdag, E. (2013). Bias in algorithmic filtering and personalization. *Ethics and Information Technology*, *15*(3), 209–227. http://doi.org/10.1007/s10676-013-9321-6.
Chadwick, A. (2013). *The hybrid media system: Politics and power*. Oxford: Oxford University Press.
Coddington, M., & Holton, A. E. (2014). When the gates swing open: Examining network gatekeeping in a social media setting. *Mass Communication and Society*, *17*(2), 1–22. http://doi.org/10.1080/15205436.2013.779717.
Foucault, M. (1979). *Discipline and punish*. New York: Vintage.

Hoskins, A., & O'Loughlin, B. (2011). Remediating jihad for Western news audiences. *Journalism, 12*(2), 199–216. http://doi.org/10.1177/1464884910388592.

Jürgens, P., Jungherr, A., & Schoen, H. (2011). Small worlds with a difference. In *Proceedings of the 3rd International Web Science Conference* (p. 21). New York: ACM. http://doi.org/10.1145/2527031.2527034.

Katz, E., & Lazarsfeld, P. F. (1955). *Personal influence.* New Brunswick, NJ: Transaction Publishers.

Latour, B. (2005). *Reassembling the social.* Oxford: Oxford University Press.

Meraz, S., & Papacharissi, Z. (2013). Networked gatekeeping and networked framing on #Egypt. *International Journal of Press/Politics, 18*(2), 138–166. http://doi.org/10.1177/1940161212474472.

Mitchelstein, E., & Boczkowski, P. J. (2009). Between tradition and change. *Journalism, 10*(5), 562–586. http://doi.org/10.1177/1464884909106533.

Napoli, P. M. (2015). Social media and the public interest. *Telecommunications Policy.* http://doi.org/10.1016/j.telpol.2014.12.003.

Newman, N., Levy, D. A. L., & Nielsen, R. K. (2015). *Reuters Institute digital news report 2015.* Oxford: Reuters Institute for the Study of Journalism. Retrieved from http://www.digitalnewsreport.org/.

Nielsen, R. K., & Schroder, K. C. (2015). The relative importance of social media for accessing, finding, and engaging with news. *Digital Journalism, 2*(4), 472–489. http://doi.org/10.1080/21670811.2013.872420.

Pariser, E. (2011). *The filter bubble.* London: Viking.

Shoemaker, P. J., & Vos, T. P. (2009). *Gatekeeping theory.* New York: Routledge.

Singer, J. B. (2014). User-generated visibility. *New Media & Society, 16*(1), 55–73. http://doi.org/10.1177/1461444813477833.

Smyrnaios, N. (2012). How does news infomediation operate online? Presented at the World Media Economics and Management Conference, Thessaloniki, Greece. Retrieved from http://nikos.smyrnaios.free.fr/Com_2012_Salonique_Smyrnaios.pdf.

Sunstein, C. R. (2009). *Republic.com 2.0.* Princeton: Princeton University Press.

Thorson, K., & Wells, C. (2015). How gatekeeping still matters. In T. P. Vos & F. Heinderyckx (Eds.), *Gatekeeping in transition* (pp. 25–44). London: Routledge.

Thurman, N. (2011). Making 'the daily me'. *Journalism, 12*(4), 395–415. http://doi.org/10.1177/1464884910388228.

Turow, J. (2012). *The daily you.* New Haven, CT: Yale University Press.

White, D. M. (1950). The 'gate keeper'. *Journalism Quarterly, 27*(4), 383–390.

Williams, B. A., & Carpini, M. X. D. (2004). Monica and Bill all the time and everywhere. *American Behavioral Scientist, 47*(9), 1208–1230. http://doi.org/10.1177/0002764203262344.

6

IS THERE A 'POSTMODERN TURN' IN JOURNALISM?

Karin Wahl-Jorgensen

This chapter considers the idea that we might helpfully draw on the conceptual tools of postmodernism to understand changes in the practices of and discourses surrounding journalism. This is a particularly urgent concern at the present moment, given the challenges to the profession and its practices. The chapter suggests that new analytical tools which have emerged in part as a result of profound changes in the profession may help us to give as much attention to instabilities, uncertainties and contestations as we have previously given to the foundational narratives of journalism and of journalism studies, and may offer new conceptual and methodological approaches for rethinking journalism and its social role and relevance as the 'primary sense-making vehicle of modernity' (Hartley, 1996).

The chapter sees evidence for a postmodern turn in a series of interlinked developments. First, the past few decades have seen a catastrophic collapse in the business model of journalism, bringing an end to the certainties and stabilities historically characterizing narratives around the profession. Second, scholars have recently begun to question the central role in democracy afforded to institutions of journalism, so central to professional discourses. Third, over the past two decades, processes of convergence have brought unprecedented changes to the production, form, content and consumption of journalism. These changes have, among other things, challenged traditional binary distinctions between objectivity and subjectivity, news and opinion, information and entertainment, producers and audiences, and professional and amateur content. By focusing on these particular changes, I do not mean to suggest that they are the only ones that need to be considered by journalism scholars. The central social role of journalism, however, stems in large part from a series of assumptions that are centrally tied to these certainties now under challenge. Journalism has historically been underpinned by its longstanding financial stability and independence; by the normative presumptions surrounding its central role in democracy; and by the ideal of objectivity in its discursive practices, which has cemented its claims to truth (e.g. McNair, 1998). These transformations highlight the fact that *the industry*, its *practices* and *products*, and its *normative rationale* are not just in flux, but are undergoing a radical redefinition in such a way that we need new conceptual tools to make sense of what we may have taken for granted, and to rethink the social role of journalism.

These changes could be seen to represent a 'postmodern turn' in journalism insofar as they challenge the conventional 'grand narratives', certainties and rationalities that underpin the profession and its practices. They inform not only the practices of journalists and their discourses about their profession, but also the preoccupations and analytical tools of journalism scholars. At the same time, the destabilization of categories wrought by the emergence of convergence and online journalism has been accompanied by a shift in the preoccupations of scholars studying journalism. In particular, emerging discourses of journalism scholarship articulate a deliberate break with the analytical categories of the modernist project.

Postmodernism as an analytical tool in journalism studies

I am here – with some degree of trepidation – taking up a dusty, unfashionable and widely criticized conceptual framework by drawing on the notion of postmodernism. I am doing so on the basis that postmodernism serves as a useful trope for describing changes in the narratives around, and practices of, journalism, despite the broad array of (largely justified) criticisms of this framework. The idea of the postmodern was originally spelled out by Lyotard in 1979 in his book, *The Postmodern Condition*, as an intervention into broader debates about the nature of knowledge in scientific fields, aimed at the ways in which realist representational worldviews are legitimated through the discourse of philosophy. First and foremost, the definition of postmodernism was established through its juxtaposition with the idea of the modern (see also Callinicos, 1989, p. 3):

> I will use the term *modern* to designate any science that legitimates itself with reference to a metadisclosure … making an explicit appeal to some grand narrative, such as the dialectics of meaning, the emancipation of the rational or working subject, or the creation of wealth … I define postmodern as incredulity toward metanarratives. This incredulity is undoubtedly a product of progress in the sciences: but that progress in turn presupposes it.
>
> (Lyotard, 1997, pp. xxiii–xxiv)

Lyotard and other proponents of postmodernism pointed to evidence of a crisis in representation, reflected in a process of destabilization in science and other emancipatory grand projects of modernity – including accounts celebrating progress and the success of liberal democracy (e.g. Crouch, 2004). Postmodernism fell out of favour in the 1990s and onwards, as scholars questioned its insistence on the decline of the grand narratives of modernity, suggesting that this account in itself constituted a grand narrative (e.g. Jameson, 1997). Furthermore, critics of postmodernism from across the political spectrum discerned a depoliticizing and individualizing impulse in the postmodern position in its dismissal of large-scale normative and political projects – ranging from the institutions of established religion to Marxism and liberalism (e.g. Callinicos, 1989; Jameson, 1991). In its position on the contingency of truth claims, postmodernism has been associated with a normative relativism which refuses moral judgements.

Through a critical engagement with the claims of postmodernism, scholars across the humanities and social sciences fields have built on its insights, developing concepts that have been influential in shaping contemporary sociological thinking. However, most scholars have held on to the idea (and grand narrative) of modernity while emphasizing profound change. Indeed, the idea of profound change has been central to social theory for much of the twentieth century. One of the most prominent earlier theorists to think through these shifts was Joseph Schumpeter (1950), who proposed that capitalist societies go through cycles of 'creative destruction'. For Schumpeter, processes of renewal operate through destruction of 'old' technologies and modes of production:

> the same process of industrial mutation ... that incessantly revolutionizes the economic structure from within, incessantly destroying the old one, incessantly creating a new one. This process of Creative Destruction is the essential fact about capitalism. It is what capitalism consists in and what every capitalist concern has got to live in.
>
> (Schumpeter, 1950, p. 83)

Schumpeter's themes of destruction and renewal have profoundly shaped recent thinking in journalism studies as scholars have grappled with understanding both failure and innovation (e.g. Bruno and Kleis Nielsen, 2012; Schlesinger and Doyle, 2015; Wahl-Jorgensen, forthcoming).

For scholars engaging with the insights of postmodernism, Schumpeter's understanding of creative destruction as part of the inevitable process of 'industrial mutilation' in capitalism has served as a useful – and often implicitly invoked – conceptual backdrop. This, for example, is evident in the work of Beck, Giddens and Lash (1994) on the notion of 'reflexive modernization', which stipulates a profound historical break and discontinuity between what the authors describe as 'first' and 'second' modern societies. This break, integral to processes of modernization, is accompanied by an 'ontological change of social organization and cultural imagination as a change in the system of reference' (Beck, Bonss and Lau, 2004, p. 10). This ontological change contributes to destabilizing the legitimation processes associated with key institutions in society. Here, we may include journalism as one such institution whose legitimacy is under threat from multiple directions. For Beck and his colleagues, the language of 'modernization' represents a deliberate challenge to the arguments associated with postmodernism (e.g. Beck, Bonss and Lau, 2004), even if many of the processes they describe are similar.

Along those lines, Bauman proposed the idea of 'liquid modernity' to describe the fluid uncertainty of flux characterizing contemporary life, and its challenges to social life and organization in a range of areas, including 'emancipation, individuality, time/space, work, and community' (2000, p. 8). As Mark Deuze (2007, 2008) has argued, in liquid modernity, journalism is witnessing profound shifts that shape the way audiences and citizens engage with the institution:

> Beyond the individualization of society, the ongoing de-institutionalization of the way individuals interact with society, and the largely self-referential nature of the creative process within journalism, it is possible to argue that the output of the news industry also contributes to an overall sense of disempowerment and disenchantment with traditional social institutions. It is thus important to note that any consideration of the future of news and political communication has to involve not only an awareness of how the social systems of journalism and politics self-organize to adapt to new circumstances while maintaining their internal power structures, but also an understanding of how the contemporary condition of liquid modernity and its sense of permanent revolution wreaks havoc on the very foundations of these institutions.
>
> (Deuze, 2008, p. 856)

What unites these approaches, then, is the idea of understanding major transitions 'in everyday life, in the character of social organization and in the structuring of global systems within the framework of modernity' (Beck, Giddens and Lash, 1994, p. vii), and thus drawing on the resources and tools that social theory has used to understand institutional structures, rather than assuming a dramatic departure from these. This is a useful cautionary note for anyone wishing to engage with postmodernism. At the same time, it is also important to note that the language of social thinkers critically engaging with postmodernists draws on equally dramatic language, liberally using phrases of revolution, break, transformation and disruption. What is clear is that the profound changes to social structures and institutions – including journalism – are uncontested and have been cemented following the postmodernists, but that the mechanisms through which these changes take place remain hotly debated.

Despite the important criticisms of postmodernism discussed here, the concept has retained a resonance for scholars across the humanities and social sciences disciplines. For scholars of journalism in particular, postmodernism is – despite its limitations and significant conceptual baggage – helpful for understanding aspects of the profound changes to the institutions, practices, texts and audiences of journalism.

I am not the first to draw on postmodernist ideas in discussing journalism; rather, these have informed a variety of projects and areas of research over the past few decades, and have frequently been deployed to analyse forms of journalistic storytelling. Ettema (1994) discerned the possibilities for a postmodern journalism which would reject metanarratives and instead represent human suffering through the focus on small, concrete and localized stories about specific individuals and their experiences. Stuart Allan (1995) critically interrogated the ideal of objectivity and the 'will to facticity' in journalism. For Allan (1995), postmodernism's critique of realist theories of representation enables us to question the truth claims of 'objective' journalistic accounts, and the ways in which they depend upon a shared and hegemonic construction of the commonsensical. Allan's (1995) use of postmodernist insights highlights the epistemological limitations of the journalistic project of objectivity, giving us a language for talking about what journalism scholars have long known: it highlights the fact that news, rather than objectively representing a reality, actively manufactures or constructs it (e.g. Fishman, 1980; Tuchman, 1978). Similarly, Bogaerts and Carpentier have written more recently about the postmodern challenge to journalism, suggesting that we should take seriously the decline of 'high modernism' in journalism, in the face of developments including broader contextual changes 'such as detraditionalization, individualization and globalization' as well as the 'end of a consensus-based politics and an increasing economic insecurity' (2013, p. 61). All of these developments have informed a decline in the epistemic authority of journalism. Bogaerts and Carpentier suggested that journalism 'holds on to its self-proclaimed authority' (2013, p. 61) in the face of contemporary challenges, through forms of boundary work defending their profession. They proposed that culturalist approaches to journalism – derived in part from the conceptual tools of postmodernism – can help scholars problematize the socially constructed nature of journalism, in terms of both texts and professional practices and identities.

If anything, critiques of the modernist ideology of objective journalism – and observations about its increasingly unstable nature in the onslaught of technological and social change – have only gained renewed relevance in recent years. Melissa Wall (2005), in examining blogs during the second Iraq War, argued that their style was characteristic of postmodern journalism understood in a slightly different sense:

> Analysis suggests that these blogs are a new genre of journalism that emphasizes personalization, audience participation in content creation and story forms that are fragmented and interdependent with other websites. These characteristics suggest a shift away from traditional journalism's modern approach toward a new form of journalism infused with postmodern sensibilities.
>
> (Wall, 2005, p. 153)

This development, she suggested, is associated with a broader shift away from a traditional alignment between journalism and the representational ideals of modernity, including 'a sense that reality could be observed and documented from an objective viewpoint, an emphasis on constant change and timeliness, and a belief in being able to represent reality accurately' (Wall, 2005, p. 154). As I will argue, Wall's (2005) analysis highlights larger trends signalling epistemological shifts in journalism. I will begin by discussing the decline of the metanarrative of progress as a fundamental rupture in discussions about the profession and its key role in society.

The decline of a metanarrative of progress in journalism

If ideas of progress have been central to the modernist project, these have been severely undermined over the past few decades in the face of a crisis in the business model of journalism, particularly in its print form (e.g. Blumler, 2010; Boczkowski, 2004; Lee-Wright et al., 2011; Siles and Boczkowski, 2012). To rehearse the well-established consensus, this crisis is in part the result of longer-standing trends of decline in newspaper readership across the Western world, but has accelerated rapidly with the changes wrought by processes of convergence and the emergence of online journalism. This, in turn, has caused the collapse of advertising revenues as well as income from sales and subscriptions. With plummeting resources and prospects, newspapers have been forced to close down shop or drastically reduce their staff, resulting in a dramatic decline in both the quality and quantity of journalism. The changing fortunes of the profession have been reflected in the everyday experiences of journalists, who are also living the realities of 'reflexive modernization', which have resulted in the increasing precarity of their careers (Elefante and Deuze, 2012).

This crisis has profoundly changed not just the realities on the ground for journalists and the organizations within which they work, but also the stories journalism scholars tell about the profession and its past, present and future. Conventional modernist accounts of journalism's history and its present were premised on an assumption of inevitable progress towards a brighter future. In 1974, James Carey wrote about the problem of journalism history, drawing on Herbert Butterfield's critique of a 'Whig interpretation' of history which emphasizes 'certain principles of progress in the past and to produce a story which is the ratification if not the glorification of the present' (Butterfield, 1965, p. 1). For Carey, conventional journalism history narrated:

> the slow, steady expansion of freedom and knowledge from the political press to the commercial press, the setbacks into sensationalism and yellow journalism, the forward thrust into muckraking and social responsibility. Sometimes written in classic terms as the expansion of individual rights, sometimes in modern terms as growth of the public's right to know, the entire story is framed by those large impersonal faces buffeting the press: industrialization, urbanization and mass democracy.
>
> (Carey, 1974, p. 3)

While Carey did not dispute the fundamental premises of the Whig interpretation, he argued in favour of a richer and more diverse cultural history of journalism. Rereading Carey's work some 30 years later, however, I would suggest that the certainties of progress have, in fact, been severely undermined by changes in the material circumstances of journalism as an institution and a profession, as well as by broader shifts in the social and political structures underpinning it.

The Whig interpretation of journalism history has nonetheless prevailed in some quarters up to the present day (see Wahl-Jorgensen, forthcoming). It has survived in the era of digital journalism through accounts celebrating the liberating potential of new technologies.[1] This view of technological change as progress towards a brighter future is exemplified by the work of scholar-advocates like Clay Shirky (2008, 2010) and David Gauntlett (2011, 2015), for whom the birth of social media and Web 2.0 heralds an unprecedented age of creativity. Shirky (2010) argued that the networked age enables twenty-first-century individuals to spend their leisure time more productively, creatively and altruistically:

> This linking together in turn lets us tap our cognitive surplus, the trillion hours a year of free time the educated population of the planet has to spend doing things they care about. In the twentieth century, the bulk of that time was spent watching television, but our cognitive surplus is so enormous that diverting even a tiny fraction of time from consumption to participation can create enormous positive effects.

Despite this reading of the exciting technological present as a harbinger of a hopeful future, scholars within journalism studies who have used qualitative methods to understand the lived experience of the profession are increasingly painting a rather different picture, calling attention to the difficulties experienced by journalists on the ground. For example, Ekdale *et al.* (2014) carried out in-depth interviews with journalists at an independently owned media company in a mid-sized US city that had recently gone through a round of lay-offs. They found that the growing 'culture of job insecurity' in the newsroom hindered adaptation to change 'as those who fear their jobs are in danger are unlikely to risk altering well-understood practices, while many others who perceive job security would rather accommodate than initiate change'. Similarly, David Ryfe's book *Can Journalism Survive?* presents a devastating picture of a profession in terminal decline, in part due to its inability to respond to the challenges of the internet, on the basis of long-term ethnographic work at US regional newsrooms:

> What did I find? The short answer is that journalists have not adapted very well. For the most part, they continue to gather the same sorts of information, from the same sorts of people, and package it in the same forms they have used for decades. Newspapers have the same look and feel they have had since the 1930s, and newspaper websites still look uncomfortably like newspapers. When journalists have tried to break from tradition, their efforts largely have come to naught. I know of no recent innovations in news that were invented in a metro daily newsroom, and no newsroom, to my knowledge, has adopted the new innovations in a comprehensive way.
>
> (Ryfe, 2013, p. 3)

Ryfe's sobering account is representative of a small, but growing body of work on the nitty-gritty everyday life of journalists who are struggling to come to terms with profound changes in their professions. Together, this body of work represents a profound challenge to the metanarrative of progress. It begins from the position that journalism, as one of the key social institutions of modernity, is under profound existential threat, and the industry that underpins it is in decline. And it suggests that the production of scholarly knowledge must take into account profound ruptures in the fabric of journalism – ruptures which are, at the same time, closely tied to broader social and political transformations. This, in turn, implies that if we abandon the quest for the certainties of progress, we are better able to see the complex and often uncomfortable realities on the ground

Challenges to the metanarrative of journalism's role in democracy

Closely associated with the decline of the metanarrative of progress is an emerging set of questions about journalism's key place in democracy, which is so central to modernism. Journalism has long been seen as a 'Fourth Estate' in liberal democratic societies, playing the role of a watchdog on concentrations of power. For example, as Street explained it, the aims of the media:

> should be, firstly to enable people to choose between those who wish to stand for office and to judge those who currently are in office and, secondly, to provide a platform for interest groups to publicize their concerns and claims. This means informing citizens about their (prospective) representatives' plans and achievements; it also means reflecting the range of ideas and views which circulate within society, subjecting those who act in the name of the people to scrutiny, to make them accountable.
>
> (Street, 2001, p. 253)

The view of journalism as an institution embodying central democratic responsibilities has served to naturalize claims about its importance – both for society as a whole and for the citizens who inhabit it. Indeed, the close relationship between citizenship and journalism has been the building block of the Whig interpretations of journalism that Carey (1974) discussed, with progress measured in terms of improvements in the ability of journalism to serve its democratic role. However, this dominant narrative has been called into question in recent years. For example, a recent special issue of *Journalism* focused on 'Decoupling Journalism and Democracy', in the context of a challenge to the dominant normative paradigm through which journalism has long been assessed – and often found wanting (Josephi, 2013). Barbie Zelizer (2013) questioned whether the shelf life of democracy in journalism scholarship has been over-extended, describing the 'journalism/democracy nexus' as closely linked to a particular understanding of modernity:

Prevalent from the late 19th century onward, their version of modernity rested on an association with rationality, certainty, consent, reasoned thought, order, objectivity, progress and universal values, all of which journalism was expected to promote in order to create the conditions needed for an optimum public life.

(Zelizer, 2013, p. 463)

For Zelizer (2013), the narrow focus on very particular understandings of both democracy and journalism – and the relationship between them – has hindered a productive engagement with a broader range of practices.

Similarly, John Nerone (2013) aptly deconstructed journalism as a modernist belief system which makes disciplining distinctions that designate appropriate forms of practice and exclude those that are found normatively wanting:

Journalism is an ism … That is, it is a belief system. In particular, it is the belief system that defines the appropriate practices and values of news professionals, news media, and news systems. All societies have some sort of news system, because any society requires a mechanism for monitoring change and deviance. But only some societies, and in particular modern societies, feature journalism as a discipline governing parts of their news system: I say parts because any form of journalism will distinguish news that falls under its discipline from other forms of news. In the modern era, for instance, journalism has designated its 'other' in various ways as gossip, tabloid news, sensationalism, partisanism, and so forth. It does not deny that these are news practices, but it does question whether these are journalism.

(Nerone, 2013, p. 447)

Nerone (2013) here calls into question foundational assumptions of the modernist metanarrative around journalism's key role in democracy, reflecting an emerging set of preoccupations amongst journalism scholars. The boundaries between normatively 'good' and 'bad' forms of news have been widely debated over the past decade or so, starting with discussions over the increasingly close relationship between politics and popular culture (e.g. Sandvoss, 2012; van Zoonen, 2005). These debates – often initiated by scholars from outside journalism studies with an interest in popular culture – have encompassed the rise of entertaining news genres and forms of satire TV such as that exemplified by the *Daily Show* that intervene significantly in public debate even if they challenge conventional modernist definitions of what constitutes journalism (Jones, 2005; Jones et al., 2009). While few observers are, in fact, willing to radically decouple democracy and journalism, this debate calls attention to the fact that the modernist narrative has blinded us to the many things that news media *also* do, sometimes very well, including entertaining the audience and providing broader opportunities for involvement.

Some of these may have little or nothing to do with democracy, but are still important for societies and social life. This, in turn, suggests that if we take heed of postmodernism's insights into the instability of categorical distinctions, we may be able to find practices of journalism – but also practices of broader forms of audience participation and engagement – in places where we haven't previously looked. For example, amongst scholars studying political communication, such an approach is evidenced in engagement with practices around political fandom (e.g. Sandvoss, 2012, 2013), as well as everyday political talk in non-political online spaces, or 'third spaces' (Graham *et al.*, 2015). Journalism scholars are similarly operating with increasingly broad definitions of what constitutes journalistic practices, encompassing everything from fashion blogging (Rocamora, 2012) to posts on Twitter, YouTube and Flickr (Poell and Borra, 2012). At the same time, as proponents of reflexive modernization and liquid modernity have argued, the instability of categories does not mean that such categories are easily dispensed with but are instead hotly contested, defended and policed – and here we can usefully draw on the emerging study of boundary work in journalism to understand the meanings and consequences of such contestations (e.g. Carlson and Lewis, 2015).

Changes in the epistemology of journalism: questioning the modernist ideology of objectivity

As discussed above, one of the main ways in which the postmodernist framework has shaped work in journalism is in the questioning of the modernist ideology of objectivity as the cornerstone of the profession. Technological change has further fuelled these debates because the affordances of new platforms and modes of communication have facilitated new forms of storytelling. This encapsulates a key paradox affecting not just journalism, but also a range of other social institutions: if technological change has always been a key engine of modernity and a driver of modernization (e.g. Beck, Bonss and Lau, 2004, p. 7; Landes, 2003), it has also at the same time wrought the dissolution of journalism as one of modern society's key institutions and discursive practices. The changes occasioned by technological transformations could be understood as a postmodern form of journalism because they have destabilized conventional: (a) physical, stylistic and genre distinctions; (b) differentiations between amateur and professional content; and (c) distinctions around the truth value of objective versus emotional content.

First of all, storytelling has been transformed in part because new genres have enabled new ways of presenting information. To some observers, this constitutes a shift in the epistemology of journalism, as formats and platforms such as blogs and Twitter have enabled journalists to develop more personal, informal and subjective styles (e.g. Papacharissi, 2014; Wall, 2005). These shifts, in turn, are aligned with a move to a form of 'subjective journalism' which privileges personal voice, alongside a broader democratization of opinion – both of which deal a blow to modernist understandings of news journalism as the voice of authority (Coward, 2013, pp. 116–17). This trend introduces a more emotionalized form of public discourse – and hence a way of knowing – which is described by both audience members and newsworkers in juxtaposition to ideals of objectivity (see Wahl-Jorgensen, 2014, 2015).

A second and closely related transformation pertains to the blurring of the line between audiences and producers of media content, and the corresponding increase in the role of the audiences in participating in the generation this content (e.g. Singer *et al.*, 2011, van Dijck, 2009).[2] These developments have variously been referred to as the rise of 'participatory journalism', 'citizen journalism' or 'produs-age' (e.g. Bruns, 2005; Hermida, 2011, p. 15), to name just a few of the labels that describe 'the act of a citizen, or group of citizens, playing an active role in the process of collecting, reporting, analyzing and disseminating news and information' (Bowman and Willis, 2003, cited in Hermida, 2011, p. 15).

What these developments share is a profound challenge to modernist conceptions of journalism. First of all, they represent an overturning both of the authority granted to the profession of journalism and of the ideal of objectivity as a privileged mode of knowledge production. Instead, they enable a particular form of subjective journalism by encouraging more personal forms of storytelling, based on the lived experience of 'ordinary people'. Along those lines, Stuart Allan (2013) has written compellingly about the epistemological consequences of the increasing place of citizen journalism in the news landscape. To Allan, citizen journalism 'may be characterized as a type of first-person reportage in which ordinary individuals temporarily adopt the role of a journalist in order to participate in newsmaking, often spontaneously during a time of crisis, accident, tragedy or disaster when they happen to be present on the scene' (2013, p. 9). Citizen journalism implies a more personal and often subjective stance, free of the constraints of objective journalism. Allan succinctly summarized the main arguments around the epistemological consequences of citizen journalism advanced by critics and proponents. Its proponents suggest that citizen journalism may serve as a welcome paradigm shift challenging the 'dry, distancing, lecture-like mode of address' of traditional journalism:

> Journalism by the people for the people is to be heralded for its alternative norms, values and priorities. It is raw, immediate, independent and unapologetically subjective, making the most of the resources of web-based initiatives … to connect, interact and share first-hand, unauthorized forms of journalistic activity promising fresh perspectives.
>
> (Allan, 2013, p. 94)

This positive reading is consistent with research on audience responses to user-generated content, which suggests that audiences tend to value it because it is seen as more 'authentic' than professional content – a view frequently shared by journalists involved in shaping and curating audience contributions. This understanding of authenticity encompasses the idea of an uncensored outpouring of personal storytelling, emotional integrity, realism, immediacy and identification. This is contrasted with the perceived professional distance of journalism, which involves a 'cold', 'detached', 'objective' and 'distanced' approach (Wahl-Jorgensen *et al.*, 2010).

For example, in describing user-generated content after Hurricane Katrina, Michael Tippett, founder of NowPublic.com, argued 'it's a very powerful thing to have that emotional depth and first-hand experience, rather than the formulaic, distancing approach of the mainstream media' (Allan, 2013, p. 94).

The epistemological shifts facilitated by the affordances of digital journalism have been further accentuated by the rise of social media, which have enabled new ways of organizing participation. Events such as Occupy Wall Street and the Arab Spring in Egypt have illustrated the ways in which the information architecture of Twitter enable the emergence of 'affective news streams' which blend opinion, fact and emotion in ways that are both public and private (Papacharissi, 2014; Papacharissi and de Fatima Oliveira, 2012). Technological change has thus facilitated a fundamental challenge to modernist boundaries between professionals and amateurs, objectivity and subjectivity, and the public and the private. As a result, it firmly questions the epistemic authority of journalism based on its claims to be a privileged provider of our collective truths rather than one of many voices.

Conclusion

This chapter has proposed that we might see evidence of a postmodern turn in journalism, associated with a series of profound transformations in the institution, its text, practices and audiences, as well as in our accounts of it as journalism scholars. By making this argument, I do not mean to suggest that we should bring back the (largely discredited) premises of postmodernism, nor do I wish to refute the continued relevance of the metanarratives that have shaped the institution of journalism for the duration of its history. Nonetheless, the chapter has suggested that both the practices of and scholarly discourses surrounding journalism present significant challenges to the modernist metanarratives that have long defined it. These have been occasioned by the collapse of the business model of journalism, the questioning of the relationship between journalism and democracy, and the changing storytelling forms and epistemologies occasioned by technological change.

While the chapter has taken seriously the criticisms and limitations of the postmodern position, it has also argued that it serves as a useful analytical tool. Ultimately, it is a tool which reminds us that our first priority as scholars should always be to question received accounts and look for what is missing, what has been taken for granted and what remains unseen. We should pay just as much attention to instabilities, uncertainties and contestations as we have previously given to the foundational narratives of journalism and of journalism studies.

The places where we have seen the most helpful challenges to the received modernist wisdom come from detailed ethnographic studies of the everyday experiences of journalists, and from critical approaches to journalism by interdisciplinary scholars with an interest in popular culture, to mention but a few examples. If, as journalism scholars, we have been disciplined to accept the metanarratives we live by, it is also our responsibility to question them with resort to the tools and questions from other disciplines and approaches. First of all, an engagement with the postmodern enables us to interrogate and move beyond the assumptions built into the received knowledge of the field, based on the certainties of modernism. Second, it enables us to develop new approaches for studying professional practices. In particular, this chapter's examination of challenges to financial viability, the democratic role and the epistemology of journalism suggest that its central societal role can no longer be taken for granted; instead, we need to pay careful attention to the precise ways in which this role is being challenged and reconsidered. To better understand challenges to the journalism industry, we need to first study the lived experiences of failure and success of journalists on the ground. In addition, accepting the challenge to the democratic role of journalism could be put to more constructive use by looking for journalism practice and the forms of participation and engagement it facilitates in new and different places. Finally, the challenge to the epistemology of journalism also implicates the privileged truth claims of its discourses. Here, we need to understand how the profession is now increasingly competing with other 'truth providers', while its ability to stake out authority is under fire now more than ever. Understanding the shifting terrain in which claims to truth are made, and how these very claims may be articulated in changing ways, is crucial in any analysis of the legitimacy of journalism. Ultimately, an understanding of the postmodern turn helps us in rethinking journalism through seeing what has previously been rendered invisible.

Notes

1   Material in this section draws on an argument made in Wahl-Jorgensen (forthcoming).
2   Material in this section is taken from Wahl-Jorgensen (2014).

References

Allan, S. (1995). News, truth and postmodernity: Unravelling the will to facticity. In B. Adam & S. Allan (Eds.), *Theorizing culture: An interdisciplinary critique after postmodernism* (pp. 129–144). London: UCL Press.

Allan, S. (2013). *Citizen witnessing*. New York: Polity Press.

Bauman, Z. (2000). *Liquid modernity*. Cambridge: Polity Press.

Beck, U., Bonss, W., & Lau, C. (2004). The theory of reflexive modernization problematic, hypotheses and research programme. *Theory, culture & society, 20*(2), 1–33.

Beck, U., Giddens, A., & Lash, S. (1994). *Reflexive modernization: Politics, tradition and aesthetics in the modern social order*. Cambridge: Polity Press.

Blumler, J. G. (2010). Foreword: The two-legged crisis of journalism. *Journalism Studies, 11*(4), 439–441.

Boczkowski, P. J. (2004). *Digitizing the news: Innovation in online newspapers*. Cambridge, MA: MIT Press.

Bowman, S., & Willis, C. (2003). *We media: How audiences are shaping the future of news and information*. Reston, VA: The Media Center at the American Press Institute.

Bruno, N., & Nielsen, R. K. (2012). *Survival is success: Journalistic online start-ups in Western Europe*. Oxford: Reuters Institute for the Study of Journalism.

Bruns, A. (2005). *Gatewatching: Collaborative online news production*. London & New York: Peter Lang.

Butterfield, H. (1965). *The Whig interpretation of history.* New York: W. W. Norton.

Callinicos, A. (1989). *Against postmodernism: A Marxist critique.* Cambridge: Polity Press.

Carey, J. W. (1974). The problem of journalism history. *Journalism History, 1*(1), 3–5; 27.

Carlson, M., & Lewis, S. (Eds.). (2015). *Boundaries of journalism.* New York: Routledge.

Coward, R. (2013). *Speaking personally: The rise of subjective and confessional journalism.* Basingstoke: Palgrave Macmillan.

Crouch, C. (2004). *Post-democracy.* Cambridge: Polity Press.

Deuze, M. (2007). *Media work.* Cambridge: Polity Press.

Deuze, M. (2008). The changing context of news work: Liquid journalism for a monitorial citizenry. *International Journal of Communication, 2,* 848–865.

Ekdale, B., Tully, M., Harmsen, S., & Singer, J. B. (2014). Newswork within a culture of job insecurity: Producing news amidst organizational and industry uncertainty. *Journalism Practice, 9*(3), 1–16.

Elefante, P. H., & Deuze, M. (2012). Media work, career management, and professional identity: Living labour precarity. *Northern Lights, 10*(1), 9–24.

Ettema, J. S. (1994). Discourse that is closer to silence than to talk: The politics and possibilities of reporting on victims of war. *Critical Studies in Mass Communication, 11*(1), 1–21.

Fishman, M. (1980). *Manufacturing the news.* Austin: University of Texas Press.

Gauntlett, D. (2011). *Making is connecting: The social meaning of creativity, from DIY and knitting to YouTube and Web 2.0.* Cambridge: Polity Press.

Gauntlett, D. (2015). *Making media studies: The creativity turn in media and communications studies.* London & New York: Peter Lang.

Graham, T., Jackson, D., & Wright, S. (2015). 'We need to get together and make ourselves heard': Everyday online spaces as incubators of political action. *Information, Communication & Society,* (ahead-of-print), 1–17.

Hartley, J. (1996). *Popular reality.* London: Arnold.

Hermida, A. (2011). Mechanisms of participation: How audience options shape the conversation. In J. Singer, A. Hermida, D. Domingo, A. Heinonen, S. Paulussen, T. Quandt, … M. Vujnovic (Eds.), *Participatory journalism: Guarding open gates at online newspapers* (pp. 13–33). Malden, MA: Wiley-Blackwell.

Jameson, F. (1991). *Postmodernism, or, the cultural logic of late capitalism.* Durham, NC: Duke University Press.

Jameson, F. (1997). Foreword. In J.-F. Lyotard (Ed.), *The postmodern condition: A report on knowledge* (pp. vii–xxii). Manchester: Manchester University Press.

Jones, J. P. (2005). *Entertaining politics: New political television and civic culture.* Lanham, MD: Rowman & Littlefield.

Jones, J. P., Gray, J., & Thompson, E. (Eds.). (2009). *Satire TV: Politics and comedy in the post-network era.* New York: NYU Press.

Josephi, B. (2013). De-coupling journalism and democracy: Or how much democracy does journalism need? *Journalism, 14*(4), 441–445.

Landes, D. S. (2003). *The unbound Prometheus: Technological change and industrial development in Western Europe from 1750 to the present.* Cambridge: Cambridge University Press.

Lee-Wright, P., Phillips, A., & Witschge, T. (2011). *Changing journalism.* Routledge.

Lyotard, J.-F. (1997). *The postmodern condition: A report on knowledge.* Manchester: Manchester University Press (first published 1979).

McNair, B. (1998). *The sociology of journalism.* Oxford: Oxford University Press.

Nerone, J. (2013). The historical roots of the normative model of journalism. *Journalism, 14*(4), 446–458.

Papacharissi, Z. (2014). *Affective publics: Sentiment, technology, and politics.* Oxford: Oxford University Press.

Papacharissi, Z., & de Fatima Oliveira, M. (2012). Affective news and networked publics: The rhythms of news storytelling on #Egypt. *Journal of Communication, 62*(2), 266–282.

Poell, T., & Borra, E. (2012). Twitter, YouTube, and Flickr as platforms of alternative journalism: The social media account of the 2010 Toronto G20 protests. *Journalism, 13*(6), 695–713.

Rocamora, A. (2012). Hypertextuality and remediation in the fashion media: The case of fashion blogs. *Journalism Practice, 6*(1), 92–106.

Ryfe, D. M. (2013). *Can journalism survive: An inside look at American newsrooms.* Hoboken, NJ: John Wiley & Sons.

Sandvoss, C. (2012). Enthusiasm, trust and its erosion in mediated politics: On fans of Obama and the Liberal Democrats. *European Journal of Communication, 27*(1), 68–81.

Sandvoss, C. (2013). Toward an understanding of political enthusiasm as media fandom: Blogging, fan productivity and affect in American politics. *Participations, 10*(1), 252–296.

Schlesinger, P., & Doyle, G. (2015). From organizational crisis to multi-platform salvation? Creative destruction and the recomposition of news media. *Journalism, 16*(3), 305–323.

Schumpeter, J. A. (1950). *Capitalism, socialism and democracy.* London: Unwin University Books.

Shirky, C. (2008). *Here comes everybody: The power of organizing without organizations.* New York: Penguin.

Shirky, C. (2010, 4 June). Does the internet make you smarter? *Wall Street Journal.*

Siles, I., & Boczkowski, P. J. (2012). Making sense of the newspaper crisis: A critical assessment of existing research and an agenda for future work. *New Media & Society, 14*(8), 1375–1394.

Singer, J., Hermida, A., Domingo, D., Heinonen, A., Paulussen, S., Quandt, T. … Vujnovic, M. (2011). *Participatory journalism: Guarding open gates at online newspapers.* Malden, MA & Oxford: Wiley-Blackwell.

Street, J. (2001). *Mass media, politics and democracy.* Basingstoke: Palgrave Macmillan.

Tuchman, G. (1978). *Making news: A study in the construction of reality.* New York: The Free Press.

Van Dijck, J. (2009). Users like you? Theorizing agency in user-generated content. *Media, Culture & Society, 31*(1), 41–58.

Van Zoonen, L. (2005). *Entertaining the citizen: When politics and popular culture converge.* Lanham, MD: Rowman & Littlefield.

Wahl-Jorgensen, K. (2014). Changing technologies, changing paradigms of journalistic practice: Emotionality, authenticity and the challenge to objectivity. In C. Zimmerman & M. Schreiber (Eds.), *Technologies, media and journalism* (pp. 264–283). New Haven, CT: Yale University Press.

Wahl-Jorgensen, K. (2015). Resisting epistemologies of user-generated content? Cooptation, segregation and the boundaries of journalism. In M. Carlson & S. Lewis (Eds.), *Boundaries of journalism* (pp. 169–185). New York: Routledge.

Wahl-Jorgensen, K. (forthcoming). A manifesto of failure for digital journalism. In P. Boczkowski & C. Anderson (Eds.), *Remaking digital news.* Cambridge, MA: MIT Press.

Wahl-Jorgensen, K., Williams, A., & Wardle, C. (2010). Audience views on user-generated content: Exploring the value of news from the bottom up. *Northern Lights, 8*, 177–194.

Wall, M. (2005). 'Blogs of war': Weblogs as news. *Journalism, 6*(2), 153–172.

Zelizer, B. (2013). On the shelf life of democracy in journalism scholarship. *Journalism, 14*(4), 459–473.

PART II

Journalism and its public relevance

7

WHAT JOURNALISM BECOMES

Mark Deuze and Tamara Witschge

Journalism worldwide is in a process of becoming a different kind of profession. Once organized in formal institutions, where contracted labourers would produce content under informal yet highly structured working conditions, today the lived experience of professional journalists is much more precarious, fragmented and networked. At the heart of the project of understanding contemporary journalism as a profession and the way it functions in society must be a conceptualization of journalism beyond its formerly distinct and boundaried organization of newswork.

The post-industrialization of journalism (Anderson, Bell and Shirky, 2012) is part of a trend benchmarked by the creative industries more generally: a gradual shift from centralized and hierarchical modes of industrial production to what Castells (2010) labels a network enterprise form of production. The networked form of enterprise is also at work in journalism, as the International Federation of Journalists and the International Labour Organization already noted in a 2006 survey among journalism unions and associations in 38 countries from all continents. The report signalled the rapid rise of so-called 'atypical' work in the media, documenting that close to one-third of journalists worldwide work in anything but secure, permanent or otherwise contracted conditions. Since then, freelance journalism, independent news entrepreneurship and casualization of labour have become even more paramount, particularly among younger reporters and newcomers in the field (as well as for more senior journalists affected by lay-offs and downsizing so common across the news industry; see Deuze, 2014; Mosco, 2009).

Today's post-industrial journalism can be seen as constituting and resulting from what is called 'liquid modernity' (Bauman, 2000) where individual practices are part of a profoundly precarious context governed by a *permanently impermanent* industry (where continuous reorganizations, managerial reshuffling, buyouts, lay-offs and innovations are the norm), working environment (where the place you work and the people you work with are constantly changing) and career (where one's job-hopping trajectory is unpredictable to say the least). In order for journalism to adapt, its practitioners have been pushed to develop new tactics, a new self-conception and new organizational structures – while older structures, routines and definitions (of news values) persist.

In this chapter, we consider how the post-industrial mode of journalism asks for new ways of conceptualizing and researching the lived experience of journalists. We argue that we need their particularly personal perspective to rethink journalism as an ensemble of people 'committing acts of journalism' (Stearns, 2013) beyond processes of 'routinizing the unexpected' (Tuchman, 1973) in news institutions large and small. In this contribution, we chart the permanent state of flux of journalism and the developments that fundamentally challenge journalism theory and research. Though much has been done already to move away from the rather stable and solid notions of what journalism is, as a field we still struggle to do justice to and capture the complexity and processes of continuous change experienced by working journalists and the organizations that use their labour. Ultimately, we propose a distinct perspective on journalism that views it as a moving object, something that *becomes* rather than *is*.

Enter the journalist

Our central argument in this chapter is that we need to theorize contemporary journalism as a rather complex and evolving ensemble of attitudes and practices of (groups or teams of) individuals involving both professional journalists and practitioners from related fields such as coders, programmers, designers and marketers (Deuze, 2008; Lewis and Usher, 2014). By way of context, we first highlight four trends transpiring in journalism that signal a shift away from the conceptualization of journalism as a more or less stable and consensual field, namely: the concurrent reorganization of working environments; the fragmentation of newswork; the emergence of a redactional society; and the ubiquity of media-making technologies. These trends, each in their own way, point to a more individual rather than institutional perspective of the journalist and a need to reconceptualize the field.

First, what Sennett (2006) calls the 'culture of the new capitalism' draws our attention to emphasis on individualized responsibilities placed in the reorganization of working and being at work. Whether contracted or independent, media workers are increasingly supposed to embrace and embody an 'enterprising' mindset, where every individual becomes a self-directed and self-disciplining brand or company. The journalist as an enterprising self reconstitutes 'workers as more adaptable, flexible, and willing to move between activities and assignments and to take responsibility for their own actions and their successes and failures' (Storey, Salaman and Platman, 2005, p. 1036). Journalism has been no exception to the trend of labour individualization (Lowrey and Anderson, 2005). However, shifting the notion of enterprise – with its connotations of efficiency, productivity, empowerment and autonomy – from the company to the individual uproots the professional identity of workers. Gall (2000), for example, has noted how the introduction of personalized contracts, though allowing individual journalists some freedom to negotiate their own terms and conditions of employment, in fact resulted in a deterioration of the working conditions of journalists: lower wages, less job security and more contingent labour relationships (variable hours, job rotation and flextime).

Second, the production of news increasingly takes place both within and outside of professional news organizations, as well as within and across multiple media forms and formats. This fragmentation of newswork is furthermore facilitated by practices of outsourcing, subcontracting and offshoring, which are paramount in broadcasting (Ryan, 2009) as well as print media – as documented by the World Association of Newspapers in its ongoing series of 'Shaping the Future' reports.[1] The practice of such functional flexibility in the workforce is common throughout the news industry. Functional flexibility relates to the division of the workforce in a multi-skilled core and a large periphery of semi-affiliated professionals. The multi-skilled core consists of a few professionals enjoying greater job security and career development who perform many different tasks throughout the organization. The peripheral group – consisting of the majority of newsworkers today – tend to be temporarily employed in subcontracted or outsourced arrangements and consists mainly of independent individual contractors working within a dynamic and often informally governed 'project ecology' (Grabher, 2002) of people both inside and outside news institutions.

Third, on a more abstract level, in today's advanced communicational democracies, society can be conceptualized as 'redactional' (Hartley, 2000). A redactional society is one where editorial practices are required for anyone's survival in the digital age and therefore cannot be considered to be exclusive to a particular professional group such as journalists employed at news organizations. Traditionally, survival in the information age was seen as dependent on being an 'informational' as well as an informed citizen (Schudson, 1995): next to being saturated in information, citizens needed to have 'a point of view and preferences with which to make sense of it' (1995, p. 27). In redactional societies, simply having access to and making sense of information is not enough and what were originally deemed as journalistic skills and competences are required for all citizens: they need to know how to gather and process vast amounts of information, weigh and sift the information at hand, and be able to do something effectively and creatively with that information (Gauntlett, 2011). As such, in this digital era, everyone, at some point, commits acts of 'journalism' (Stearns, 2013, p. 2), using what are deemed journalistic techniques and bearing the responsibility for their consequences.

The last trend that frames newswork in terms of the individual is the pervasive and ubiquitous role that (ever-developing) technologies play in the changing nature of journalistic work and organization. Today's printing press is the desktop or laptop personal computer equipped with broadband internet access and standard outfitted with easy-to-use publishing tools, open source software applications and converged hardware (camera, microphone, keyboard). These technologies have resulted in converged journalism within newsrooms as well as facilitating the production of all aspects of journalism outside of newsrooms. This features centrally the multi-skilled journalist who performs a greater variety of tasks – including those that were traditionally performed by others (whether designers, marketers, publishers or editors) (Lee-Wright and Phillips, 2012).

Structures beyond the individual

In the precarious individualized context of contemporary journalism, it is not stretching too far to signal a gradual de-professionalization process taking place (Witschge and Nygren, 2009), as the profession is under tremendous pressure due to a variety of factors, such as: market demands and financial expectations; a precarious and atypical division of labour which fragments the profession; an ongoing erosion of its values and practices through the intervention of technology (including the advent of algorithms, drones, robotics and software to select, organize, report and publish the news); an altogether unstable and fluctuating trust in the public sector generally (Van de Walle, Van Roosbroek and Bouckaert, 2008); and a concomitant decline of trust in journalism specifically (McNair, 2003).

At the same time, traditional professional standards and norms can still be found throughout the industry, and we see among most journalists, regardless of contractual arrangement, an inherent drive to do the job well – a commitment to quality which suggests a dedication to the profession and the 'craft' that is journalism (Hanitzsch and Mellado, 2011; Willnat, Weaver and Choi, 2013; Witschge, 2013). This furthermore suggests how intrinsic values continue to drive practices in the field, both within and outside of the newsroom. The drive to do the job well is not exclusively connected to the organizational arrangement of newswork, but rather lies at the individual, personal level that indicates a commitment beyond the institution (Russo, 1998). To gain insight into the interaction between professional norms and self-understanding of journalists in an age of de-professionalization and precarity, journalism needs to be understood beyond its traditional institutional and organizational boundaries. What journalism is and what being a journalist means in both ideological and praxeological terms are no longer dependent on work done inside institutions.

Taking up the call to move beyond newsroom-centricity (Wahl-Jorgensen, 2009) or to 'blow up' the newsroom (Anderson, 2011), we do not suggest that the profession and its attendant organizations do not play a role any longer. We do argue that one does not necessarily have to be a salaried employee of a news organization in order to be part of the journalism system (in fact, most working journalists today do not enjoy such employment anymore). It rather depends on one's participation in communicating the foundational elements (the building blocks) of that system. Understanding journalism in this way, Scholl and Weischenberg propose a model for the systematic identification of factors that constitute a journalism system (1998, pp. 21–2). They identify different levels of analysis through which we can access what journalism is, ranging from macro to micro levels: systems, institutions, messages and actors.

Adding social and belief systems as a fifth factor to Weischenberg's 'onion-model' (1992), Shoemaker and Reese (2014) summarize this approach as a hierarchy-of-influences model of media work and include the following dimensions. First, social systems in which content is influenced by the social systems or ideologies of societies, generally assumed to be more or less coherent belief systems particular to dominant groups. Within journalism as a profession, this relates to its occupational ideology consensually shared by journalists which allows them to self-organize and maintain their discipline as a profession. Second, social institutional influences on newswork, where content is influenced by such factors as markets, audiences, advertisers, and interest groups, referring to the power exerted on (and, in some instances, over) journalists by a variety of institutions and actors in society, including the government, sources, clients, interest groups, audiences, employers and other media organizations (such as advertising, public relations and marketing communications). Third, they distinguish the organizational level, pointing at the goals and policies of individuals as part of one or more larger social structures (such as news organizations, client companies and networks) and how power is exercised within such structures. Fourth, everyday routines in newswork are the constraining and enabling influences of work practices in the particular context of what Ulrich Beck (2000) called the 'brave new world' of work. Routines are patterned practices that organize how media professionals perceive and function within the social world of (competitor-)colleagues and their professional group as a whole. Fifth, the individual level of newsworkers, which includes the attitudes, training and background of the journalist that impact the various ways in which she or he participates (and shapes) the process of journalism.

We below explore how, on each of the above levels, developments are at work that significantly disrupt the way we can conceptualize journalism.

Understanding journalism as individuals and institutions in their context

In the current media environment, we need an understanding of not only how disruption functions at each level of influence on the work journalists do, but also – and perhaps most importantly – how journalists as individuals and groups enact agency within this system. Where the institution was once dominant in organizing journalistic work and facilitating (and constraining) communication about journalism, this is no longer sufficient to understand journalism as it is practised in so many new places by so many more actors under such widely differing circumstances. We set the investigation of journalism in the context of what Susan Keith (2011) calls the 'media milieu' within which journalists work, which, if anything, has to be understood as an industry in transition – a post-industry indeed.

Journalism theory has to be benchmarked by a critical assessment of the role, work and milieu of individual journalists, while recognizing the object of study – journalism – as dynamic: requiring an ontology of 'becoming' rather than of 'being' (Chia, 1995). With Robert Chia, we propose a perspective on journalism that privileges 'reality as a processual, heterogeneous and emergent configuration of relations' (1995, p. 594). We discuss below how on each of the above identified levels of analysis – social systems, social institutions, organizations, routines and individual journalists – the changes and challenges in the field of journalism ask for specific considerations in our methodology and theory.

Social system

At the level of the social system, we need to critically examine journalists' occupational ideology, that is the conceptualization of their profession and role that is consensually shared by journalists, allowing them to self-organize and maintain their discipline as a profession without formal boundaries. In journalism's self-understanding as well as societies' conceptualizations of the profession, journalism's function in society is very much connected to its importance to democracy, which has led to a highly consensual understanding of journalism (Hallin, 1992). Scholars and journalists alike often use a normative notion of journalism as providing the 'social cement' of democracies as a point of departure in their work (Josephi, 2013).

Even though the professional context of contemporary journalism and the state of the news industry are profoundly precarious, the consensual definition and understanding of journalism prevails, affecting our scholarly capacity to analyse and critique journalism (Zelizer, 2013). In this state of flux, it is important to consider the way in which journalism studies views journalism's role in society and democracy, and particularly whether this is still apt. A key to re-orienting journalism studies to the rapidly changing human condition may be found in the late twentieth century (and onwards) project of re-theorizing modernity itself, benchmarked by the suggestion that modernity has entered a new phase, phrased as a second, reflexive network, or liquid modernity. Bauman's work on all aspects of life in liquid modern times warrants specific attention. Bauman defines a liquid modern society as 'a society in which the conditions under which its members act change faster than it takes the ways of acting to consolidate into habits and routines. Liquidity of life, and that of society, feed and reinvigorate each other' (2005, p. 1).

If we consider Bauman's understanding of modernity, it is important to note that journalism is not only taking place in, but also helps constitute this 'liquid modern society', where uncertainty, flux, change, conflict and revolution are the permanent conditions of everyday life. In this view, newswork not only contributes to, but also is susceptible to the qualities of liquid life. In this context, work has a generally temporary character, experienced as a distinct break from the routine of traditional work-life (premised on long-term, open-ended contracts with a single employer who shares responsibilities such as social benefits and healthcare). The atypical nature of newswork directly feeds into the lived experience of liquid modernity in terms of its structural condition of temporariness (Deuze, 2007).

Media and news organizations play an important role in exposing and amplifying this liquid state of modernity. The speed and multitudes of this social system gains form in such phenomena such as 24/7 news, online happening anywhere at any time, covered by millions of social media users, live blogging news organizations and a host of freelance roaming correspondents. At the same time, we can identify counter-movements, such as the emergence of 'slow' news (Le Masurier, 2015), new genres of long-form journalism (such as longreads on tablet PCs) and transmedia journalism (Moloney, 2012), and numerous news start-ups around the world advocating a type of journalism that is based on quality and depth rather than speed or breaking news (such as *De Correspondent* in the Netherlands, *The Conversation* in Australia and elsewhere, and *Mediapart* in France). In this sense we see that journalism is both part of and constituting the social context: both the acceleration and slowing down of news production are symptoms of and responses to a profession in liquid modern times.

Such developments do not take place in a vacuum and we need to understand journalism as product of as well as response to its environment. Given its central role in society many actors try to exert influence on journalistic reporting (McQuail, 2013) and given the economic and market forces at hand, journalism is always under pressure. As self-proclaimed gatekeepers, journalists rely on their occupational ideology and news culture as a defence against such actors and forces. At the same time, elements of this ideology are used to usher in disruptive innovation and transformation in the field. Through definitional debates, which happen not just at the level of the profession, but also very much so at the level of public discourse on journalism, and through the processes of legitimizing or excluding particular participants in these discussions, journalists have established (largely informal) barriers of entry to the profession.

In interaction with the actors surrounding journalism, whether it is the public, sources or political and economic powers, five ideal-typical values give legitimacy and credibility to what journalists do: public service, objectivity, autonomy, immediacy and ethics (Deuze, 2005). In this discourse, journalists provide a public service as watchdogs or newshounds, active collectors and disseminators of information. They argue that what sets them apart is their strive to be impartial, neutral, objective, fair and (thus) credible. They report the need to be autonomous, free and independent to do their work effectively. Inherent to their concept of news is a sense of immediacy, actuality and speed. And last, they argue that another identifying feature is that they have a sense of ethics, validity and legitimacy.

Viewing these, what we can consider 'high modern', values against the accelerated 'liquid modern' context society at large, we can view a clear contrast. This tension comes even more to the fore in current debates about the nature of such age-old values as objectivity, truth and autonomy. The amplification and acceleration of more or less new news genres, forms, products and services today point towards the fact that the occupational ideology of journalism allows for many different 'journalisms' to flourish.

For journalism studies, it is important to understand the challenge posed by the gap between the consistency of the profession's ideology and the proliferation of a diverse range of journalisms, often valorized by ideological claims. Questions of what journalism is are paramount, boundary work is rife throughout the profession and academe, but who is in and outside of the definition of journalism is by no means uncontested. Each of the definitions is legitimized through ideological stances, furthering what journalism should be or should do. With such divergent practices grounded in a consensual ideological stance on journalism, journalism seems to encapsulate possibly opposing practices.

The challenge for journalism studies is to understand the ontology of *becoming* in the context of an ideology of *being*: understanding that journalism is not something that 'is', but rather 'becomes' through a diversification of practices and subsequent boundary work. As such, it is important to let go of the desire to make claims about 'the' profession, what it is (or what it should be) and what it means to a working journalist, and instead develop a heightened sensitivity towards mapping and articulating divergent practices, definitions as well as ideological interpretations that in turn produce many different *journalisms* on a social systemic level.

Social institution

Viewing how journalism is constituted or shaped by institutional factors and actors, we need to consider how the professionalization of journalism to some extent contributed to the difficulties it currently faces when looking for new business models (as an industry as well as to support individual careers). The professional understanding of autonomy shapes its interaction with and resistance to a fundamental re-imagining of practice, and particularly of the institutional framework(s) in which such practice takes place. Currently, faced with disruptive challenges on many fronts, the news business requires its workers to increasingly shoulder the responsibility of the company (or companies, in the case of those with patchwork careers, carrying a portfolio of multiple clients), altering the role of journalists in their institutions. In this context, Witschge and Nygren ask the question whether the development in journalism on an institutional level is indeed 'going towards a de-professionalization where journalists become "media workers" or "content producers" in the media companies' (2009, p. 42).

The traditional conceptualization of journalism as an institution that is beset at all sides by forces trying to exert influence over it, we argue, does not help us understand the current practices of journalism which includes cross-media and transmedia storytelling, projectized workstyles and portfolio careers, business and editorial convergence, entrepreneurship and entrepreneurialism, and what Henry Jenkins calls 'convergence culture' (2004), where the cultures of production and consumption increasingly converge in new creative processes (in journalism exemplified by trends towards more user-centred design, audience interactivity and citizen reporting).

Considering the variety of institutions and societal actors that impact journalism production, content and use, we need to acknowledge the broad range of actors involved, disrupting the once considered more or less coherent and contained practice of professional journalism. In the current digital and networked media ecosystem, the roles played by different professional disciplines in the making of news – media makers, financial executives, advertising creatives, communication managers, including marketing and sales practitioners – are increasingly intertwined.

In journalism, the roles of content, sales and marketing are converging. Emblematic of this is the emergence of the 'enterprising professional' in journalism – from the editors whose job descriptions increasingly include human resource management and policy making (rather than strictly editorial work) to the budding reporters trying to make a living as 'entrepreneurial' journalists (Briggs, 2011). Entrepreneurialism is a relatively recent phenomenon, and in journalism coincides with a gradual breakdown of the wall between the commercial and editorial sides of the news organization. The breakdown of the wall separating these two sides is important in understanding what journalism becomes, as it was once deemed fundamental. As Robert Picard (2010) suggests, the building of the wall was core to the process of professionalization of journalism. It was a process that simultaneously separated journalists from business decisions and removed them from any responsibility for the organization's actions and sustainability, and led to journalists generally enjoying editorial autonomy in their work. With the growing prominence of entrepreneurialism as a value for working journalists both within and outside legacy news organizations, it is safe to assume that on an institutional level, journalism is much more interwoven with a host of other actors, values and priorities than it is generally made out to be (both in terms of its self-perception and in academic conceptualizations of the field). This in turn broadens the conversation about journalism – what it is and what it should be.

These developments force us to rethink journalism as a stable institution amidst other discrete institutions, wherein journalists were either seen as 'cogs in the machine' or, conversely, as active agents resisting change. Instead, it makes more sense to focus on journalism and the work of journalists as praxis, at once conditioned by existing social arrangements and facilitating transformation and emergence. Such a perspective on institutional change 'emphasizes agents' ability to artfully mobilize different institutional logics and resources, appropriated from their contradictory institutional environments, to frame and serve their interests' (Seo and Creed, 2002, p. 240). Through praxis, inside-outside distinctions in newswork become less relevant, as we would be looking at what journalists do and where (and how) journalistic work gets done, and how practitioners give meaning to what they do individually and collectively.

News organization

The scholarly understanding of journalism as a boundaried, institutional practice can be traced to the understanding of journalism as squarely located in the newsroom. The relative stability of the ideal-typical values of journalism's ideology and the consensus about their validity has legitimized the dominant structure of the news industry, which consolidated journalists (and, therefore, debates on what journalism is) in newsrooms. But today's newsroom is an excellent example of a liquid modern concept: in many ways, it looks exactly like the newsrooms of newspapers and broadcast news organizations of the mid-twentieth century, with the important difference that most newsrooms today are either largely empty (because of mass lay-offs and outsourcing practices) or are transforming into integrated operations where content, sales, marketing and a host of other functions converge.

Besides the newsroom becoming an increasingly fluid object, it is important to note that most of the actual reportorial work gets done elsewhere. With the rise of 'post-industrial' journalism (as embodied in an increasingly distributed workforce consisting of individual entrepreneurial journalists, freelance editorial collectives and a worldwide emergence of news start-ups), the 'new' newsroom is fragmented, dispersed, networked and therefore anything but stable. For journalism scholars, this means that they need to reconsider their object of study: from an easily located and neatly organized space to a dispersed, fragmented network of workers, undocumented labourers, citizen volunteers and anything in between. That this can prove to be a challenge becomes clear when we think of how, throughout history, scholars of journalism and the news have supported the dominance of certain interpretations of (the role of) journalism by focusing on specific organizational arrangements within particular privileged settings. As Karin Wahl-Jorgensen (2009, p. 23) puts it, the 'newsroom-centricity' in journalism studies has meant that:

> Scholars have tended to focus on journalists' culture as it emerges within the limited areas of newsrooms and other centralized sites for news production, usually paying scant attention to places, spaces, practices and people at the margins of this spatially delimited news production universe.

What determines the outcomes of newswork in its contemporary arrangement must be grounded in a critical realist understanding of the constantly shifting and changing members and memberships of news organizations. Membership in journalism is not just determined by being 'in' the newsroom or standing at the outside (with hopes of getting in). When considering the disruptions and developments in the field at the level of the news organization, it becomes apparent that this, in the digital age, is not so much a *place* as a *process* that involves networks of people, technologies and spaces. There is a high degree of flux, blurring the in/out boundary of the newsroom and its environment. In fact, the new ways in which newswork is organized asks us to move beyond the binary opposition of inside and outside the newsroom, as this notion becomes ever more obsolete and, as a concept, may obfuscate rather than illuminate.

Routines

Another mechanism of organizing newswork is through everyday routines: patterned practices that organize how media professionals see and operate. These, too, are increasingly challenged and disrupted, impacting the way in which journalism is practised. And here, too, do we see an important challenge for journalism studies to come to terms with and get a grip on the nature and impact of the changes. This is far from straightforward, as the scholarly understanding on the professional routines that make up newswork in newsrooms has been consolidated in journalism education where such routines are fixed elements in the coursework for print, broadcast and online sequences.

As such scholarly understanding of the profession feeds straight into the practice of journalism. Cottle (2007, p. 10) notes how the emphasis on 'organizational functionalism' that still dominates journalism education privileges routines and patterned ways of doing newswork over differentiation and divergence. Though studying the patterned practices that organize how media professionals do their work made sense given the generally prescheduled nature of much of the news (consider conferences and press releases, set dates in a parliamentary cycle, fixtures in sports, opening and closing of markets, and so on), this is no longer sufficient. Much of the reporting today is not necessarily done in this way (or at such places), and in many cases reporting takes place virtually (using data as source) or completely online – for example, by net-native social news organizations such as *Reported.ly* in the US and *Bellingcat* in the UK. Focusing on the routines that long stabilized journalistic production no longer suffices in mapping and explaining the diversity of journalistic work.

Beyond the online, mobile and virtual character of much of today's reporting and storytelling the nature of the contemporary news organization is changing so fast that it seems safe to assume that routines are anything but stable in these environments. Whereas legacy media newsrooms are converging and integrating people, units and departments, a host of new organizational forms emerge around the world, consisting of (online and offline) editorial collectives, news start-ups and pop-up newsrooms, including managerial innovations. A specific example of an emerging organizational form in journalism is the introduction of agile development sequences in renowned news companies such as the *Washington Post*, NPR, *Politiken* and the BBC. 'Agile' refers to a set of management principles commonly used in software development, and in the context of news production stipulates fast-paced projects with short design cycles, working in temporary teams based on the integration of people from different parts of the company – reporters, assignment editors, designers, developers, market research and management.

These new forms of news organization not only challenge the output, but also demand new routines to develop. Beyond the fact that a focus on routines belies an everyday practice that is perhaps not as stable or solid than it has been made out to be, contemporary changes brought about by disruption and innovation force us to re-evaluate conceptualizations of 'routine' as an organizational function. This is then an ultimate challenge for journalism scholars: without throwing the baby out with the bathwater, how can we conceptualize newswork doing justice to both routinized and fluxional work practices, and the convergence between such practices?

Individual journalists

Our discussion of contemporary newsrooms indicates that at the level of individual journalists working in journalism, an important observation must be made: the number of salaried and contracted journalists working in the setting of the newsroom is declining. The scope of lay-offs in journalism has been nothing but astounding in the last decade. Figures reported by journalism unions and trade associations in developed countries around the world in recent years suggest their members see their colleagues being fired (and not replaced), understaffing on the rise, and more and more journalists working on contingent bases (International Labour Organization, 2006). Professionals today increasingly have contracts, not careers in journalism, and stress and burnout are on the rise (O'Donnell, Zion and Sherwood, 2015; Reinardy, 2011). As is clear at all the different levels of analysis, precarity has come to be part of the lived experience in journalism.

Of the people left in the profession, some still enjoy a permanent contract (including benefits and protections) with a formal news organization. These generally senior staffers work side-by-side with a host of competitor-colleagues in roles that are anything but stable or structural: (unpaid or underpaid) interns, temp workers, part-timers and independent contractors. In a development similar to other professions – particularly those across the creative industries – permanent jobs are disappearing from journalism, and generally unpaid internships and other forms of free labour now determine access to what one day may be some kind of formal working arrangement.

All this is accompanied by the rising cost of entry into journalism: a trade school diploma is a bare minimum – for jobs in the national quality news media, in practice a high-level university education is required. Student grants in most of the developed world have been cut, their duration has been shortened and they have been converted into loans. The majority of newcomers in the profession start as a freelancer or otherwise independent journalist (and the majority of journalists keep working that way). For freelance journalists, tariffs have declined structurally over the past decade. In fact, a growing number of part-timers, freelancers and other free agents in the news business do not earn the majority of their living wage with journalistic work, instead opting for a hybrid, cross-subsidized practice (Vinken and IJdens, 2013, p. 4; Weischenberg, Malik and Scholl, 2006, p. 350).

For journalism studies, this brings the challenge of capturing the diversity of work practices and the range of workers in this industry: the atypical journalists mentioned above tend to be ignored by scholarly surveys of journalist populations around the globe. The same goes for the work they do, how they go about doing it and what being a journalist means to them. The journalism population is changing. With the accelerating dynamic of reorganizations and reshuffling, buyouts and lay-offs, new owners and managers, new work arrangements and budget cuts, journalism has become less accessible to everyone. In fact, journalism increasingly seems to be the playing field of a wealthy class consisting only of those who can afford to work for years or even for the majority of their careers below or around the minimum wage in the largest and therefore most expensive cities, where the main news media organizations are mostly located. It is thus more important than ever to capture who is working in journalism, under which circumstances the work gets done, what kind of work is produced, and ultimately with what impact on society and citizens' self-governance.

Clearly, the make-up of the profession is changing: on the one hand, the profession is greying, as those contracted with legacy media organizations have often had the benefit of a long career; on the other hand, younger journalists enter the profession in large numbers (as journalism programmes are still very popular among students at the undergraduate as well as graduate levels), but they leave the profession relatively quickly as well, as a comparison of surveys conducted between 1996 and 2011 among journalists in 31 countries shows (Willnat, Weaver and Choi, 2013, p. 4). This process is a mirror of the revolving door effect long plaguing the careers of women (and ethnic minorities) in professions dominated by white/male workers (Jacobs, 1989). It begs the question what kind of people – in terms of demographics, socioeconomic class and personality type – can survive and thrive beyond the revolving door. To understand journalism, it is important to capture who populates it (and also who does *not*), to gain insight into the conditions they work under and ultimately how this informs the type of journalism that is produced.

Discussion and conclusion

This chapter highlights how post-industrial modes of journalism face disruptions along different dimensions, arguing that these disruptions fundamentally challenge the dominant ways of conceptualizing, theorizing and analysing journalism practices. Journalism theory has treated journalism predominantly as a stable object, which means it is unable to deal with the complexity and continuous change and state of becoming in the field. Ultimately, our exploration of the disruptive developments suggests that we need to view journalism as a moving object. In other words, we need to ask what journalism becomes rather than what journalism is (Deuze, 2005). We have considered how the becoming of journalism is currently evolving at the levels of the social system, social institutions, news organizations and the individual journalist. Viewing the developments in journalism through these access points, it becomes clear how the context, institutions, practices and population of journalism are significantly changing.

For scholars in this field, it is of critical importance to not just capture a snapshot of journalism at a particular time, freezing certain phenomena as if they are stable, but rather to focus on the 'becoming' of journalism: to show the process through which journalism is constituted within its social context, to acknowledge the variety of actors involved in this process, and to trace the changing definitions of who is and who is not considered a journalist, as well as the precarious and shifting nature of newswork. The ultimate aim of such research and the resulting theories is not to 'pin down' journalism and its role in society, but rather to reflect on and make space for the multitude of ever-shifting practices and their varying impacts. Such research has to rely not only on a variety of vantage points, as we have argued here, but also on a variety of methods and theoretical perspectives to consider the becoming of journalism. Moreover, to do justice to its complexity, such triangulation needs to allow for varying definitions to co-exist, to allow various insights, even (or especially) when they contradict each other. It is in this space of doubt and insecurity that a deeper and more complex understanding of journalism in the digital age can come into being (see also Costera Meijer, 2016).

Such explorations, as we aimed to inspire here, will show that what happens at the level of the individual, organization, institution and social system does not always paint a coherent and neat picture of a stable and clearly boundaried profession. One of the tensions that such research will bring up, and that we would like to highlight in our concluding paragraph, is that to be a professional, working journalist in the twenty-first century means, to most, having to go and perform beyond journalism. When focusing, as we have suggested, on the becoming of journalism – tracing the lived experience of individual journalists in its organizational, institutional and social context – we see that many (if not most) journalists today are engaged well beyond what any profession could ask for. Normally the profession asks for a certain type of commitment, but journalists in the digital age have to be committed beyond any of this, as their work is insecure, their pay limited, the people's trust precarious, and their working time stretches beyond the boundaries of a print deadline or broadcast schedule. With the limited institutional protections and privileges of the profession, this means that their drive becomes increasingly personal. This personal, affective and emotional engagement with newswork that in the period of 'high modernism' (Hallin, 1992) could be related back to journalists 'living and breathing the news' needs to be reconsidered with the changing institutional, organizational and social definitions of what journalism is. One of the main questions that journalism scholars need to consider is what journalism becomes in the profoundly precarious industry, working environment and career context in which individual journalists currently operate.

Note

1   See, for example, http://www.wan-ifra.org/reports/2009/03/12/outsourcing-revisited; and for an overview, http://www.wan-ifra.org/microsites/research-shaping-the-future-of-news-publishing.

References

Anderson, C. W. (2011). Blowing up the newsroom: Ethnography in an age of distributed journalism. In D. Domingo & C. Paterson (Eds.), *Making online news* (pp. 151–160). New York: Peter Lang.

Anderson, C. W., Bell, E., & Shirky, C. (2012). *Post-industrial journalism: Adapting to the present.* New York: Tow Center for Digital Journalism, Columbia University.

Bauman, Z. (2000). *Liquid modernity.* Cambridge: Polity Press.

Bauman, Z. (2005). *Liquid life.* Cambridge: Polity Press.

Beck, U. (2000). *The brave new world of work.* Cambridge: Polity Press.

Briggs, M. (2011). *Entrepreneurial journalism*. New York: CQ Press.

Castells, M. (2010). *The rise of the network society* (3rd ed.). Cambridge, MA, & Oxford: Blackwell.

Chia, R. (1995). From modern to postmodern organizational analysis. *Organization Studies* 16(4), 579–604.

Costera Meijer, I. (2016). Practicing audience-centred journalism research. In T. Witschge, C. W. Anderson, D. Domingo & A. Hermida (Eds.), *Sage Handbook of Digital Journalism* (pp. 546–561). London: Sage.

Cottle, S. (2007). Ethnography and news production: New(s) developments in the field. *Sociology Compass, 1*, 1–16.

Deuze, M. (2005). What is journalism? Professional identity and ideology of journalists reconsidered. *Journalism, 6*(4), 443–465.

Deuze, M. (2007). Journalism in liquid modern times: An interview with Zygmunt Bauman. *Journalism Studies, 8*(4), 671–679.

Deuze, M. (2008). The professional identity of journalists in the context of convergence culture. *Observatorio, 2*(4). Retrieved from http://obs.obercom.pt/index.php/obs/article/view/216.

Deuze, M. (2014). Journalism, media life, and the entrepreneurial society. *Australian Journalism Review, 36*(2), 119–130.

Gall, G. (2000). New technology, the labour process and employment relations in the provincial newspaper industry. *New Technology, Work and Employment, 15*(2), 94–107.

Gauntlett, D. (2011). *Making is connecting*. Cambridge: Polity Press.

Grabher, G. (2002). The project ecology of advertising: Tasks, talents and teams. *Regional Studies, 36*(3), 245–262.

Hallin, D. (1992). The passing of the 'high modernism' of American journalism. *Journal of Communication, 42*(3), 14–25.

Hanitzsch, T., & Mellado, C. (2011). What shapes the news around the world? How journalists in 18 countries perceive influences on their work. *International Journal of Press/Politics, 16*, 404–426.

Hartley, J. (2000). Communicational democracy in a redactional society. *Journalism, 1*(1), 39–47.

International Labour Organization. (2006). *The changing nature of work: A global survey and case study of atypical work in the media industry*. Research report. Retrieved from http://www.ifj.org/pdfs/ILOReport070606.pdf.

Jacobs, J. (1989). *Revolving doors: Sex segregation and women's careers*. Palo Alto: Stanford University Press.

Jenkins, H. (2004). The cultural logic of media convergence. *International Journal of Cultural Studies, 7*(1), 33–43.

Josephi, B. (2013). De-coupling journalism and democracy: Or how much democracy does journalism need? *Journalism, 14*(4), 441–445.

Keith, S. (2011). Shifting circles: Reconceptualizing Shoemaker and Reese's theory of a hierarchy of influences on media content for a newer media era. *Web Journal of Mass Communication Research, 29*. Retrieved from http://www.scripps.ohiou.edu/wjmcr/vol29/29.html.

Le Masurier, M. (2015). What is slow journalism? *Journalism Practice, 9*(2), 138–152.

Lee-Wright, P., & Phillips, A. (2012). Doing it all in the multi-skilled universe. In P. Lee-Wright, A. Phillips & T. Witschge (Eds.), *Changing journalism* (pp. 63–80). London: Routledge.

Lewis, S., & Usher, N. (2014). Code, collaboration, and the future of journalism. *Digital Journalism, 2*(3), 383–393.

Lowrey, W., & Anderson, W. (2005). The journalist behind the curtain: Participatory functions on the internet and their impact on perceptions of the work of journalism. *Journal of Computer-Mediated Communication, 10*(3). Retrieved from http://jcmc.indiana.edu.

McNair, B. (2003). *Sociology of journalism.* London: Routledge.

McQuail, D. (2013). *Journalism and society.* London: Sage.

Moloney, K. (2012). *Transmedia journalism as a post-digital narrative.* Denver: University of Colorado Press.

Mosco, V. (2009). The future of journalism. *Journalism, 10*(3), 350–352.

O'Donnell, P., Zion, L., & Sherwood, M. (2016). Where do journalists go after newsroom job cuts? *Journalism Practice, 10*(1), 35–51. doi: 10.1080/17512786.2015.1017400.

Picard, R. (2010, January 2). The biggest mistake of journalism professionalism. *The Media Business.* Retrieved from http://themediabusiness.blogspot.nl/2010/01/biggest-mistake-of-journalism.html.

Reinardy, S. (2011). Newspaper journalism in crisis: Burnout on the rise, eroding young journalists' career commitment. *Journalism, 12*(1), 33–50.

Russo, T. C. (1998). Organizational and professional identification: A case of newspaper journalists. *Management Communication Quarterly, 12*(1), 72–111.

Ryan, K. M. (2009). The performative journalist: Job satisfaction, temporary workers and American television news. *Journalism, 10*(5), 647–664.

Scholl, A., & Weischenberg, S. (1998). *Journalismus in der gesellschaft: Theorie, methodologie und empirie.* Opladen: Westdeutscher Verlag.

Schudson, M. (1995). *The power of news.* Cambridge, MA: Harvard University Press.

Sennett, R. (2006). *The culture of the new capitalism.* New Haven, CT: Yale University Press.

Seo, M. G., & Creed, W. E. D. (2002). Institutional contradictions, praxis, and institutional change: A dialectical perspective. *Academy of Management Review, 27*(2), 222–247.

Shoemaker, P. J., & Reese, S. D. (2014). *Mediating the message in the 21st century: A media sociology perspective.* New York: Longman.

Stearns, J. (2013). *Acts of journalism: Defining press freedom in the digital age.* New York: Free Press.

Storey, J., Salaman, G., & Platman, K. (2005). Living with enterprise in an enterprise economy: Freelance and contract workers in the media. *Human Relations, 58*(8), 1033–1054.

Tuchman, G. (1973). Making news by doing work: Routinizing the unexpected. *American Journal of Sociology, 78*(1), 110–131.

Van de Walle, S., Van Roosbroek, S., & Bouckaert, G. (2008). Trust in the public sector: Is there any evidence for a long-term decline? *International Review of Administrative Sciences, 74*(1), 45–62.

Vinken, H., & IJdens, T. (2013). *Freelance journalisten, schrijvers en fotografen.* Tilburg: Pyrrhula.

Wahl-Jorgensen, K. (2009). News production, ethnography, and power: On the challenges of newsroom-centricity. In E. Bird (Ed.), *Journalism and anthropology* (pp. 21–35). Bloomington: Indiana University Press.

Weischenberg, S. (1992). *Journalistik: Theorie und praxis aktueller medienkommunikation. Band 1: Mediensysteme, medienethik, medieninstitutionen.* Opladen: Westdeutscher Verlag.

Weischenberg, S., Malik, M., & Scholl, A. (2006). Journalismus in Deutschland 2005. *Media Perspektiven, 7,* 346–361.

Willnat, L., Weaver, D., & Choi, J. (2013). The global journalist in the twenty-first century. *Journalism Practice, 7*(2), 163–183.

Witschge, T. (2013). Transforming journalistic practice: A profession caught between change and tradition. In C. Peters & M. Broersma (Eds.), *Rethinking journalism: Trust and participation in a transformed news landscape* (pp. 160–172). London: Routledge.

Witschge, T., & Nygren, G. (2009). Journalism: A profession under pressure? *Journal of Media Business Studies, 6*(1), 37–59.

Zelizer, B. (2013). On the shelf life of democracy in journalism scholarship. *Journalism, 14*(4), 459–473.

8

THE JOURNALIST AS ENTREPRENEUR

Jane B. Singer

The rise of 'entrepreneurial journalism' – the creation of publicly relevant content by journalistic enterprises that have emerged and evolved outside of legacy news organizations – is fundamentally a response to industry disruption. Veteran journalists who suddenly find themselves unemployed are rethinking their career options; so too are new journalists who have struggled to find jobs at all or been disappointed by the ones they have found.

Both groups recognize the allure of an open-access, interconnected platform that undermines capital-intensive business models but invites low-cost experimentation, and growing numbers of journalists have joined the staffs of digital news start-ups or become media entrepreneurs themselves. They have quickly encountered a need to transform themselves into savvy businesspeople and to identify the relevance of traditional journalistic norms and practice for sustainably competitive enterprises. Doing so often requires learning new skills and taking on unfamiliar occupational roles. The many resulting challenges include maintaining editorial independence while meeting commercial demands within a nascent organization; identifying, enticing, engaging and retaining audiences; and identifying and implementing viable financial strategies that are also journalistically sound.

Entrepreneurial journalists are thus forced to revisit what often are deeply held views about what journalism is, should be and might become. This chapter explores the implications for practitioners and publics, as well as for the scholars who seek to understand them. As the volume of influential journalism produced outside traditional newsrooms continues to grow, exploring its relevance to democratic society becomes increasingly vital.

Entrepreneurial journalism

Although entrepreneurialism has fascinated business scholars for decades (Kuratko, 2005), its connection to journalism is relatively new, and the term 'entrepreneurial journalism' remains more a label than an identifiable practice (Anderson, 2014). There is some consensus that the term should not stretch to encompass freelancers, who have relatively little power or flexibility (Baines and Kennedy, 2010; Drok, 2013), but it has rarely been defined more explicitly even within industry discourse. Most references to entrepreneurial journalism are vague enough to accommodate a variety of constructed meanings, typically drawing on a listing of characteristics or comparisons to traditional journalistic practice or forms (Vos and Singer, 2016).

Despite the imprecision, consideration of news production as an entrepreneurial enterprise has accelerated as traditional media models have come under increasing pressure, driven in part by a technological environment hospitable to innovation and thus appealing not only to individuals but also to media institutes and foundations (Compaine and Hoag, 2012). The financial environment, while dreadful for traditional media companies, has also benefited news start-ups; one example is the recent rise of 'impact investing', in which an investor's explicit intention is to generate a positive social impact as well as a financial return (Bugg-Levine and Emerson, 2011; Clark, Emerson and Thornley, 2014). Crowdfunding has also gained ground as a revenue stream during this time (Bennett, Chin and Jones, 2015; Carvajal, Garcia-Aviles and Gonzalez, 2012), enabling distributed funding for journalistic projects. 'Journalism has long been considered a public service, more of a calling than a profession. Now it is also a business opportunity', writes Mark Briggs. 'The ability to adapt to a changing environment will separate success from failure' (2012, pp. xxi, 38).

Yet with a few high-profile exceptions, most journalistic start-ups have struggled; indeed, sustainability has been so elusive that 'survival in itself must be recognised as a form of success' (Bruno and Nielsen, 2012, p. 102). One suggested reason is that journalists tend to over-estimate the demand for, and hence the economic value of, high-quality journalism and to under-estimate how much competition exists for users' time, attention and money (Picard, 2000). In case studies of three US news start-ups that sought to replace community coverage lost because of newspaper shutdowns or cutbacks, Naldi and Picard (2012) found 'formational myopia': unrealistic expectations about demand for journalists' services and the economic value of their work. Each start-up tried to import professional newspaper practices and norms, a hierarchical and cost-intensive endeavour poorly suited to the digital world. None met the goals of 'providing broad coverage and community impact using significant numbers of professional journalists' (2012, p. 91).

More broadly, the success of technological innovation hinges on the extent of overlap among the needs of customers, content producers and financiers; the likelihood of success increases when those needs converge or can be accommodated. Innovations 'will succeed only if the market believes that they create value that is currently absent' and cannot be supplied by cheaper or simpler alternatives (Picard, 2000, p. 61). Yet such alternatives, many of them free, have proliferated in the digital space. Traditional media content was created in 'technical, economic, political and information environments that no longer exist' (Picard, 2011, p. 8). The industry challenge is to provide a value that consumers want in unique or distinctive ways appropriate to a digital network.

Normative challenges compound the fiscal ones. Of particular concern has been the potential to breach the celebrated 'wall' separating editorial and commercial considerations. Indeed, media ethicist Stephen Ward (2009) has depicted issues of independence and conflicts of interest for journalists who double as fundraisers as 'the looming ethical problems of an entrepreneurial age'. He urges rigorous editorial oversight and construction of 'guidelines for protecting independence, responding to public skepticism, and managing conflicts of interest'.

The extent to which entrepreneurial journalism diverges from the conception of journalism as a public service that enables an informed electorate to make sound civic choices – the journalist's view of democracy (Gans, 2003) – is another normative concern. Hanitzsch, for example, explicitly distinguished a market orientation, associated with giving audiences what they want to know 'at the expense of what they should know' (2007, p. 375), from the conceptualization of journalism as independent watchdog. Market-driven journalism (McManus, 1994) addresses audiences as clients and consumers rather than citizens, and the digital environment that hosts most entrepreneurial efforts has long been portrayed as an arena where journalistic practices are notably vulnerable to market influence (Cohen, 2002).

Framework for comparison: the business model canvas

The picture of something called 'entrepreneurial journalism', then, seems to depict numerous issues swirling in the background while the subject in the foreground remains blurry. A tool from the world of business studies can help sharpen the focus and provide a framework for comparing entrepreneurial culture with that of traditional journalism.

The business model canvas enables planners to visualize and describe the building blocks of a business plan, and to identify potential trade-offs among them (Osterwalder and Pigneur, 2010). It is especially valuable to entrepreneurs because of its emphasis on interdependency among components, facilitation of communication with diverse stakeholders, broadly holistic approach to innovation, and encouragement of creativity and experimentation (Trimi and Berbegal-Mirabent, 2012). Moreover, it affords centrality to customers and the value delivered to, and perceived by, those customers. The canvas thus is an ideal tool for exploring the contemporary news environment, in which journalists are developing and using new tools for understanding media audiences (Lee, Lewis and Powers, 2014; Usher, 2013), engaging with them (Lewis, Holton and Coddington, 2014; Loosen and Schmidt, 2012) and retaining them (Tandoc, 2015; Vu, 2014).

The designers of the canvas identify nine interrelated building blocks (Osterwalder and Pigneur, 2010). The following brief descriptions are based on theirs, with media context added as appropriate. Although all nine are highlighted in the discussion below, this chapter focuses primarily on those explicitly involving customers and the creation of a product those customers will see as valuable, the components most directly relevant to the ways in which journalism studies scholars might seek to understand entrepreneurial journalism.

Key canvas components for entrepreneurial journalism

Customer segments are the people or organizations that an enterprise intends to reach and serve. Entrepreneurs must start by considering who might find their product or service valuable. Some businesses seek to serve a mass market and do not distinguish among customer segments within that aggregate. Others target specialized niche markets or make different offers to different components of a larger market; a bank with both commercial and individual customers is one example of the latter. For media organizations, customers include advertisers as well as readers (or viewers, listeners or users).

Relationships with those customers can be personal or automated, motivated by audience acquisition, retention or expansion goals. Interactive technologies facilitate new relationships. For example, user communities may be formed to facilitate knowledge exchange and problem solving, or users may be engaged in ways that co-create value, such as by providing reviews or other content.

The creation and maintenance of these segments and relationships depends on creating clear *value propositions*. Each product or service offered must be of value for one or more customer segments, creating benefits that constitute the reason potential customers turn to one company over another. A value proposition solves a customer problem or satisfies a customer need ideally better than competitors or other available options. Values may be quantitative, such as a better price or faster service, or qualitative, such as more attractive design or higher associated status.

Other canvas components

Channels describe how a company communicates with its customers to deliver a value proposition, including mechanisms for sales and distribution as well as the actual message itself.

A consideration of *revenue streams* enables entrepreneurs to address a key question: for what value is each customer segment truly willing to pay? Media companies have traditionally relied on advertisers and audiences, who buy their content one way or another, but other options include usage fees, licensing and event hosting. And although news outlets typically set a fixed price for their product, other pricing mechanisms are available, such as those based on the number or quality of features.

Producing these revenue streams requires identification of *key resources*, the assets needed to create value and to reach and keep customers, and *key activities*, the most important actions an enterprise must take to operate successfully. Key resources can be physical (the printing press or delivery trucks), financial (cash or credit lines), intellectual (brands, proprietary knowledge or copyrights) or human (particularly crucial in knowledge-intensive or creative industries such as publishing). Activities typically include those related to production (designing, making and delivering a product or service) and problem solving to address customer needs. Such activities often require *key partnerships,* as alliances enable businesses to reduce risk and uncertainty, acquire resources economically or take advantage of economies of scale. Networks of suppliers and partners are cornerstones of many business models, though often challenging for journalists accustomed to the enclosed, linear and competitive processes of traditional news production.

And finally, businesses must consider their *cost structure*: the cost of successfully undertaking all the previous components. Some business models, such as those of discount airlines, are cost-driven; others, such as high-end hotels, are value-driven, typically offering customers considerable personalized attention. Many business models fall in between, seeking to offer good quality at a cost that customers will consider reasonable – not necessarily an easy proposition, as many mainstream news organizations can attest.

Each of these areas poses challenges for journalists as they move to engage in, or compete with, an entrepreneurial media culture. Doing so demands that they rethink well-defined, well-understood and broadly supported articulations about journalistic roles, norms and practices. The rest of this chapter explores those challenges, using the canvas components as a framework for positing that an entrepreneurial approach is not only novel but can also directly conflict with what journalists know or believe about what they do. Many of the issues are inextricably linked with the broader trend towards a world in which digital forms of information are increasingly dominant, creating new technological, financial and social mandates for journalists wherever they work.

The discussion here focuses on individual journalists seeking to re-invent themselves as entrepreneurs, with challenges to news organizations also touched on as appropriate. The emphasis is, therefore, on practitioner norms, roles and self-perceptions. It is worth noting, however, that these organizations as social institutions also face significant economic and cultural disruption from news start-ups, disruption that inevitably affects those journalists who continue to work in their newsrooms as well as those who no longer do.

The challenges of entrepreneurial journalism

For entrepreneurial journalists, the core challenge can be summed up this way: rightly or wrongly, journalists tend to view their distance from the economic realities of the news industry as both a mark and a guarantor of their editorial autonomy, and therefore of their ability to serve the public interest honestly and impartially. Such a normative stance may indeed retain its social value, but it presents obstacles that go beyond those any entrepreneur necessarily faces in turning an idea into a profitable, sustainable business.

Customer segments and customer relationships

The most obvious customer segments for news organizations and their employees are information consumers and advertisers. An additional 'customer' is the outlet's owner, director or publisher; the broad structural shift from individual- or family-owned media companies to large, publicly traded corporations has also meant keeping boards of directors and, ultimately, stockholders sweet. Though that level of influence is generally segregated from newsroom operations, the relationship is rarely made explicit in either formal or informal codes of newsroom practice (McManus, 1997).

More explicit are norms describing – or, more accurately, circumscribing – journalists' relationships with advertisers. The so-called 'wall' between editorial and commercial operations constitutes a fundamental normative understanding for journalists in societies that put a premium on an independent press, dictating that considerations of, let alone direct relationships with, this crucial customer segment be kept wholly outside the newsroom (Borden, 2000). While it's true that this barrier has been breached with some regularity over the years, particularly as economic pressures on media organizations have mounted – and native advertising has raised additional concerns, including the possibility of journalists producing advertising copy (Carlson, 2015) – direct connections between advertisers and journalists are still considered verboten in most newsrooms.

Traditional journalists do acknowledge a relationship with news audiences ... up to a point. That relationship, however, is a one-directional one: it consists primarily of journalists producing and providing information in the public interest, broadly and often vaguely defined. Despite the overarching goal of service to society, journalists have only rarely seen their role as extending to an active facilitation of civic discourse, as those who tried to instigate public journalism projects in highly resistant newsrooms learned (McDevitt, 2003).

Moreover, the traditional news audience is a 'mass' audience, a faceless public acknowledged to have a wide range of interests but thought to share a concern with matters judged (mostly by the journalist) to be of civic importance. The actual composition of this audience was largely unknown except in the aggregate to journalists in twentieth-century newsrooms. Unless they worked in very small communities, those producing the news tended to see readers, viewers or listeners as an undifferentiated and amorphous mass, people with whom journalists had remarkably little contact for a century and more. Some of this distance has closed in a digital era, thanks to the pervasiveness of web analytics, which provide information about the popularity and use of items on a website (Tandoc and Thomas, 2015), as well as comment threads and social media. The latter two, in particular, have brought audience members closer and made more of them individually identifiable. But many journalists continue to keep their distance.

Entrepreneurs, in contrast, must know a great deal about their customers, and precise, concrete and detailed knowledge is the best kind. Entrepreneurial journalists are no exception. To succeed, they must understand how the people they hope to attract and retain currently get information, what kinds of information those people want and need, what delivery mechanism they prefer, and how much as well as in what ways they might be willing to pay. A vague conception of an amorphous public in need of something broadly defined as in their own interest is woefully inadequate. Moreover, the best, if not the only, way to obtain such information is through personal communication: The entrepreneurial journalist has no newsroom walls, no separate marketing or circulation departments, to serve as an audience interface.

The nature of the entrepreneurial audience is also likely to differ from the one for legacy news outlets. Most start-ups will have a niche rather than a mass audience for reasons related to logistics and available resources, as well as to the nature of existing and emerging news markets. The mass market is already served by legacy outlets and others with strong brand name recognition; the emerging market clearly exhibits a trend towards personalization (Thurman, 2011). This is especially true for online news; digital media in general are really good at niche, and mobile technologies in particular are really good at personal (Newman and Levy, 2014). So journalists seeking to launch their own outlets – almost certainly through a digital medium, given the high cost of physical infrastructure – need skills in understanding and courting an audience quite different from the one they are accustomed to serving through their well-understood roles with legacy organizations.

Not only must members of this niche audience be actively wooed as readers but they must also be wooed as contributors – and as advertisers. Contributors first: the people interested in a niche topic are apt to be knowledgeable about it, and a start-up enterprise is unlikely to have the resources for coverage thorough enough to engage such people over time without help – their help. Yet the literature is replete with descriptions of how uneasy journalists have been with various forms of user-generated content or contributions from audiences to news websites (Hermida and Thurman, 2008; Lewis, Kaufhold and Lasorsa, 2010; Singer, 2010). Many legacy outlets remain unconvinced that such contributions are worthwhile at all, as witnessed by the growing number deciding to cut off commenting ability. Even those who see their own articles as the beginning of a conversation may find the notion of having a relationship with readers uncomfortably weird (Singer and Ashman, 2009).

But entrepreneurial journalists unavoidably need to find 'outsiders' who can contribute reliably, cogently, credibly and ideally frequently. Once located, they must be engaged, nurtured and perhaps even compensated. Doing these things requires relationship skills that go far beyond what journalists may have developed with traditional sources, whose only role was to provide information that was routed through, and vetted by, the journalist.

And, of course, traditional media audiences are seen as clearly distinct from advertisers. Journalists serve audiences, vaguely defined though they may be. Advertisers, in contrast, have historically been kept well outside the purview of the newsroom lest they taint journalistic work and output. Yet for an entrepreneurial journalist whose enterprise relies in whole or in part on an advertising-based revenue model (as most do; see Sirkkunen and Cook, 2012), pursuing and securing advertisers is at least as important as pursuing and securing audiences. Who are the most likely advertisers? Commercial entities in the same market niche as the audience, whose employees likely constitute not only part of that audience but also a key word-of-mouth publicity channel – as well as information sources for stories.

Customers and relationships with them, then, are central to any successful business model, yet raise a variety of normative issues for entrepreneurial journalists. Those who have considered these issues more thoroughly stress the importance of having clear ethical guidelines and being transparent with all constituencies about what those guidelines entail (Briggs, 2012). But walking the walk can be difficult amid the ambiguity and the unfamiliar pressures raised by start-up enterprises. The multiple challenges highlight the unfamiliarity of this territory for most journalists, forcing decisions about roles, relationships, practices and skills that likely are quite novel to them. In the traditional newsroom, journalists interact with colleagues and sources, dealing minimally with audiences and not at all with advertisers. As entrepreneurs, they must put a premium on sustainable ethical relationships with everyone.

Value propositions

The value proposition for journalists within a news organization rests on their professional expertise, defined through the editorial content they contribute. Of crucial importance here (notorious newsroom scandals notwithstanding) are normative principles exercised in maintaining credibility, which at least in theory attracts and retains audiences. And important to their self-perception is, again, this broadly defined notion of journalism as a calling in service to democracy, to the creation and sustenance of an informed citizenry able to govern itself wisely precisely because of information that journalists provide (Gans, 2003; Kovach and Rosenstiel, 2007).

The skills and norms in producing a credible story remain valuable, but sadly, as already suggested, not as universally valuable as those who possess them tend to believe. Many of the start-ups that have enjoyed big success are less about serious reporting and close attention to professional ethics than they are about edginess and trend-riding and visuals and speed, with a few kittens tossed in. (Yes, BuzzFeed really has had a 'Beastmaster' on its editorial team – and several Associate Beastmasters, too.) Journalists have little experience in, and often little appetite for, producing the material that attracts the mass audiences that legacy media once drew.

Indeed, both the number and range of competitors for entrepreneurial journalists are enormous. Not least is competition from their former employers, legacy outlets that despite their economic woes still have an established brand reputation as information providers, long-term relationships with audiences and advertisers, and the clout and the resources to hold the powerful to account when they choose to do so. Despite well-documented challenges to all those institutional advantages, they remain substantial; elite news organizations, in particular, continue to derive value from serving a vital civic role in their societies. News start-ups have virtually none of the resources that enable legacy players to maintain this journalistic value: not the brand name or reputation, not the relatively extensive (and expensive) staffs, not the institutional relationships with diverse constituencies and often not the deep pockets either.

Entrepreneurial journalists also face challenges from audiences themselves. As the ability to disseminate information has become widely shared, people have proved willing and able to rely on one another to stay in the know. While the journalist-as-middleman may still be appreciated for purposes of verification or analysis, he or she is no longer necessary to make information available in the first place.

More broadly, considering the competition in a traditional media world was much like looking in the mirror. Competitors generally had comparable goals and values, perhaps with a different approach to meeting them, but still roughly similar in terms of structure, skills and practices. The value proposition for any given outlet involved doing things 'better', somehow, than the competition: maybe one had excellent sport coverage, while the other was known for its business reporting. Needless to say, the nature of competition is vastly diversified today. We live in media. We are surrounded by it, part of it, immersed in it all the time (Deuze, 2012).

Quite rationally, most entrepreneurial journalists have responded by seeking to establish themselves within a particular topical or geographical niche. Hyperlocal news sites, created to serve geographically defined communities particularly in the USA, have based their value proposition on differentiating their content – in terms of quantity, quality or diversity – from that of legacy outlets. They have employed various funding models, including private investment, foundations and employee ownership, but most rely heavily on advertising. Scholars examining these start-ups have concluded that while the goal of filling a gap in local civic discourse is admirable, the long-term sustainability of these enterprises – which have high content creation costs but generally low uptake among audiences or advertisers – is uncertain if not unlikely (Kurpius, Metzgar and Rowley, 2010).

Most other journalism start-ups cover a topical niche, offering narrow-interest content serving special-interest audiences (Cook and Sirkkunen, 2013). Their value lies in the provision of deep knowledge about a narrowly defined domain, emphasizing perspective, analysis and storytelling skills over 'news' (Haque, 2009). Monetizing that value, however, is far from straightforward. As a study of journalism start-ups in Western Europe pointed out, they operate in extremely uncertain circumstances, dependent on fickle users, fluctuating advertising models and investor whims (Bruno and Nielsen, 2012). Most have chosen to avoid direct competition with legacy news outlets that command stronger brands, larger newsrooms and the ability to produce more original content than any start-up can manage. Instead, they have focused on diverse markers of quality – in content, in curation, in user involvement and in the use of multimedia or interactivity.

This extensive consideration of customers and value propositions serves to highlight some of the core difficulties journalists face in reconceptualizing and re-inventing themselves as entrepreneurs. The following section more briefly adds additional implications related to the other business model canvas components. It is worth quickly noting that while larger start-ups may have the wherewithal to employ people specifically to deal with business or IT matters, smaller ones commonly count on everyone – journalists included – to pitch in.

Other business model canvas components

Journalists working in a traditional newsroom understand *channels* mainly as modes and mechanisms of content delivery, from the broadcast tower, to the newspaper delivery truck, to the mysterious bits and bytes that constitute the website. Whatever the actual channel, its creation happened a long time ago and its maintenance is someone else's job – someone else with whom the journalist may never cross paths. An entrepreneurial journalist must be savvy enough about the tools to know not just what they can do but also what they might reasonably be expected to do a year from now. That's notoriously difficult even for experts, and few journalists are experts. Moreover, those channels must be adeptly used not just in the service of content, the journalist's traditional remit, but also for marketing and delivering the product to both audiences and advertisers.

At a more esoteric level, channels must fit with audience behaviours, and for traditional media, these remain broadly recognizable: I go to the store and buy a newspaper, I turn on the TV news while I'm eating dinner. Online audience habits are far less easily segmented and involve far less loyalty, shifting rapidly as new devices, new software and new content offerings become available. And for a journalism start-up, of course, there are no habits at all – entrepreneurs must create and nurture them from scratch if their enterprise is to survive.

Money – *revenue streams* and *cost structures* in business model parlance – also matters. In traditional news organizations, newsroom salaries and infrastructure often constitute the largest expense, which is one reason journalists have been so vulnerable in tough times. Here's something that hasn't changed: content creation is likely still the biggest expense. Although it's the area of a media start-up budget that the entrepreneurial journalist likely understands most fully, the temptation to spend more than is wise is great, as indicated above. The entrepreneur needs to think hard about every cost: how big it is, what value it adds and how central that value is to success or even survival.

The next questions, of course, are where that money will come from and how to ensure that more comes in than goes out. The start-up sector is even more massively unstable than the traditional media sector. Potential financial backers must be effectively pitched, and because people are constantly asking them for money, they have bullshit detectors to rival those of any journalist. Advertisers must be convinced to climb on board. Audiences must be convinced to contribute time or money or both, in a media environment where so much great stuff, including stuff from well-established providers, is available for free.

While journalists in traditional newsrooms are well aware that the content they produce is for sale, their involvement with that transaction is quite deliberately nil. Start a business, and the learning curve promises to be steep and sharp. Adding to the difficulty, the revenue streams that dominate traditional media business models – advertisers and audiences – almost certainly need to be supplemented. Experts have universally insisted that diverse revenue sources are imperative to the survival of media start-ups (Bruno and Nielsen, 2012; Kurpius, Metzgar and Rowley, 2010;

Sirkkunen and Cook, 2012). Money comes from investors and donors, event hosting and consulting, design work and syndication, and more.

Generating that revenue requires resources. Journalists tend to think of themselves as the *key resources* of any news organization. Remember that resources also can be physical, financial and intellectual, but for journalists, the real key is the human resource – them, and through them the sources they nurture, the information they gather and the skills they apply in turning that information into a story. As already described, a key mistake of many journalism start-ups has been sinking too much money into hiring journalists to the detriment of other vital resources. Smoothly functioning technology, for instance, is imperative across multiple platforms of both production and delivery. What do journalists know about hardware and software? Some know a lot. Many know very little beyond the basics.

The same goes for the *key activities* of running a business. Traditional journalistic activities have been expanding steadily since journalists went online two decades ago. They expanded into different modes of communication. They expanded, gingerly, into the scary realm of audience interaction. They continue to expand content delivery across new platforms, from mobile to wearables to virtual reality. Undeniably, journalists are doing more and different things today than they were in 2006 or in 1996, but aside from promoting content on social media, few of those things relate to the business side of the house. Worse, journalists have been socialized from their days at university (where journalism schools had nothing whatsoever to do with business schools) to see as alien such activities as identifying revenue sources, assessing competitors, marketing content or pitching to investors. All are expressly outside the remit of the people who consider themselves journalists.

Even developing content, the one activity that journalists do have experience with, is a challenge. It's a big step from having an idea to assessing its economic viability and then creating a sustainable business around it. The increasing use of web analytics to provide detailed traffic data constitutes a start, as suggested above; for the first time, journalists know exactly which stories attract an audience and which do not. But at a conceptual level, journalists know relatively little about what people are interested in reading or viewing and even less about what they are interested enough to pay for.

And finally, there are *key partnerships* to consider. In a traditional world, journalists' content partners include sources and, well, sources. Even with the rise of social media, it's safe to say that journalists continue to see users primarily as sources of information, either as providers of tips that reporters then pursue or as sources to be interviewed in more depth by, yes, the reporter. Few journalists have any real partners beyond the occasional joint byline – with another journalist.

Yet no one can go it alone in an entrepreneurial world. Partnerships, including with others who provide similar content, are vital. And entrepreneurial journalists must rely on collaboration not just with audiences and with other journalists but also with advertisers, other providers of revenue and resources, and even competitors. Negotiating these partnerships is not easy. What do you create yourself? What do you buy and what are you unable to buy because you bought that other thing? What do you share, how and with whom?

These components of a successful business model (Osterwalder and Pigneur, 2010) have served to highlight some of the reasons why the transition from an employee of a legacy news organization to a media entrepreneur is so very challenging for most journalists. The last section of this chapter summarizes the issues and suggests key questions for empirical exploration by journalism studies scholars.

Conclusions

Over the past decade, as legacy media have experienced so much financial pressure and so many journalists have left (or been unable to enter) traditional newsroom employment, there has been an uptick in consideration of news production as an entrepreneurial enterprise. Journalists have sought to turn what they know and love into a going, growing business. Many have brought with them traditional views of what news is or should be, along with a perhaps overly optimistic perception of the market for it. Journalists, by and large, really do believe in the power of a free press and in the value of a well-informed public to civic and community life. And they believe that they know – and know best – how to provide that value.

Yet making the transition from employee to owner of a news organization requires knowing about business plans, revenue generation, spreadsheets, profit and loss statements, accounting procedures, staffing and partnerships, just for starters. It requires being about attracting not only audiences but also advertisers, sponsors, donors or angel investors. One way or another, it requires being able to talk about money and to understand it at a level far beyond personal finance – all that b-school stuff that journalists jeered at in college and beyond as they pursued their own higher and nobler calling.

And at the end of the day, journalists do still have that higher calling. If they are to remain relevant in contemporary society, they do still have to maintain trust in the credibility of the information they provide, and they do still have to do that in part by maintaining editorial autonomy from the financial decisions they make and the influence of people involved in them. A start-up that loses the trust of any of its core constituences gets no second chance. For the entrepreneurial journalist, that is a challenge made even more complex by the extent to which one and the same person may be an advertiser, a donor and a reader.

The point of dwelling on the challenges facing entrepreneurial journalists has not been to discourage innovation or downplay the urgent need for it. Rather, it has been to highlight the reality that for journalists, the obstacles – concrete and cultural – to launching their own media enterprise are many. As Bruno and Nielsen (2012) point out, mere survival is a notable achievement. Even enterprises that attract sizeable investments and millions of readers struggle to survive: in March 2015, technology news start-up GigaOm abruptly shut down, for example, after an 11-year run that attracted 6.4 million readers.

Entrepreneurial journalism thus raises many intertwined questions, including those familiar from other fundamental shocks to journalism as those over age 20 knew it. Who am I as a journalist? What value do I offer – to whom, how and how much? What do I do? What is my role in society? What hats can I not live without? What new ones do I need and how do I get them to fit without chafing? Which relationships are the ones that matter? How can I nurture them? How can I safeguard them from corruption in various guises? If success isn't leading the newscast, or maybe not even serving that nebulous thing called democratic society, then what exactly is it and how do I attain it?

These are questions that journalism scholars can help answer through empirical investigation and that journalism educators can help the media entrepreneurs of tomorrow work through. At the moment, data-driven studies of entrepreneurial journalists are rare, and the skills I've belaboured here are largely missing from our classes. Business skills are especially notable for their absence, not least because both students and instructors tend to see them as irrelevant and distracting at best, and nefarious at worst. In today's hyper-competitive media environment, however, they are fundamentally relevant to both the public and the profession that seeks to continue serving it.

References

Anderson, C. W. (2014). The sociology of the professions and the problem of journalism education. *Radical Teacher, 99*, 62–68.

Baines, D., & Kennedy, C. (2010). An education for independence: Should entrepreneurial skills be an essential part of the journalist's toolbox? *Journalism Practice, 4*(1), 97–113.

Bennett, L., Chin, B., & Jones, B. (2015). Crowdfunding: A *New Media & Society* special issue. *New Media & Society, 17*(2), 141–148.

Borden, S. L. (2000). A model for evaluating journalist resistance to business constraints. *Journal of Mass Media Ethics, 15*(3), 149–166.

Briggs, M. (2012). *Entrepreneurial journalism: How to build what's next for news.* Washington, DC: CQ Press.

Bruno, N., & Nielsen, R. K. (2012). *Survival is success: Journalistic online start-ups in Western Europe.* Oxford: Reuters Institute for the Study of Journalism.

Bugg-Levine, A., & Emerson, J. (2011). *Impact investing: Transforming how we make money while making a difference.* San Francisco: Jossey-Bass.

Carlson, M. (2015). When news sites go native: Redefining the advertising-editorial divide in response to native advertising. *Journalism, 16*(7), 849–865.

Carvajal, M., Garcia-Aviles, J. A., & Gonzalez, J. L. (2012). Crowdfunding and non-profit media: The emergence of new models for public interest journalism. *Journalism Practice, 6*(5–6), 638–647.

Clark, C., Emerson, J., & Thornley, B. (2014). *Collaborative capitalism and the rise of impact investing.* San Francisco: Jossey-Bass.

Cohen, E. L. (2002). Online journalism as market-driven journalism. *Journal of Broadcasting & Electronic Media, 46*(4), 532–548.

Compaine, B., & Hoag, A. (2012). Factors supporting and hindering new entry in media markets: A study of media entrepreneurs. *International Journal on Media Management, 14*(1), 27–49.

Cook, C. E., & Sirkkunen, E. (2013). What's in a niche? Exploring the business model of online journalism. *Journal of Media Business Studies, 10*(4), 63–82.

Deuze, M. (2012). *Media life.* Malden, MA: Polity.

Drok, N. (2013). Beacons of reliability: European journalism students and professionals on future qualifications for journalists. *Journalism Practice, 7*(2), 145–162.

Gans, H. J. (2003). *Democracy and the news.* New York: Oxford University Press.

Hanitzsch, T. (2007). Deconstructing journalism culture: Toward a universal theory. *Communication Theory, 17*(4), 367–385.

Haque, U. (2009, 27 July). The nichepaper manifesto. *Harvard Business Review.* Retrieved from https://hbr.org/2009/07/the-nichepaper-manifesto.

Hermida, A., & Thurman, N. (2008). A clash of cultures: The integration of user-generated content within professional journalistic frameworks at British newspaper websites. *Journalism Practice, 2*(3), 343–356.

Kovach, B., & Rosenstiel, T. (2007). *The elements of journalism: What newspeople should know and the public should expect.* New York: Three Rivers Press.

Kuratko, D. F. (2005). The emergence of entrepreneurship education: Development, trends and challenges. *Entrepreneurship: Theory and Practice, 29*(5), 577–598.

Kurpius, D. D., Metzgar, E. T., & Rowley, K. M. (2010). Sustaining hyperlocal media: In search of funding models. *Journalism Studies, 11*(3), 359–376.

Lee, A. M., Lewis, S. C., & Powers, M. (2014). Audience clicks and news placement: A study of time-lagged influence in online journalism. *Communication Research, 41*(4), 505–530.

Lewis, S. C., Holton, A. E., & Coddington, M. (2014). Reciprocal journalism: A concept of mutual exchange between journalists and audiences. *Journalism Practice, 8*(2), 229–241.

Lewis, S. C., Kaufhold, K., & Lasorsa, D. L. (2010). Thinking about citizen journalism: The philosophical and practical challenges of user-generated content for community newspapers. *Journalism Practice, 4*(2), 163–179.

Loosen, W., & Schmidt, J. H. (2012). (Re)-discovering the audience: The relationships between journalism and audience in networked digital media. *Information, Communication & Society, 15*(6), 867–887.

McDevitt, M. (2003). In defense of autonomy: A critique of the public journalism critique. *Journal of Communication, 53*(1), 155–160.

McManus, J. H. (1994). *Market-driven journalism: Let the citizen beware?* Thousand Oaks, CA: Sage.

McManus, J. H. (1997). Who's responsible for journalism? *Journal of Mass Media Ethics, 12* (1), 5–17.

Naldi, L., & Picard, R. G. (2012). 'Let's start an online news site': Opportunities, resources, strategy, and formational myopia in startups. *Journal of Media Business Studies, 9*(4), 69–97.

Newman, N., & Levy, D. A. L. (2014). *Reuters Institute digital news report 2014: Tracking the future of news.* Oxford: Reuters Institute for the Study of Journalism. Retrieved from http://reutersinstitute.politics.ox.ac.uk/sites/default/files/Reuters%20Institute%20Digital%20News%20Report%202014.pdf.

Open Society Foundations. Retrieved from http://www.opensocietyfoundations.org/sites/default/files/digitization-media-business-models-20110721.pdf.

Osterwalder, A., & Pigneur, Y. (2010). *Business model generation: A handbook for visionaries, game changers, and challengers.* Hoboken, NJ: John Wiley & Sons.

Picard, R. G. (2000). Changing business models of online content services: Their implications for multimedia and other content producers. *International Journal on Media Management, 2*(2), 60–68.

Picard, R. G. (2011). Mapping digital media: Digitization and media business models.

Singer, J. B. (2010). Quality control: Perceived effects of user-generated content on newsroom norms, values and routines. *Journalism Practice, 4*(2), 127–142.

Singer, J. B., & Ashman, I. (2009). 'Comment is free, but facts are sacred': User-generated content and ethical constructs at the Guardian. *Journal of Mass Media Ethics, 24*(1), 3–21.

Sirkkunen, E., & Cook, C. (2012). *Chasing sustainability on the net.* Tampere: Tampere Research Centre for Journalism, Media and Communication. Retrieved from http://www. submojour.net/.

Tandoc, E. C. (2015). Why web analytics click: Factors affecting the ways journalists use audience metrics. *Journalism Studies, 16*(6), 782–799.

Tandoc, E. C., & Thomas, R. J. (2015). The ethics of web analytics: Implications of using audience metrics in news construction. *Digital Journalism, 3*(2), 243–258.

Thurman, N. (2011). Making 'the daily me': Technology, economics and habit in the mainstream assimilation of personalized news. *Journalism, 12*(4), 395–415.

Trimi, S., & Berbegal-Mirabent, J. (2012). Business model innovation in entrepreneurship. *International Entrepreneurship and Management Journal, 8*(4), 449–465.

Usher, N. (2013). Al Jazeera English online: Understanding web metrics and news production when a quantified audience is not a commodified audience. *Digital Journalism, 1*(3), 335–351.

Vos, T. P., & Singer, J. B. (2016). Media discourse about entrepreneurial journalism: Implications for journalistic capital. *Journalism Practice, 10*(2), 143–159.

Vu, H. T. (2014). The online audience as gatekeeper: The influence of reader metrics on news editorial selection. *Journalism, 15*(8), 1094–1110.

Ward, S. J. A. (2009, 15 September). *Journalism in the Entrepreneurial Age.* Center for Journalism Ethics, School of Journalism and Mass Communication, University of Wisconsin-Madison. Retrieved from http://ethics.journalism.wisc.edu/2009/09/15/journalism-in-the-entrepreneurial-age/.

9

A JOURNALISM OF CARE

Kaori Hayashi

Debates on ethics are nothing new for journalism. Indeed, many of the foundational discussions around objectivity that characterized the 'high modern' period of journalism (Hallin, 1992), especially in the Anglo-American context, centred around the value and necessity of such ideal forms of conduct. Notions that came to act as industry-wide technical and discursive standards, such as factuality, fairness, non–bias, independence, non-interpretation, neutrality and detachment, were also rhetorical claims whose ethical underpinnings helped establish and defend journalism as a profession and practice (Ward, 2005). Against this more familiar backdrop, this chapter explores an alternative ethos, that of a 'journalism of care', to articulate a vision of journalism that sets its underpinnings not in abstract truths, but in its relevance to the public.

A journalism of care is a journalism that incorporates in its ethical foundation feminist values inherent to the ethic of care. In this respect, it is meant to be a critical review of the Anglo-American type of libertarian journalism ethics that still pervade a contemporary age marked by diverse societies; it calls for more inclusiveness and integration of those who are forced to live as 'social others'. Above all, a journalism of care problematizes how the right of free speech, which tends to be taken for granted in large parts of the world, is virtually irrelevant to many 'social others' in society, particularly those most in need of it. I argue that the idea of care can act as a prompt to respond to actual feelings of those who are being left out, segregated or abandoned due to a lack of resources to speak up. A journalism of care can also serve as a social institution that provides the public with a more comprehensive picture of the world, as well as binding people together who are otherwise increasingly spread out in modern mass society.

In this chapter, I illustrate some of these challenges by focusing on the suffering of residents living in radiation-contaminated areas in Fukushima. In all cases, journalistic approaches based on more conventional libertarian ethics, especially notions emphasizing the centrality of free speech, provide little guidance. In this respect, practitioners have much to gain if they embrace more differentiated and reflexive questions to underlie codes of conduct, such as 'how can individual journalists be best equipped to act professionally *and* morally in particular cases?' or 'how can free speech be best realized within intangible social and cultural restrictions (moral guidelines)?' Similar issues were raised around the shooting at the offices of the French satirical newspaper *Charlie Hebdo* in January 2015. The paper had been publishing non-concessional, hostile expressions towards Muslim communities and had received death threats from Muslim extremists. In the eyes of a majority of Western countries, the shooting was an attack on freedom of speech, a symbolic act of aggression against the Western values of liberal democracy. However, debates were ignited later on about whether the paper's outright rights-based attitude should be protected, particularly in consideration of the social context in which its expressions were directed – often towards underprivileged minorities in Western society who were subject to discrimination. Questions remain as to how far one should take context into consideration in terms of the execution of fundamental human rights, especially in an era of globalization in which people from different value systems meet in the public sphere, owing to the rising mobility of ordinary citizens and availability of communication tools. Subsequently, I hope to propose a vision for how we can best re-incorporate the idea of care into society to reinvigorate the modern democratic polity in an age of abundant digital communication.

Care as a challenge to libertarian values

Critical reflections on libertarian ethics have been reiterated particularly in the face of increased market pressures and commercialism in the media industry since the late nineteenth century. Considered the standard, libertarian ethics are the most globally prevalent form of journalism ethics, driven by the belief that they enhance individual freedom and choice, and thus bring about social mobility, progress and change. In other words, libertarian journalistic activities uphold notions of individual freedom and autonomous command of will, along with scientific impartiality and objectivity, as well as endorsing the function of the 'marketplace of ideas', in which only truth survives (Siebert, 1956).

However, an increasing number of critics argue that the guidelines offered by libertarian ethics may not so much serve for the betterment of journalism, but instead prove harmful to society. According to these views, libertarian ethics – with their emphasis on individualism – sow sensationalism, tabloidization or else irresponsible horse-race reporting, all of which contribute to producing cynical and disengaged citizens (Steiner and Okrusch, 2006). In addition, with the rapid proliferation of digital media, the significance of a discursive journalism ethics that lauds individual autonomy and freedom may have unintended consequences: citizens are now encouraged to contribute to the 'news', but rather than facilitating public integration and solidarity, such conversations often result in people articulating 'facts' in their own interest, opining their own views in infinite cyberspace. Rather than bringing citizens together, such informational abundance can produce even more fractured publics. More fundamentally, questions have also been raised in the face of globalization, particularly from non-Western countries, concerning the validity of seemingly universal journalism professional ethics that are rooted in libertarianism (Ward, 2013; Ward and Wasserman, 2010). In short, continuing to embrace libertarian ethics as foundational to journalism's future going forth raises multiple concerns.

In an effort to overcome the limitations of libertarian ethics, recent studies on media and media ethics have focused on the concept of an openly inclusive news culture that takes care of a community as a point of departure, aiming to contribute to its good. Such a culture accommodates practical everyday-life information as well as interactive conversations and communication, aided by new digital technologies. In general, a considerable number of media and journalism studies scholars have called for the re-examination of the conventional type of libertarian norms, especially in light of the broadening horizon of the participatory spaces brought about by the internet (see Allan, 2013; Silverstone, 2006; Waisbord, 2013). My aim is to join this tide of exploration into new realms of journalistic ethics and activities and add a feminist perspective, especially in light of the ethics of care and empathy that call for human solidarity (Hayashi, 2011).

To develop my argument for a journalism that supports the ethic of care, it is essential to discuss its virtues and contemporary significance. First proposed by Carol Gilligan in 1982 in the field of developmental psychology, the ethics of care has since been redefined and re-interpreted as a theory of feminism. A number of political theorists and ethics researchers contend that its values are fundamental to the enlightenment and enrichment of human life in the contemporary capitalistic world of freedom and diversity (Held, 2006, pp. 18–19). After reviewing these values, I demonstrate the contradictory nature of freedom of speech within contemporary Japanese society. By contrasting this with the idea of care, I clarify and discuss the difference and significance a journalism of care can make compared with conventional journalistic activities in a free society.

The ethic of care and its relevance to journalism

The ethic of care, as proposed by Gilligan (1982), is a multi-faceted set of ethics developed using insights from developmental psychology. Gilligan observed that girls develop their moral sensibilities differently from boys and attributed this phenomenon to the existence of two distinct 'moral projects' based on gender differences. The division is based upon the social reality that women are traditionally relegated to the domestic sphere and given the responsibility of caring for other people, especially those who are vulnerable, such as infants and the elderly. She argued that women defined themselves in the context of human relationships and judged themselves in terms of their capability to carry out care responsibilities; meanwhile, men equated their maturity with attaining personal autonomy and respecting the prevailing sense of social fairness. She thus concluded that, for women, 'the moral problem arises from conflicting responsibilities rather than from competing rights.

The care ethics require for its resolution a mode of thinking that is contextual and narrative rather than formal and abstract' (Gilligan, 1982, p. 19).

The two different moral spheres are based on the gendered stereotypes of adulthood, and Gilligan criticized the idea that the feminine sphere, which upholds relationships and care, is regarded as subordinate and inferior to the masculine sphere, which upholds autonomy and individual rights. Indeed, the social system favours 'the separateness of the individual self over connection to others, and leaning more toward an autonomous life of work than toward the interdependence of love and care' (Gilligan, 1982, p. 17). She therefore argued that both moral theories are equally important and deserve attention. Other care theorists have also attempted to extend the scope of the ethic of care well beyond gender, acknowledging criticisms that an ethical schema that attributes women to the domain of private or intimate relationships actually does more harm than good to women themselves by confirming the stereotypical division of social roles. Such argumentation will not suffice as a practical ethic in society at large.

In recognizing the weakness in their (initial) arguments, care theorists contended that one main feature of the ethic of care is its critical stance towards liberal individualism and other liberal human conceptions, such as those upon which the Rawlsian *theory of justice* is based. These liberal theories presuppose that human beings are autonomous, mature and rational from the outset, and thus uphold the contractual model of human relations (e.g. Held, 2006; Kittay, 1999). Therefore, those who need care (children, the elderly and the sick) and their carers (mainly women) are excluded from this modern social framework; when they are taken into account, they are given special treatment, at best as 'exceptions'. In contrast to such views of human beings, the ethic of care features a 'compelling moral salience of attending to and meeting the needs of the particular others for whom we take responsibility' (Held, 2006, p. 10). My intention is to introduce care ethics to journalism, to provide this field with an alternative set of values, by emphasizing the state of humans' fundamental dependence on others (Kittay, 1999).

Journalism, a modern institution established upon liberal/libertarian thoughts, also presupposes an independent and rational image of human beings; that is, every mature adult should know what to say if he or she wants to say something. Care ethics, meanwhile, is based on the fact that every human being is, at least for a certain period (i.e. childhood), vulnerable and frail. It focuses its ethical mandate on sharing the responsibility of looking after those who need care. In this sense, care ethicists see it as their task to elicit appropriate words from vulnerable persons. It is on this premise that I would like to rethink journalism practices. This endeavour can help to enrich and diversify news coverage by both expanding the scope of journalism and deepening its insight into the lives of human beings.

In particular, the following paradox must be addressed: whereas the ability to speak out is attributed to the presupposed autonomy and independence of a person from his or her social context, the need to speak out only arises precisely because people are frail, embedded in and dependent upon a web of social relations.

Journalism has been linked to the ethics of care, although the potential of such connection has not been fully exhausted. Vanacker and Breslin (2006, pp. 204ff), for instance, offer a useful categorization by identifying three areas in which care ethics can contribute to the study and practice of journalism ethics: (a) it can provide more attention to global, cosmopolitan media ethics; (b) it challenges established professional norms and practices in journalism; and (c) it offers guidelines for particular coverage, such as reporting on crime victims. Related scholarship on cosmopolitanism also offers helpful contributions. Although many such studies do not directly mention the ethic of care, their underlying idea is deeply related to this concept in that they view the media as an actor responsible for engaging the audience to help those who live in poverty and danger to include them in the larger society. Chouliaraki (2013), for example, strongly advocates and argues for this more active role in a global age of diversity. The media play and should play, she argues, the central role in disseminating 'shared vulnerability as a cause for solidary action upon all humanity' (Chouliaraki, 2013, p. 111). Thus, the media serve as an indirect but fundamental care provider to developing countries in a world with widening gaps in regional wealth (see Chouliaraki 2006, 2013; Silverstone, 2006).

In a similar vein, studies on disaster reporting also frequently share the view of care ethicists. Cottle (2013), for example, observed that journalists purposefully produce news reports with a subtle idea of an 'injunction to care' to induce audience engagement. By analysing the professional accounts and testimonies of TV news correspondents and reporters involved in recent disaster reporting, he suggests they may contribute to the wider cultural currents of cosmopolitanism and compassion. Pantti (2013) notes the recent trend to pay more attention to citizen-created imagery for events such as the Arab uprisings and the Japan tsunami disaster, aided by digital technologies, has become a resource for the cosmopolitan commitment of the audience, which remains largely overlooked (see also Pantti, Wahl-Jorgensen and Cottle, 2012).

Apart from cosmopolitanism and globalization, initiatives have also been undertaken to introduce the ethics of care to a more local, everyday type of practical journalism. Pech and Leibel (2006, p. 150), for instance, criticized the traditional dominant liberal model of journalism, arguing that its conventional practices promote an impoverished view of what humans can and should be to one another in interactive human webs. They proposed a journalism with an emphasis on an ethic of care that embraces communal solidarity and 'a sense of our human connectedness with other human beings, among members of its audience' (Pech and Libel, 2006, p. 152). Similarly, Steiner and Okrusch demonstrated the limit of normative thinking based on liberal enlightenment and commitment to 'formalist, rights-based ethics that insist on neutrality, distance, and objectivity' (2006, p. 114). Reporting on the public journalism movements of the 1990s that incorporated common values, such as care, connection and attachment, at a local level, they invited journalists 'to listen to "different voices" and borrow care ethics' optimism in citizens' eagerness to take on responsibilities as agents of care' (2006, p. 118). Craig and Ferré (2006, p. 127) discussed the Christian concept of *agape* and related it to journalism's original task of 'speak[ing] up for people who are ill-treated'. In this sense, they showed its useful-ness, particularly in life-and-death issues, such as reporting on suicide.

While these types of discussions resonate with the idea of the ethics of care in the realm of media and journalism studies, the more conventional approach when discussing ethics is to depart from a libertarian point of view instead. Central to such a perspective is the idea of free speech, the values it is said to promote and the ends it is assumed to achieve. In the following, I problematize this fundamental assump-tion of journalism by considering how the right of 'free' speech is exercised from the perspective of socially ill-treated or overlooked people.

Freedom of speech: a right for 'heroes'

The idea and value of the right of free speech in a democracy are no doubt funda-mental and indispensable. It enables journalists to report in as balanced a fashion as possible, to include diverse viewpoints and to serve people's right to be informed so that they can appropriately judge public affairs and make decisions. In this sense, the right of free speech has been understood as a fundamental institution for democratic society. However, I argue that this understanding is too simplistic and optimistic in a contemporary modern society for three reasons.

First, people in general are socially embedded and thus are not as free as the the-ory presupposes. In addition, the optimism underlying it was born and bred largely in more individualistic Western society, which means that its tenets are harder to apply in highly consensual, group-oriented societies such as Japan. Second, the opti-mism of the free speech theory falls short in concrete cases of crisis and disaster when people are frail and exposed to life-or-death situations. Finally, those who have needs to speak up are often those who are deprived of necessary resources to do so, such as education or money. In the following, I explain these three points based on the case of Japan. Japan belongs to the Western advanced industrial world espousing liberal democracy and guarantees the basic right of freedom of speech to its citizens, as stated in Article 21 of the Japanese Constitution: 'Freedom of assembly and association as well as speech, press and all other forms of expression are guar-anteed. No censorship shall be maintained, nor shall the secrecy of any means of communication be violated.'[1]

Constitutional scholars have held the view that this right takes precedence over all other basic rights guaranteed in the Constitution. They speak of it rigorously and proudly as a symbol of post-war Japan. Masami Itō, one of the most renowned scholars in Japanese constitutional law as well as a former Supreme Court judge, has stated:

> It is the very principle of democracy that government should be conducted through the will of the majority of citizens. Furthermore, this majority will should be formed as the result of the public being exposed to every kind of political expression (even opinions held by only a minority of citizens and considered repugnant by the majority) and allowed to choose freely from

these diverse opinions. ... *The freedom of expression is therefore directly related to the essence of democracy and can be judged to have a value demanding greater Constitutional protection than economic rights, which are not directly related to the basic principle of this form of governance.*

(Itō, 1974, p. 22, emphasis added)

This statement is likely in line with mainstream thoughts held in other advanced liberal nations in the world. Far stricter conditions would have to be applied before the right of free speech could be limited than would apply in the case of other constitutionally guaranteed rights, given that the right of free speech is exceptionally fundamental to the proper functioning of a democratic polity. However, considered from the view of daily living, such statements of ideals seem didactic or even hollow.

One of the reasons for this widening gap between the perceptions of ordinary citizens and the theoretical debates on the significance of the right of free speech is that this right remains largely seen from the anachronistic perspective of nineteenth-century crackdowns on public speech (O'Neill, 2002, pp. 92ff). In the nineteenth century, newspapers were censored or forced to cease publication whenever they attempted to criticize those in power. Particular forms of thought and expression were placed under severe restrictions. This was true of Japan as much as it was of Western countries. In the 1870s, the Meiji government enacted strict penalties for defamation and issued a decree to regulate the publication of newspapers.[2] This move was in response to the rise of the Freedom and People's Rights Movement (*Jiyū Minken Undō*) and the growing role of newspapers in the expression of political opinions.

However, the present-day situation is different. Those heroes of the media (newspaper publishers at the time) who risked themselves by standing up to the powerful are no longer suppressed. Instead, they have grown into major media corporations with considerable power of their own. They are the major beneficiaries of the constitutionally guaranteed right to free speech and have come to wield substantial influence in society. The long-fought struggle of these heroes for the right of free speech has left the ordinary citizen in the background. These heroes use that right as a means to assert their own authority in the name of 'standing up to the powerful'.

As the right of free speech is enjoyed mostly by the powerful heroes of the mass media, many ordinary citizens feel that this right bears little relation to their everyday lives. At least for ordinary citizens living in wealthy liberal welfare societies, communicating through language is not so much about confronting those in power as about maintaining social relations. Human beings are inevitably situated and embedded in a particular local community or field, from which they develop their identities, self-awareness and feelings. They partake in communal narratives and subconsciously embed mechanisms of self-monitoring and self-regulation within themselves. In short, human beings live as social beings, not as individuals isolated from an external world. Moralities are induced in such interrelated social webs. The ethic of care works with such conception of persons as relational and contextual beings rather than as the self-sufficient independent individuals of dominant liberal existence. In other words, people are not individuals who stand in society separately and alone by drawing a clear line from others and the outer world; they are deeply socialized.

This scenario is particularly true in a society such as Japan's, which respects both the hierarchical seniority principle and conventional local communitarian dynamics as well as orienting itself heavily on consensus building within and across groups.

Free speech in disaster-hit Fukushima

Having this in mind, I now turn to a case that highlights the themes raised above. The Great East Japan Earthquake on 11 March 2011 caused unprecedented damage in the northeastern part of Japan: fatalities exceeded 15,000 and, at the time of writing, more than 2,500 people remained missing and 320,000 evacuees still lived in temporary housing. Worst of all, half of these 'refugees' were evacuees from the radiation-contaminated zones near the Fukushima Daiichi Nuclear Power Station.

In the aftermath, a book that collected the testimony of 61 people from the local area, most of whom were forced to leave their homes to avoid nuclear contamination, was published under the editorship of journalist Masayuki Takada, who was a freelancer at the time. In the preface, Takada described the book's role as follows:

> Although it may only be 61 of the several million potential voices, this book is packed with the silent voices of those many from Fukushima who could not speak out. It is full of their sorrow, anger, resignation, despair, struggles and hopes.
>
> (Takada, 2011, p. 7)

In describing the plight of these refugees, journalists realized that traditional journalistic norms and practices – encouraging practitioners to be objective and neutral – manifested themselves as insufficient in these disastrous circumstances, where sensitivity, empathy and advocacy comprised the unwritten mandate of their activities. The issue over the so-called low-dose nuclear contamination, which is invisible, intangible and whose long-term impact on human bodies is debated by experts and scientists, undermined the capacity of traditional journalism. As radiation had no smell or colour, residents were often made to believe that they would be able to lead a normal life, even when data indicated that the nuclear dose in Fukushima was substantially higher than that in other areas in Japan.

In response, a number of journalists launched blogging sites to foster interactive dialogues with local residents, whereas others openly advocated anti-nuclear protests. These practices were all formerly uncommon among corporate journalists in Japan.

The case of Fukushima shows that the shorter the distance between the speaker and those who will be affected by his or her speech, the smaller the chance to exercise this right freely. By bringing information out in the open and writing everything, much possible suffering may result. One of the 61 voices included in the book is that of Hikaru Yaginuma, a reporter for *Fukushima Minpō*, a small local newspaper in Fukushima whose readership consists predominantly of ageing people living in the countryside. In addition, a number of its readers once made their living working for the very nuclear plants that exploded and forced them to evacuate. Furthermore, the earthquake and explosion seriously affected the newspaper itself. Its subscriptions declined after the large-scale evacuation from the area, and a number of delivery stations went out of business. Yaginuma reflected on his continued local reporting and attempt to write about local interests:

> I don't think we can follow the journalistic stance of the national media. We became news by the national media over and over. After the news, we all were left out in the cold, but we have to go on living after the storm.
> (Yaginuma, in Takada, 2011, pp. 269–70)

In their coverage of the earthquake and nuclear accident, local reporters such as Yaginuma were overwhelmed by the simple task of 'representing' the various views of those living in the area. Their capacity to engage in the task of 'opinion formation', as the national press did, was limited because they experienced first hand the opinions and feelings of local residents. In their understanding, then, their tasks as journalists were not to monitor power or to form public opinion, but rather to listen to those whose voices were not much heard in public, even if these voices were unlikely to be printed. Referring to the thoroughly anti-nuclear editorial stance adopted by *Tokyo Shimbun*, a newspaper circulated mostly in the densely populated urban Tokyo Metropolitan area, Yaginuma had the following to say:

> What would happen if we published that (same) kind of opinions in Fukushima? … We are residents of the local area. *Tokyo Shinbun* is a Tokyo newspaper and can afford to be outright anti-nuclear. But *Fukushima Minpō* and our rival *Fukushima Minyū* are Fukushima local newspapers.
> (Yaginuma, in Takada, 2011, p. 265)

One might expect those most directly affected by the disaster to hold the strongest opinions. However, with the desperate and confused face of each local resident in mind, Yaginuma abrogated the task of encapsulating conflicting interests and divergent feelings and refrained from any attempt at the formation of a singular opinion. Local journalists were as aware as anyone of the dangers of nuclear power and had suffered more than others as a result of the accident. Nevertheless, they refrained from taking any overt position either for or against nuclear power, choosing to be silent while the debate raged on in Tokyo. One might be tempted to see this simply as an inferior quality of provincial local journalism compared with competitive, advanced national journalism, but such a view would be an oversimplification at best. As explained above, it was extremely difficult for these local voices to be formed into a set of coherent opinions that could be presented in the national media. The local journalists confronted a cacophony of diverse statements, none of which could gain much attention alone, and any third party could not faithfully represent the thoughts and feelings of those who suffered the most. Clearly, simply guaranteeing the formal right to freedom of speech does very little in such cases.

The voice of the frail

Articulating one's thoughts is in fact not an everyday, taken-for-granted routine, at least not to many social groups and cultures (Taylor, Gilligan and Sullivan, 1995). In the words of Toru Mōri, an expert in constitutional law, 'Japanese constitutional law emphasizes the importance of the freedom of expression but has failed to observe the fact that only a small minority of the population is able to exercise that right' (2008, p. 46). One of the great ironies of the nuclear issue is that those most directly affected by it (the evacuees of Fukushima) are the least able to speak out, as they may have depended on the presence of the nuclear industry in one way or another for their livelihood in communities where there are no other major industries. As a large part of the population in Fukushima lived on incomes from the electric utility Tokyo Electric Power Company (TEPCO) and its related industry, criticisms against TEPCO may be potentially taken as personal criticisms against their neighbours or friends. The victims of the disaster were all aware that any critical statement about the nuclear power plant might cause harm to the lives of their loved ones. The irony cannot therefore be resolved by the strictest adherence to the right to free speech.

Takako Shishido, who voluntarily evacuated from the city of Date (close to the site of the accident but outside areas that received evacuation orders for avoiding radioactive contamination) to Sapporo, was a victim who did not remain silent and suffered from having articulated her opinion. She had the following to say about how national television stations approached the residents:

> Speaking out while revealing your face and name is not something just anyone can do … Your words could destroy another person's life. It happened once. I was asked by a television station to introduce them to someone, and I did. It was really painful thinking about what might happen to that person because I introduced her. What if she lost her job or had something nasty said about her?
>
> (Shishido, in Takada, 2011, pp. 70–1)

Shishido herself was prepared to reveal her story in public out of desperation. In the interview, however, she described how many people in Fukushima were unable to do the same because of personal relationships. For people living in small rural communities, especially women, speaking up can be extremely difficult.[3] Her case showed it was irresponsible for the media to thrust microphones in their faces and expect them to make statements about the issues of nuclear contamination and temporary evacuation. The more directly affected a person is, the more vulnerable he or she is to the consequences of making statements in public.

In another case reported by the internet news site Ourplanet TV, Ruri Sasaki testified that:

> On the surface I look absolutely normal. But in my mind I worry whether this piece (of vegetable) is ok or not … But we are running out of our energy to articulate and problematize our everyday lives. We are all tired.[4]

Sasaki, who had been blogging in the aftermath of the disaster continued, describing everyday life in Fukushima:

> One day, a friend of mine couldn't stand seeing the ugly sight of the laundry hanging inside the house. So she made up her mind to hang them outside, thinking it does not matter anymore whether the risk of getting cancer rises because of it. Having finished hanging the laundry outside, she felt relieved not having to see laundry inside the house. But then, after she collected the dried laundry from outside, she couldn't have her kids wear them out of fear, and washed them all over again. But the next day she still wanted to hang the laundry outside because she couldn't stand to see them in the house. But she felt guilty and washed them again … she feels full of guilt every day with these mundane events. I may as well give this [blogging on the website] up. I got criticized by many people, and sometimes I hurt somebody unintentionally. So I might as well remain silent.

In the uncertain state brought by low-dose nuclear contamination, voices of accusations slowly faded and local residents were silenced.

Mass media journalism, if left alone, often tends to neglect paying attention to the ordinary lives of the voiceless. When it does, it is not out of empathy or active engagement to help, but for the sake of professional curiosity and/or perceived standards of journalistic excellence. The profession tends to be indifferent to routines that iterate inside homes or small local communities. This is potentially damaging, as the mass media still exercises enormous influence over the speech and expression space in a modern industrialized society such as Japan, but its 'objective and balanced' reporting can be irresponsible towards those who need care. Without engaging in people's lives, media reporting easily becomes aloof from society and even redundant. We therefore need to rethink alternative logics, including the proposed ethics of care and empathy. Only through this foundation will we be able to realize actual diversification or multiplicity of views.

Conclusion: towards a journalism of care

Regarding a journalism of care, it is the underlying idea and particularly the professional attitudes of journalists that matter. A journalism of care does not put its professional priority on being balanced or impartial. It also does not dwell on utilitarian ways of thinking of the social significance of news in terms of relevance to the largest possible number of people. Rather, a journalism of care is rooted in the fundamental human capacity to have empathy with those in need of care and takes sides with them, even if they belong to the absolute minority in number. It can be therefore called advocacy journalism in that it supports a particular group of people, although it might not support their ideology.

A good case in point is the recollection by Jirō Yuasa, a TV cameraman in Japan, on his production of a documentary programme. Yuasa produced a film in 2008 that explicitly supported action to legalize medicine that heals a particular type of intractable disease, despite the fact that only as few as 300 people in Japan were suffering from it:

> My report (about the disease and medicine) was clearly one-sided and trivial in number. I wouldn't give any excuses if somebody reproaches me for being biased as a journalist. If you see the program, it clearly supports the side of the patients who are ailing from the disease called mucopolysaccharidosis.
>
> (Yuasa, 2008, p. 145)

Despite opposition inside the TV station, he produced the programme and then succeeded in mobilizing the health ministry to legalize the medicine. As a result, the programme helped cure the 300 patients. As such, a journalism of care is a response to our moral obligation to help and respect others. Its journalistic mandate prioritizes why a topic should be reported rather than the maintenance of an ethics of neutrality.

Thus, the 'ethics of care' does not necessarily deny the right to 'freedom of speech and expression'. On the contrary, the ethics of care re-emphasizes the social meaning of the right to freedom of speech and expression, which citizens obtained as a modern achievement of the bourgeois revolution. It relates the right of freedom of speech more realistically to the lives of people, clarifying its democratic significance and demonstrating its responsible exercise while presenting a more concrete path to make every voice matter (Couldry, 2010).

Those women who evacuated from Fukushima and could not speak out, as mentioned above, and the local newspaper, which could not collate the voices of Fukushima into one, represent the daily reality of people who do not fit the typical, modernist view of rational human beings. The reason why those people cannot fully make use of their 'freedom of speech' is not mental weakness, immaturity or irrationality. Ironically, those who refused to evacuate from Fukushima remained in a contaminated area to protect the very essence of their lives, that is, their own web of social life with their family, relatives and friends. In the situation where a group of people is abandoned in a place in which the most fundamental right would not be guaranteed, speaking up on their own becomes increasingly difficult, even in an age with social media and the internet. Although many of the voices of the minority can only be raised by those people themselves, they have to overcome numerous obstacles and hardships to air their voices in the public space, particularly in communities or groups where consensual behaviours are expected, as seen in such cases as Fukushima. Consequently, the vulnerable are forced into a negative spiral where it is impossible to even come out to the public sphere, similar to the situation of the voices of the subaltern, as discussed by Spivak (1988).[5]

Apart from illuminating the erstwhile uncertain path towards attaining a society that realizes freedom of speech and expression, particularly for those who are regarded as social 'others', the ethics of care can also be a sophisticated professional ethic for journalism. At a time when we increasingly face difficulties in commanding a comprehensive view of society as a whole, given that it is becoming increasingly diversified and stratified, it is too easy to omit particular types of voices while prioritizing others. Journalists should therefore be trained accordingly to *listen* to distant voices that remain unnoticed and unheard, and act responsibly for them by giving them a chance to express their emotions and thoughts, even though they may sound irrational, ambivalent or irrelevant.

Framed in the perspective of care, mass media journalism and the role of professional reporters, both of which are said to be 'in crisis' in the digital age, take on a significant new meaning. In other words, the ethics of care teaches that professional journalists who hold an overwhelming advantage in terms of resources, such as expressive ability, investigative skills, financial resources and prestige, have a responsibility to pay attention to the voices of the minority and those who are in absolutely disadvantaged positions. The ethics of care teaches that even where digital media have advanced and all people can publicize their words themselves, the job of 'speech and expression professionals' will never disappear. It gives renewed significance to professional journalism in the highly competitive digital information age in which everybody and anybody can potentially articulate their voice.

Acknowledgements

I am grateful to Chris Peters and Marcel Broersma for their comments on and suggestions on an earlier version of this work. I also thank Yujin Yaguchi for his constructive comments and advice.

Notes

1 The Constitution of Japan. English translation: http://japan.kantei.go.jp/constitution_and_government_of_japan/constitution_e.html.
2 The Meiji government was the first central government for the Empire of Japan after the restoration of the Shogunate government in 1868. It introduced Western polity systems, such as the Parliament and the Constitution. The concept of journalism was also introduced during this regime.
3 Many women who married into families in Fukushima were expected to stay in communities to take care of their aged parents-in-law. Young women in Fukushima also avoided appearing in public for fear of becoming unable to bear healthy children due to exposure to radioactive contamination, a rumour that spread at the time.
4 http://fukushimavoice.net/2013/05/676.
5 Perceiving refugees from Fukushima as the subaltern is an idea presented by Kuniko Sakata of Tohoku University at the Spring Research Symposium II held by the Japan Society for Studies in Journalism and Mass Communication.

References

Allan, S. (2013). *Citizen witnessing: Revisioning journalism in times of crisis.* Cambridge: Polity Press.

Chouliaraki, L. (2006). *The spectatorship of suffering.* London: Sage.

Chouliaraki, L. (2013). Mediating vulnerability: Cosmopolitanism and the public sphere. *Media Culture & Society, 35*(1), 105–112. doi: 10.1177/0163443712464564.

Cottle, S. (2013). Journalists witnessing disaster: From the calculus of death to the injunction to care. *Journalism Studies, 14*(2), 232–248. doi: 10.1080/1461670X.2012.718556.

Couldry, N. (2010). *Why voice matters: Culture and politics after neoliberalism.* London: Sage.

Craig, D. A., & Ferré, J. P. (2006). Agape as an ethic of care for journalism. *Journal of Mass Media Ethics, 21*(2–3), 123–140.

Gilligan, C. (1982). *In a different voice: Psychological theory and women's development.* Cambridge, MA: Harvard University Press.

Hallin, D. C. (1992). The passing of the 'high modernism' of American journalism. *Journal of Communication, 42*(3), 14–25.

Hayashi, K. (2011). *'Onna-Kodomo' no journalism: Care no Rinri to tomoni.* Tokyo: Iwanami shoten.

Held, V. (2006). *The ethics of care: Personal, political, and global.* Oxford: Oxford University Press.

Itō, M. (1974). *Gendai Shakai to Genron no Jiyuū.* Tokyo: Yūshindō.

Kittay, E. F. (1999). *Love's labor: Essays on women, equality and dependency.* New York: Routledge.

Mōri, T. (2008). *Hyōgen no Jiyu: Sono Kōkyōsei to Morosa nitsuite.* Tokyo: Iwanami shoten.

O'Neill, O. (2002). *A question of trust.* Cambridge: Cambridge University Press.

Pantti, M. (2013). Getting closer? *Journalism Studies, 14*(2), 201–218. doi:10.1080/14616 70X.2012.718551.

Pantti, M., Wahl-Jorgensen, K., & Cottle, S. (2012). *Disasters and the media.* New York: Peter Lang.

Pech, G., & Leibel, R. (2006). Writing in solidarity: Steps toward an ethic of care for journalism. *Journal of Mass Media Ethics: Exploring Questions of Media Morality, 21*(2–3), 141–155. doi: 10.1080/08900523.2006.9679730.

Siebert, F. S. (1956). The libertarian theory. In F. S. Siebert, W. Schramm & T. Peterson (Eds.), *Four theories of the press: The authoritarian, libertarian, social responsibility, and Soviet communist concepts of what the press should be and do* (pp. 39–71). Urbana, IL: University of Illinois Press.

Silverstone, R. (2006). *Media and morality: On the rise of the mediapolis.* Cambridge: Polity Press.

Spivak, G. C. (1988). Can the subaltern speak? In C. Nelson & L. Grossberg (Eds.), *Marxism and the interpretation of culture* (pp. 271–313). Chicago: University of Chicago Press.

Steiner, L., & Okrusch, C. M. (2006). Care as a virtue for journalists. *Journal of Mass Media Ethics: Exploring Questions of Media Morality, 21*(2–3), 102–122. doi: 10.1080/ 08900523.2006.9679728.

Takada, M. (Ed.). (2011). *@Fukushima. Watashitachi no nozomu monoha. (@Fukushima. What we hope).* Tokyo: Sangakusha.

Taylor, J. M., Gilligan, C., & Sullivan, A. (1995). *Between voice and silence: Women and girls, race and relationships.* Cambridge, MA: Harvard University Press.

Vanacker, B., & Breslin, J. (2006). Ethics of care: More than just another tool to bash the media? *Journal of Mass Media Ethics, 21*(2–3), 196–214.

Waisbord, S. (2013). *Reinventing professionalism: Journalism and news in global perspective.* Cambridge: Polity Press.

Ward, S. J. (2005). *Invention of journalism ethics: The path to objectivity and beyond.* Montreal: McGill-Queen's Press.

Ward, S. J. (2013). *Global media ethics: Problems and perspectives.* Oxford: Blackwell.

Ward, S. J., & Wasserman, H. (Eds.). (2010). *Media ethics beyond borders: A global perspective.* New York: Routledge.

Yuasa, J. (2008). Kyakkan kōsei hōdō de shakai ha kawarunoka? In T. Hanada (Ed.), *'Ko' to shiteno Jānarisuto (Can society change with objective fair reporting?, Journalist as Individuals)* (pp. 10–153) Tokyo: Waseda University Press.

10

FROM PARTICIPATION TO RECIPROCITY IN THE JOURNALIST–AUDIENCE RELATIONSHIP

Seth C. Lewis, Avery E. Holton and Mark Coddington

The relationship between journalists and their audiences has long been a particularly fraught one, marked by a tension between dependence and resistance, reliance and resentment. Journalism is an inherently public activity, one that requires an audience to be practised. Since journalism around the world began to professionalize in the late nineteenth and early twentieth centuries, that connection between journalism and its audience – often mythologized as 'the public' – has taken on an even greater importance (Anderson, 2013). Journalists have increasingly seen themselves as performing a service for that public, beholden to the public interest rather than corporate directives or powerful interests, especially during the 'high modern' era that dominated late twentieth-century journalism in the USA (Hallin, 1992). At the same time, however, journalists have viewed this public, so crucial to their own professional self-perception, as incomprehensible, uninformed and irrational. They have continually resisted the input and influence of that audience as a threat to their own professional autonomy (Gans, 1979; Schlesinger, 1978; Sumpter, 2000).

Fast-forward a few decades. Much has changed in a contemporary mediascape characterized by mobile phones, social media and networked platforms (Howard, 2015; Rainie and Wellman, 2012; Westlund, 2015). These new(er) technologies allow for more blended forms of information production, distribution and consumption, as ambient awareness systems – 'broad, asynchronous, lightweight and always-on' (Hermida, 2010, p. 297) – contribute to the hybridization of media forms and functions (Chadwick, 2013). Altogether, 'the tenuous distinction between producers and consumers of content has faded' (Papacharissi, 2015, p. 29), even while it is equally apparent that much of the information recognized as 'news' in society is still produced by many of the same legacy institutions that have dominated the scene for decades, making news organizations and their journalists stubbornly central to media work in the public interest (Anderson, 2013). The boundaries of journalism do not simply go away. They are perpetually tested and negotiated, making them as salient now as ever because their contours reveal fundamental contests over what counts as journalism and who counts as a journalist (Carlson and Lewis, 2015; cf. Loosen, 2015). The question then becomes how might barriers as well as connections between journalists and audiences require a reconsideration of this producer–user relationship? According to what set of norms, values or expectations might such a re-evaluation take place? And, crucially, how might a reconfigured relationship between journalists and audiences contribute to the larger work of resituating journalism's relevance for the various publics that journalism normatively serves?

Establishing a case for reciprocity

The participatory affordances of digital media, including blogs, social media and comment sections, have led several media executives and observers to call for the development of forms of journalism that are marked by robust, collaborative participation via networked publics (e.g., Gillmor, 2004; Rosen, 2006; Rusbridger, 2010). As Boczkowski (2010) and others have noted, many of the factors that shielded twentieth-century journalists from their audiences – lack of competition, insulation from market pressures and relatively weak tools to measure audience desires – have been altered or undone by increasing corporatization, a growing market logic and the development of sophisticated information systems for tracking digital audiences. Altogether, the digital media environment has complicated notions of 'distance' between journalists and audiences in relation to expectations of and practices towards one another (directly) and among others (indirectly) in networked spaces (Loosen and Schmidt, 2012). In addition, prominent efforts have been made to encourage journalists to engage their audiences more regularly and meaningfully, beginning with the public journalism movement in the 1990s. With its emphasis on ensuring that the public's expressed agenda informed journalists' news coverage, public (or civic) journalism helped refocus some of journalists' attention on the importance of building relationships with audiences, though it failed to achieve broad, lasting implementation in American journalism (Nip, 2008).

Practically speaking, in the past decade most news organizations have become familiar with some degree of audience participation in the news process, even if they prefer to keep it comfortably at arm's length (Singer *et al.*, 2011). As Wall (2015, p. 807) sums up in her synthesis of the literature on citizen/participatory journalism, 'this phenomena is now so intertwined with the workings of the professional news media that it is hard to imagine citizen journalism – or whatever one wants to call it – disappearing'. Indeed, there is evidence that at least some journalists, some of the time, have come to see openness and participation as necessary elements of the news process, with potential for diversifying discourse and connecting users with news organizations and each other (Lewis and Usher, 2013; Reich, 2011; Robinson, 2011; Singer, 2010). But, often within those same newsrooms, journalists also hold deeply constrained views of participation that conceive of it as a fundamentally one-way process that should remain under journalists' control and serve their purposes (Jönsson and Örnebring, 2011; Usher, 2014). Journalists are moving closer to embodying in practice a truly public-centred mindset that they claim to espouse, but they remain deeply limited in the degree and forms they will allow that participation to take.

We propose that the concept of reciprocity offers a novel perspective for re-imagining this fractured relationship. Reciprocity – a principle of mutual exchange and giving in community that is linked with the core social attributes of trust and social capital – has taken on a broad range of forms both positive (Wellman and Gulia, 1999) and negative (Perugini et al., 2003) within contexts both online (Pelaprat and Brown, 2012) and offline (Putnam, 2000). When developed in relation to journalism, reciprocity can work within communities to encourage an active, participatory construction and sharing of news in which networks of community members and journalists work together to circulate information and sustain discussion (Lewis, Holton and Coddington, 2014). Reciprocity is not a cure-all for the mistrust and disregard that often plague the relationship between journalists and their audiences; these issues have deep roots in professional ideology (Lewis, 2012) and therefore cannot be undone by infusing a single social value into that relationship.

Still, we argue that reciprocity offers a useful new lens for imagining what the journalist–audience relationship could be, not only in reconceiving it broadly, but also in evaluating what participatory journalistic initiatives might work and why. We intend in this chapter to articulate how reciprocity might inform a rethinking of the journalist–audience dialectic, one that explores how it can be reformed rather than simply explaining its pathologies. Reciprocity does not, however, lead us towards a utopian ideal for journalism. Rather, the contingency in its development allows more space to critically examine the varied directions in which reciprocal relationships among journalists and their communities may take shape.

Reciprocity as a concept

Reciprocity is among the most universal of social norms and is inscribed in many civil laws and accepted in many cultures: 'one should help those who have helped him/her in the past and retaliate against those who have been detrimental to his/her interests' (Perugini et al., 2003, p. 252). While both positive and negative, reciprocity is generally understood as exchange between two or more actors for mutual forms of benefit. As such, it is considered a fundamental feature of human sociality throughout history. In the prosocial sense of sharing kindness in response to kindness received, reciprocity is a key starting point in establishing and maintaining personal relationships (Gouldner, 1960). Scholars have gone so far as to suggest that humans – or 'homo reciprocus', as the sociologist Howard Becker (1956) described the species in *Man in Reciprocity* – are, by nature, evolutionarily wired for reciprocity, and that reciprocal exchanges thus form the very basis for social cohesion and cooperation (see Molm, 2010). It is in this overall sense of mutualized gift-giving that reciprocity is deemed critical not only to interpersonal relations, but also to the broader development of community, as members in a given locale or network take a greater interest in and learn to rely upon one another (Putnam, 2000). Beyond the offline social contexts familiar to Putnam's analysis of social capital and the role that reciprocity plays in fostering it, the social function of reciprocity is likewise important for digitally mediated spaces (Pelaprat and Brown, 2012).

However, despite such wide agreement about reciprocity as a social norm, there is less clarity in the literature – chiefly of importance to social psychology – regarding the conceptual definition of reciprocity (Perugini *et al.*, 2003). Does it describe tit-for-tat exchanges conducted repeatedly between two parties? Or more like anonymous, one-off interactions? Is reciprocity as much about perception as practice, and is it equally about prosocial and antisocial forms of exchange? In taking up these and related questions, Perugini *et al.* (2003) developed survey scale measures, validated cross-culturally, that delineated first between beliefs and behaviours related to reciprocity and second between positive and negative forms of reciprocity. The upshot, they found, was that reciprocity could be understood as a 'subjectively internalized mechanism' that could be reliably measured via individual differences (2003, p. 275). And, as such, reciprocity could be manifest both in perception (i.e. a personal belief in the role of reciprocity in one's life) and in practice (i.e. a set of behaviours, or intended behaviours, suited to one's particular opportunities for interaction).

To this explication of reciprocity at the level of social psychology, behavioural sociologists have contributed structural approaches for modelling forms of what Molm (1994) called 'reciprocal exchange'.[1] Such exchanges may be direct or indirect in nature (Molm, 2010). In direct exchanges, benefits flow between two actors in one of two forms: unilaterally in reciprocal exchanges (A gives to B, and B gives to A, but *without* any guarantee of something in return) or bilaterally in negotiated exchanges (A and B give to each other only on agreement, as in a contract). In indirect exchanges, individuals give benefits to one another and eventually receive benefits in return, *but not necessarily from the same person* (Molm, 2010). Such distinctions between direct and indirect (or generalized) exchanges have been studied for decades (e.g. Lévi-Strauss, 1969), but recent attention has been given to the importance of reciprocity for understanding the dynamics of (online) communities: their formation and evolution, their network ties, the trust and goodwill that exist among members, and so forth (e.g. Ammann, 2011; Gaudeul and Giannetti, 2013; Lauterbach *et al.*, 2009). Reciprocity in online and offline settings is of great social value beyond the exchange of beneficial acts themselves. As Molm, Schaefer and Collett (2007) point out, the value of reciprocity lies both in *instrumental* and *symbolic* outcomes. Instrumental values are those goods (such as gifts, conversation, attention and favours) that are gained through reciprocity. Symbolic values are the positive thoughts, perceptions and behaviours that may be communicated by reciprocity or observed by others.

To sum up the literature: more than a taken-for-granted social norm, reciprocity is manifest in individual-level perceptions and practices, whether in positive or negative forms; and it also represents a set of structured exchanges, whether direct or indirect, involving gifts that may be instrumental or symbolic. Seen in this light, reciprocity is a multi-faceted concept of belief and behaviour, evident in various forms of interaction and leading to varied outcomes for individuals and society. Moreover, a key outcome is the contribution that reciprocity makes to the formation and perpetuation of community, including (perhaps especially) in the context of online communities (Ammann, 2011; Gaudeul and Giannetti, 2013; Pelaprat and Brown, 2012). But while reciprocity has been examined within the realm of online social interactions, the concept has yet to receive broad treatment in media and journalism studies.

Indeed, in the communication literature, the concept of reciprocity is often subsumed within or sidelined by related matters of trust and social capital – as in the case of examining whether social network sites foster social capital (Valenzuela, Park and Kee, 2009). This relative neglect of reciprocity, as a distinct object of focus, points to an opportunity for (social) media research broadly (Lewis, 2015): how might reciprocity, as a key concept of social exchange, help scholars conceptualize a networked media environment increasingly characterized by the giving, sharing and re-circulating of information among peers? More to the point of this chapter, what might the concept of reciprocity, taken more purposefully, reveal about the social exchanges of journalism – namely, the growing variety and intensity of interactions that may be facilitated between/among journalists and audiences in social and digital media spaces?

Reciprocal journalism as a concept

Seeking to contribute both to the conceptualization of reciprocity as well as its application to journalism studies, we previously introduced the notion of *reciprocal journalism*: 'a way of imagining how journalists might develop more mutually beneficial relationships with audiences across three forms of exchange – direct, indirect, and sustained types of reciprocity' (Lewis, Holton and Coddington, 2014, p. 229). Such a definition assumes that journalists can exhibit positive forms of reciprocity to stimulate more meaningful and mutually beneficial exchanges with audiences, and that such exchanges may be direct and indirect, according to Molm's (2010) structural theory of reciprocity. Additionally, we argued for recognizing sustained reciprocity as a third form, one that includes both direct and indirect reciprocity, but does so by extending them across temporal dimensions. Below, we briefly describe each of these three forms of reciprocity and their potential application in journalism.

Direct reciprocity is the basic building block of online community. Individuals develop a sense of connectedness as they engage in unilateral (that is, non-binding) forms of reciprocal exchange, giving without a guaranteed response and yet with hopeful expectation of something valuable in return. Retweeting, liking, favouriting, commenting: each of these common forms of sharing and participating online invites direct reciprocity. When such actions are rewarded, as in the case of bloggers linking among each other (Ammann, 2011), trust, bonding and affinity may more readily develop (see Molm, Schaefer and Collett, 2007). For journalism, direct reciprocity can take the form of journalists simply responding to tweets and comments; Andy Carvin, for instance, famously relied on Twitter conversations with activists, protesters and other sources on the ground to help him contextualize and verify information during the 2011 Arab Spring (Hermida, Lewis and Zamith, 2014). Audiences, in this sense, may be more willing to exchange information directly with journalists if they perceive that they might be heard and, in some cases, receive information in return.

If direct reciprocity implies exchanges between journalists and audiences in a one-to-one fashion, *indirect reciprocity* points to exchanges that are witnessed by others and intended for community benefit, in a one-to-many fashion. This more generalized form of reciprocity occurs as the beneficiary of an act returns the favour not to the original giver, but rather to another member of the social network (Molm, Schaefer and Collett, 2007). As Person A gives to Person B who gives to Person C and so on, such gestures benefit group members and also signal to other people (that is, potential group members) the kind of bond developing within the group. Reciprocity, or merely the observation of it, thus contributes to a pay-it-forward dynamic in successful communities (Lauterbach *et al.*, 2009). Hashtags, for example, can represent a form of indirect reciprocity: even while perhaps responding directly to another user on Twitter, users can relay hashtagged information that may facilitate more generalized communication among a set of users following that hashtag, potentially developing broader 'news streams' of affective, personalized storytelling (Papacharissi, 2015). Tweets around #Egypt during the Arab Spring, for instance, led to certain actors and frames being crowdsourced to prominence, thereby contributing to the gatekeeping and framing functions of journalism (Meraz and Papacharissi, 2013). Moreover, take the example of the #Ferguson hashtag that sprang up in response to protests surrounding police violence in Ferguson, Missouri in 2014 (see Bonilla and Rosa, 2015). Beyond helping community members inform and coordinate with one another – akin to a direct reciprocity function – the hashtag also served as a megaphone and discussion forum for broader national conversations around race and police brutality. People went from directly relaying information back and forth to others in a geographically bounded network, to relaying information and ideas to others outside the network in the hope that it would facilitate a more generalized response of understanding and conversation. Thus, for journalism, indirect reciprocity points to opportunities for more publicly visible interactions that encourage further contribution from others and transcend barriers of time and space.

The longer and more enduring such exchanges become, the greater potential they have for developing *sustained reciprocity*. In journalism, as in other social interactions online, direct and indirect reciprocity can be enacted almost immediately, especially in moments of crisis, but they also may not last much longer than that, limiting the long-term impact of exchanges of goodwill. For reciprocity to reach its fullest potential and contribute most meaningfully to community dynamics, it should be perpetuated over time. As Molm, Takahashi and Peterson (2000) point out, when people value the continuation of a relationship, they are less likely to exploit one another. For journalism, this means imagining interactions with audiences, whether online or offline, that carry greater expectation for the future – an expectation that such interactions will continue, for one thing, and that they will remain mutually beneficial. Sustained reciprocity may be most actionable at the level of community journalism (Robinson, 2014). Such journalists, understanding the nuances of their audiences, can more readily develop carefully patrolled spaces for community members to interact with journalists and with each other (Lewis, Holton and Coddington, 2014). To cite one example: the *Houston Herald*, a newspaper serving a small community in Houston, Missouri, has emphasized reciprocal discussions and information sharing with and among community members on its Facebook page. That, in part, has helped develop the *Herald*'s social media presence over time, leading to a Facebook following larger than the town's population (Mayer, 2012).

Overall, then, reciprocal journalism resituates journalists in the network. It casts them in a community management role: journalists may catalyse reciprocal exchange directly with audiences/users, indirectly among community members and repeatedly over time. And as a practice with roots in a social-psychological concept, reciprocal journalism involves not just behaviour, but motivation as well. Simply posting tweets with a community-based hashtag or responding to reader comments and inquiries does not constitute reciprocal journalism if it is not undertaken with a motivation to give something of value with the expectation of receiving something similar in return. It is important to note that these actions *may* do such things; there is little evidence that journalists *actually* do such things within a reciprocal mindset, particularly given what we know about their general reluctance to engage with audiences (Singer *et al.*, 2011). As yet, there is little empirical research regarding reciprocity in and for journalism. In one study, Borger and colleagues (2014) found support for the reciprocal journalism model as they examined participatory news projects from the audience perspective. The citizen participants, they noted, expected something in return from journalists for their contributions; consequently, projects often failed when such expectations were not met and users quit participating. Such findings suggest that reciprocity may play a crucial 'bridging' role between journalists and audiences: users are more likely to remain engaged when they feel that someone on the other side is returning the favour. What is yet to be understood, however, is what reciprocity in journalism looks like from the perspective of journalists.

Reciprocity from the perspective of journalists

Taking up the challenge to unpack the nature of reciprocal journalism from the producers' vantage point, we surveyed a large pool of US newspaper journalists and editors (hereafter referred to as 'journalists') in February 2014. Using a randomized, stratified sample drawn from the media contact service Cision, we collected 546 completed surveys that included responses to open-ended questions about journalists' engagement with readers that asked respondents to think about how they engaged with audiences, directly and indirectly, on a daily basis and over time. From those responses, we were able to glean the various lenses through which these journalists view reciprocity in journalism and, in some cases, how they demonstrate reciprocity in their professional routines.

In terms of *direct reciprocity*, which most journalists surveyed recognized as an important and relatively new trend in the news creator–news consumer relationship, journalists tended to view such exchanges as another extension of their professional engagement with readers. Where emails replaced telephone calls, tweets and Facebook posts have begun to supplant emails. Many journalists reported working diligently to return phone calls within a day or two, to respond the same day to emails and to respond within hours to messages sent via social media platforms. While many journalists noted that face-to-face interactions helped to develop the strongest connections with their sources and readers, they acknowledged the power to enhance those ties with social media responsiveness. Indeed, those surveyed listed 'responsiveness', 'speed of responses', 'following up quickly', 'allowing audiences to teach us' and 'deeper engagement', alongside other more traditional tenets of good journalism such as accuracy, consistency, truthfulness and balance.

Notably, while several journalists reported that audiences continued to use phone calls, emails and social media channels to seek praise or to express concerns about particular stories or reporting techniques, many said they spend a sizeable portion of their time building relationships through direct reciprocity in their communities, both online and offline. At the local level, journalists described themselves as the 'face of the community', frequently finding ways to attend community events, seek audience input on stories, listen and respond to critiques, and make engagement with their readers a 'casual, intimate feeling of reciprocated benefit'. Others noted that they attempt to respond 'thoughtfully' and 'politely' to reader comments and posts on Facebook, and to thank readers for providing information or sharing their stories through retweets, favourites and mentions on Twitter.

These same journalists made it clear, though, that when it came to inappropriate or vulgar comments from audiences, they either ignored them or removed them from public feeds. This, as one journalist put it, 'is in the best interest of our community'. Such actions – those performed with the greater good of the community, not just the individual, in mind – fall more closely under the category of *indirect reciprocity*. For smaller, more local publications, journalists valued their direct interactions with readers as a means to illustrate for their community of readers the depth of their dedication to their craft. By being amenable to public concerns and critiques and actively listening and responding to public input, these journalists argued that others might witness or hear about their actions and take more positive, and potentially more engaged, approaches to the newspaper. In terms of social media, journalists reported fairly heavy monitoring of reader comments and posts, frequently serving as secondary gatekeepers when they deemed information irrelevant or inappropriate. Still, the majority of journalists took an optimistic approach to indirect engagements on social media, using them as platforms to extend the discourse around stories by asking questions, providing extra links or creating hashtags as a means of inviting a larger crowd into the conversation. They saw maintenance of social media channels as a challenge saddled side-by-side with opportunities to expose larger, more diverse audiences to their content. In order to reach those audiences, journalists said they needed to create welcoming environments built on relationships and exchanges that others could easily see.

They also noted that direct and indirect forms of reciprocity needed to be repeated consistently. As one journalist wrote: 'I have found that good relations [with readers] come over time.' In this sense, *sustained reciprocity* was deemed critical in the process of building trust, loyalty and longevity in readership. While some journalists argued that sustained reciprocity was as simple as responding to tweets and occasionally engaging in hashtags or live conversations on Twitter or Facebook, others again noted the importance of face-to-face interactions. One journalist at a local newspaper said that he worked hard to remember birthdays and other milestones of his readers, reaching out to them when he could or bringing up such dates when he bumped into them in public. Such attention to detail, he said, was a cornerstone of 'building a relationship of trust and credibility'.

In sum, the US journalists we surveyed, especially those working for locally oriented and mostly smaller publications, suggested that reciprocity in its various forms is an integral part of building and maintaining a sense of community with and among their audience. While some expressed a reluctance to engaging more deeply with their readers, the overwhelming majority related reciprocity with opportunities to build trust and social capital both directly with individuals in their network and indirectly within their communities broadly. Altogether, this reinforces what social scientists have long argued: that (prosocial) reciprocity is a key ingredient for meaningful, sustainable communities (Becker, 1956; Gouldner, 1960; Molm, 1997; Molm, Schaefer and Collett, 2007; Putnam, 2000), including emerging forms of community online (Ammann, 2011; Gaudeul and Giannetti, 2013).

Concluding discussion: the future of reciprocity in participatory journalism

Overall, the literature suggests that journalists have a conflicted relationship with audiences. After so long ignoring them as part of their professional purview in gatekeeping what counted as news, journalists are increasingly aware of who reads, watches and listens – both in the aggregate sense of quantified audiences (as they learn of user preferences via digital metrics) and in the more individualized sense of social media interactions (as they learn of user preferences via comments directed at them via Twitter, Facebook and so on). This chapter has focused on the latter sense, considering how the journalist–audience relationship might be re-imagined through networked technologies, ones that, both in their technical affordances and their cultural milieu, encourage more relational forms of exchange among users in the network. Such a perspective repositions journalists as network-based actors – as community organizers who engage rather than simply town criers who publicize.

The literature suggests that such a shift is already occurring to some degree, as news organizations begin to recognize the generative potential of user participation in the news process; yet, those same newsrooms find it challenging to overcome deeply held roles and routines that prioritize professional control over open participation (Lewis, 2012; Robinson, 2011; Usher, 2014).

While there is no one solution to resolving that tension, this chapter has suggested that the concept of reciprocity may offer a starting point for reconceptualizing the journalist–audience dialectic: what it is now, what it may become and how it may be evaluated in the future. Reciprocity is more than a Golden Rule social norm. It represents a complex set of perceptions and practices, generally thought to be (though not always) positive; it also represents a set of social exchanges that may be either direct or indirect, involving 'gifts' that may fulfil an instrumental function (as in the exchange of information) or a symbolic function (in contributing to good-will and cultural capital). A particularly salient outcome of positive reciprocity is the development of strong community, as much in online as in offline relationships. On these points, the literature is clear. Extending this to the particular case of journalism, therefore, reciprocity may offer a vantage point for considering how reciprocal beliefs and behaviours, manifest in various types of reciprocal exchanges between journalists and audiences, may contribute to an improved ecology of engagement and collaboration between the two. Such an ideal arrangement we conceptualized as *reciprocal journalism*, which envisions journalists developing more fruitful exchanges of mutual benefit with audiences (Lewis, Holton and Coddington, 2014). Such reciprocity may surface in direct (one-to-one) and indirect (one-to-many) forms; as they are observed by audiences and sustained over time, they can contribute to improving both journalist–audience relationships and larger community dynamics in which they operate. There is, it would seem, great potential for reciprocal journalism. Yet, is such a utopian view possible or even desirable?

As noted by some journalists we surveyed, reciprocity presents complications for professionalism. Of particular concern, journalists discussed institutionally enforced priorities or boundaries as well as ethical considerations when considering how to engage with audiences (or not). While some reported that email and social media interactions were either organizationally monitored or mandated (or both in at least one case), others were more worried about the potential outcomes of reciprocating with audiences. As one journalist put it: 'I'll certainly help readers, both those I know and those I don't, but that help doesn't trump news judgment.'

Such concerns, coupled with evidence that news audiences increasingly expect reciprocity from journalists (Borger, Hoof and Sanders, 2014), highlight some of the disconnect between what audiences want and what journalists are willing or able to give in reciprocal exchange. In many newsrooms, journalists already feel harried and stretched thin, as lay-offs force those left behind to produce more with less, particularly in a 'hamster wheel' climate that prioritizes content churn over quality (Starkman, 2010). Add to that growing demands for journalists to incorporate digital, mobile and social media throughout their work, ratcheting up the technical complexity of cross-media news work (Lewis and Westlund, 2015), as well as broader challenges in shifting the journalistic mindset from publishing a product to providing a service (Picard, 2014). Suggesting that journalists, in addition to all that, take on more frequent, more purposeful and ultimately more time-consuming forms of engagement through various forms of reciprocity – well, the notion may not sit well with many journalists, to say the least.

Moreover, recall that reciprocity has a negative as well as a positive component to it (Perugini *et al.*, 2003), meaning that reciprocal exchanges may be prosocial and antisocial in nature: building trust in one instance and undermining it in the other. Consider, for instance, how many social media exchanges are far from 'mutually beneficial', insofar as they feature forms of hate, revenge and trolling. In a less scalding but still concerning sense, the very patterns of reciprocity that foster community may also limit the diversity of individuals and ideas within communities. There are well-documented problems of homophily on social media and the Web generally, which tend to reinforce insularity and a general reluctance for people to reach beyond their social networks to encounter diverse people and viewpoints (Zuckerman, 2013). If reciprocity in its various forms serves to perpetuate communities of like-minded users, it may, at the same time, marginalize other voices and possibilities for cross-pollination. In the case of journalism, for example, niche publications or community news organizations may successfully develop rapport and reciprocity with audiences over time, but those same patterns of familiarity may make it intimidating for new members to join the conversation without feeling out of the loop, much like online forums that prioritize the contributions of veterans over new users.

For journalists, reciprocity may serve a deleterious purpose in a different way: though it is public-centred, it may not be oriented towards the public interest. Instead, journalists might approach reciprocal relationships as ones of consumption in which audiences are expected to reciprocate by providing page views, subscriptions or other economic functions rather than by participating as a civically engaged public. To the extent that reciprocal journalism is advocated on the organizational level, it has a particular potential to take on this commoditized version of reciprocity as a way to meet corporate and financial aims.

Merely having and holding an audience should not be the ultimate aim of reciprocal journalism. Rather, it should be viewed as one of a number of promising approaches that journalists may take, given the expanding opportunities of social media, to develop greater connection with and among community members. More broadly, reciprocal journalism poses a fundamental rethinking of journalism and its place in relation to audiences or 'people formerly known' as such (Rosen, 2006): users in the network who not only can participate in the media environment, but who may also expect something from journalism and journalists that is quite different from more familiar conceptions of the professional self. Indeed, reciprocity forces journalists to honestly and substantively grapple with the following questions: 'what does my audience actually want when they reach out to me or rely on my work?' and 'am I actually giving it to them?' That is, a reciprocal perspective challenges journalists to not rest on lazy assumptions about their democratic importance (cf. Peters and Witschge, 2015), but to proactively unscramble audience needs apart from journalists' assumptions about them. In this sense, reciprocal journalism could serve as a kind of diagnostic tool: a means of measuring the degree of journalists' receptivity to and understanding of audiences with whom they interact – a starting point for assessing the meaningfulness of the thing called participatory journalism. It is true that many journalists may lack the resources – or simply the time – needed to reciprocate as a regular part of their work. Nevertheless, merely recognizing the generative role of reciprocity in communities may set in motion a new kind of professional imagination about journalists and their audiences.

Note

1 This section draws on material published in Lewis, Holton and Coddington (2014).

References

Ammann, R. (2011). Reciprocity, social curation, and the emergence of blogging: A study in community formation. *Procedia – Social and Behavioral Sciences, 22*, 26–36.

Anderson, C. W. (2013). *Rebuilding the news: Metropolitan journalism in the digital age*. Philadelphia: Temple University Press.

Becker, H. (1956). *Man in reciprocity*. New York: Praeger.

Boczkowski, P. J. (2010). *News at work: Imitation in an age of information abundance*. Chicago: University of Chicago Press.

Bonilla, Y., & Rosa, J. (2015). #Ferguson: Digital protest, hashtag ethnography, and the racial politics of social media in the united states. *American Ethnologist, 42*(1), 4–17. doi:10.1111/amet.12112.

Borger, M., Hoof, A. V., & Sanders, J. (2014). Expecting reciprocity: Towards a model of the participants' perspective on participatory journalism. *New Media & Society*. doi:10.1177/1461444814545842.

Carlson, M., & Lewis, S. C. (Eds.). (2015). *Boundaries of journalism: Professionalism, practices and participation*. New York: Routledge.

Chadwick, A. (2013). *The hybrid media system: Politics and power*. Oxford: Oxford University Press.

Gans, H. J. (1979). *Deciding what's news: A study of CBS Evening News, NBC Nightly News, Newsweek, and Time*. New York: Pantheon.

Gaudeul, A., & Giannetti, C. (2013). The role of reciprocation in social network formation, with an application to LiveJournal. *Social Networks, 35*, 317–330.

Gillmor, D. (2004). *We the media: Grassroots journalism by the people, for the people*. Sebastopol, CA: O'Reilly Media.

Gouldner, A. W. (1960). The norm of reciprocity: A preliminary statement. *American Sociological Review, 25*, 161–178.

Hallin, D. C. (1992). The passing of the 'high modernism' of American journalism. *Journal of Communication, 42*(3), 14–25.

Hermida, A. (2010). Twittering the news: The emergence of ambient journalism. *Journalism Practice, 4*(3), 297–308. doi:10.1080/17512781003640703.

Hermida, A., Lewis, S. C., & Zamith, R. (2014). Sourcing the Arab Spring: A case study of Andy Carvin's sources on Twitter during the Tunisian and Egyptian revolutions. *Journal of Computer-Mediated Communication, 19*(3), 479–499. doi:10.1111/jcc4.12074.

Howard, P. N. (2015). *Pax technica: How the internet of things may set us free or lock us up.* New Haven, CT: Yale University Press.

Jönsson, A. M., & Örnebring, H. (2011). User-generated content and the news: Empowerment of citizens or interactive illusion? *Journalism Practice, 5*, 127–144.

Lauterbach, D., Truong, H., Shah, T., & Adamic, L. (2009, 29–31 August). *Surfing a web of trust: reputation and reciprocity on CouchSurfing.com.* Paper presented at the International Conference on Computational Science and Engineering, Vancouver.

Lévi-Strauss, C. (1969). *The elementary structures of kinship.* Boston: Beacon Press.

Lewis, S. C. (2012). The tension between professional control and open participation: Journalism and its boundaries. *Information, Communication & Society, 15*(6), 836–866. doi:10.1080/1369118X.2012.674150.

Lewis, S. C. (2015). Reciprocity as a key concept for social media and society. *Social Media and Society, 1*(1). doi:10.1177/2056305115580339.

Lewis, S. C., Holton, A. E., & Coddington, M. (2014). Reciprocal journalism: A concept of mutual exchange between journalists and audiences. *Journalism Practice, 8*, 229–241. doi:10.1080/17512786.2013.859840.

Lewis, S. C., & Usher, N. (2013). Open source and journalism: Toward new frameworks for imagining news innovation. *Media, Culture & Society, 35*, 602–619. doi:10.1177/0163443713485494.

Lewis, S. C., & Westlund, O. (2015). Actors, actants, audiences, and activities in cross-media news work: A matrix and a research agenda. *Digital Journalism, 3*(1), 19–37. doi:10.1080/21670811.2014.927986.

Loosen, W. (2015). The notion of the 'blurring boundaries': Journalism as a (de-)differentiated phenomenon. *Digital Journalism, 3*(1), 68–84. doi:10.1080/21670811.2014.928000.

Loosen, W., & Schmidt, J.-H. (2012). (Re-)discovering the audience: The relationship between journalism and audience in networked digital media. *Information, Communication & Society, 15*(6), 867–887. doi:10.1080/1369118X.2012.665467.

Mayer, J. (2012). Newspaper Facebook post serves as town megaphone. *Journalism + Community* [Blog post]. Retrieved from http://joymayer.com/2012/07/27/newspaper-facebook-post-serves-as-town-megaphone/.

Meraz, S., & Papacharissi, Z. (2013). Networked gatekeeping and networked framing on# Egypt. *International Journal of Press/Politics, 18*(2), 138–166.

Molm, L. D. (1994). Dependence and risk: Transforming the structure of social exchange. *Social Psychology Quarterly, 57*, 163–76.

Molm, L. D. (1997). *Coercive power in social exchange.* New York: Cambridge University Press.

Molm, L. D. (2010). The structure of reciprocity. *Social Psychology Quarterly, 73*(2), 119–131.

Molm, L. D., Schaefer, D. R., & Collett, J. L. (2007). The value of reciprocity. *Social Psychology Quarterly, 70*(2), 199–217.

Molm, L. D., Takahashi, N., & Peterson, G. (2000). Risk and trust in social exchange: An experimental test of a classical proposition. *American Journal of Sociology, 105*(5), 1396–1427.

Nip, J. Y. M. (2008). The last days of civic journalism: The case of the *Savannah Morning News. Journalism Practice, 2*, 179–196.

Papacharissi, Z. (2015). Toward new journalism(s): Affective news, hybridity, and liminal spaces. *Journalism Studies, 16*(1), 27–40. doi:10.1080/1461670X.2014.890328.

Pelaprat, E., & Brown, B. (2012). Reciprocity: Understanding online social relations. *First Monday, 17*(10). Retrieved from http://firstmonday.org/ojs/index.php/fm/article/view/3324.

Perugini, M., Gallucci, M., Presaghi, F., & Ercolani, A. P. (2003). The personal norm of reciprocity. *European Journal of Personality, 17*, 251–283.

Peters, C., & Witschge, T. (2015). From grand narratives of democracy to small expectations of participation: Audiences, citizenship, and interactive tools in digital journalism. *Journalism Practice, 9*(1), 19–34. doi:10.1080/17512786.2014.928455.

Picard, R. G. (2014). Twilight or new dawn of journalism? Evidence from the changing news ecosystem. *Digital Journalism, 2*(3), 273–283. doi:10.1080/21670811.2014.895531.

Putnam, R. D. (2000). *Bowling alone: The collapse and revival of American community.* New York: Simon & Schuster.

Rainie, L., & Wellman, B. (2012). *Networked: The new social operating system.* Cambridge, MA: MIT Press.

Reich, Z. (2011). User comments: The transformation of participatory space. In J. B. Singer, A. Hermida, D. Domingo, A. Heinonen, S. Paulussen, T. Quandt, … Z. Reich (Eds.), *Participatory journalism: Guarding open gates at online newspapers* (pp. 96–117). Malden, MA: Wiley-Blackwell.

Robinson, S. (2011). 'Journalism as process': The organizational implications of participatory online news. *Journalism & Communication Monographs, 13*, 137–210.

Robinson, S. (2014). Introduction: Community journalism midst media revolution. *Journalism Practice, 8*(2), 113–120. doi:10.1080/17512786.2013.859822.

Rosen, J. (2006, 27 June). The people formerly known as the audience. *PressThink* [Blog post]. Retrieved from http://archive.pressthink.org/2006/06/27/ppl_frmr.html.

Rusbridger, A. (2010, 19 November). The splintering of the fourth estate. *The Guardian.* Retrieved from http://www.theguardian.com/commentisfree/2010/nov/19/open-collaborative-future-journalism.

Schlesinger, P. (1978). *Putting 'reality' together: BBC News.* London: Constable.

Singer, J. B. (2010). Quality control: Perceived effects of user-generated content on newsroom norms, values and routines. *Journalism Practice, 4*, 127–142.

Singer, J. B., Domingo, D., Heinonen, A., Hermida, A., Paulussen, S., Quandt, T., … Vujnovic, M. (2011). *Participatory journalism: Guarding open gates at online newspapers.* Malden, MA: Wiley-Blackwell.

Starkman, D. (2010). The hamster wheel: Why running as fast as we can is getting us nowhere. *Columbia Journalism Review.* Retrieved from http://www.cjr.org/cover_story/the_hamster_wheel.php.

Sumpter, R. S. (2000). Daily newspaper editors' audience construction routines: A case study. *Critical Studies in Media Communication, 17*, 334–346.

Usher, N. (2014). *Making news at the New York Times.* Ann Arbor: University of Michigan Press.

Valenzuela, S., Park, N., & Kee, K. F. (2009). Is there social capital in a social network site?: Facebook use and college students' life satisfaction, trust, and participation. *Journal of Computer-Mediated Communication, 14*(4), 875–901. doi:10.1111/j.1083-6101.2009.01474.x.

Wall, M. (2015). Citizen journalism: A retrospective on what we know, an agenda for what we don't. *Digital Journalism, 3*(6), 797–813. doi:10.1080/21670811.2014.1002513.

Wellman, B., & Gulia, M. (1999). Net surfers don't ride alone: Virtual communities as communities. In M. A. Smith & P. Kollock (Eds.), *Communities in cyberspace* (pp. 167–194). London: Routledge.

Westlund, O. (2015). News consumption in an age of mobile media: Patterns, people, place, and participation. *Mobile Media & Communication, 3*(2), 151–159. doi:10.1177/205015791456336.

Zuckerman, E. (2013). *Rewire: Digital cosmopolitans in the age of connection.* New York: W.W. Norton & Company.

11

THE GAP BETWEEN THE MEDIA AND THE PUBLIC

Pablo J. Boczkowski and Eugenia Mitchelstein

Media play a fundamental role in modern democracies (Habermas, 1996;Thompson, 1995) by relaying information to individuals (Downs, 1957; Druckman, 2005; Graber, 2006), setting an agenda of common concerns for the citizenry (McCombs and Shaw, 1972), acting as watchdogs to powerful actors in the public and private sectors (Waisbord, 2000), and providing an arena for public deliberation (Page, 1996).The production and consumption of news are enmeshed in everyday life, and the importance of media as information providers, as well as the impact of news content on the audiences it reaches, has long attracted the attention of scholars and cultural commentators. One of the longstanding debates among both scholars and practitioners is whether there is a gap between the kinds of stories that the media present as the most important of the day and those that members of the public want to learn the most about (Dean, Pertilla and Belt, 2007; Gans, 2004; Mindich, 2005; Shoemaker and Cohen, 2006; Singer, 2011; Zaller, 1999).

There is a certain level of consensus that mainstream news organizations privilege stories about politics, economics and international matters (public affairs news) over articles about topics such as crime, entertainment, sports and the weather (nonpublic affairs news) (Fishman, 1980; Jones, 2009; Schudson, 2003;Tuchman, 1978). This pattern of editorial choice arises from occupational and organizational dynamics that have been central to modern journalism (Bennett, Lawrence and Livingston, 2007; Cook, 1998; Davis, 1995; Gitlin, 1980; Williams and Delli Carpini, 2012). But studies about the preferences of the public have usually generated conflicting findings. Some scholars have noted that consumers tend to gravitate towards public affairs news (Huang, 2009; Jensen, 1990; Patterson, 1994; Schramm, 1947; Shoemaker and Cohen, 2006; Stone and Boudreau, 1995), while others have argued the opposite (Bird, 2003; Bogart, 1989; Graber, 1984; Hamilton, 2004; Prior, 2007; Tewksbury, 2003).These conflicting views about the preferences of the public have led to a discussion about whether there is a news gap between the media and the public. If members of the public have a large appetite for public affairs news, then there should be no gap. If, on the contrary, they are more interested in non-public affairs stories, then a news gap should emerge. Such questions have always been pressing, but their familiar contours may be being redrawn even more starkly in the digital era. At the very least, the meaning of this 'news gap' would be completely different in the contemporary media environment, for two reasons. First, news outlets no longer operate in monopoly or oligopoly conditions, and face increased competition for audience attention and advertising income with many new content providers. Second, journalism's jurisdictional space is threatened both by new entrants, such as aggregators, algorithms and amateur content providers, and by the increased information available, in real time, about audiences' preferences. In this environment, the gap could threaten – or at least modify – the social relevance of journalism in the digital age.

In the reminder of this chapter, we describe our efforts to study the news gap empirically and engage in middle-range theorizing about the factors that shape it. We also discuss its implications for broader conceptual debates at the intersection of journalism and society.

Studying the news gap

Discussions about the existence of a news gap are not new. For instance, three-quarters of a century ago Robert Park, a leading figure of the Chicago School of sociology and a former newspaper reporter, wrote: 'The things which most of us would like to publish are not the things that most of us want to read. We may be eager to get into print what is, or seems to be, edifying, but we want to read what is interesting, (Park, 1981 [1940], p. xxii). Thus, despite the fact that the notion of a possible news gap has existed for a long time, there have been very limited empirical studies into whether this perceived gap actually exists and, if so, its magnitude and the variables that affect it. Furthermore, most of the existing empirical studies about the news gap have suffered from three main limitations.

First, most of the research relies on aggregate measures of consumer behaviour such as surveys, circulation reports and ratings data (Bartels, 1993; Price and Zaller, 1993; Tewksbury, 2003). While these measures were the best ones available in the media environment of 20 years or more ago, there are now more granular and precise metrics that capture consumer behaviour at the story level of analysis.

Second, the majority of the existing studies have looked at the news choices of either journalists or consumers, but not at both concurrently. This is related to a lack of integration of studies on media production and consumption within the academy. Given the amount and variety of information that journalists – in particular those who work for digital media enterprises – possess about their users, and the possibility that this information may factor into editorial decision making, it is critical that studies of the news gap examine the choices of journalists and consumers concurrently (Lee, Lewis and Powers, 2014; MacGregor, 2007; Singer, 2011; Thorson, 2008).

Third, most research on the news gap has relied on cross-sectional data, implicitly assuming that the patterns that characterize one point in time also apply to others. This has led to the image that the editorial preferences of journalists and consumers are static. However, related studies show that these preferences can be altered under a wide array of circumstances, including the occurrence of political events, natural disasters and other contextual transformations (Berkowitz, 1992, 2000; Boyle et al., 2004; Holbrook, 1996; Schudson, 1998; Williams and Delli Carpini, 2000).

To help overcome these limitations, we undertook a series of studies that examine the concurrent news choices of journalists and consumers at the story level of analysis. Moreover, two of these studies collected longitudinal data on these choices, which enabled us to test the assumption of whether these choices are dynamic or not. The data were collected from the following 20 news sites between spring 2007 and fall 2012 – different sites were examined in different periods:[1] Clarín.com and Nacion.com in Argentina; Folha.com in Brazil; Welt.de and Tagesspiegel.de in Germany; Eluniversal.com.mx and Reforma.com in Mexico; Elmundo.es and Elpais.es in Spain; Guardian.co.uk and Times.co.uk in the UK; and Abcnews.com, Cbsnews.com, Chicagotribune.com, CNN.com, Foxnews.com, News.yahoo.com, Seattlepi.com, Usatoday.com and Washingtonpost.com in the USA. We selected these sites because they converge and diverge on a number of critical dimensions. On the one hand, they are all affiliated with leading media that play a major role in setting the political and social agendas in their respective countries. On the other hand, they differ by being based in countries that have diverse media histories, structures and regulatory regimes; they are representative of different ideological viewpoints; and they also vary by having ties to different kinds of parent organizations – print, television, cable, and online. We also selected different periods for data collection. In most cases, we examined news choices during relatively normal political activity. However, we also gathered information during major scheduled political events (the 2008 and 2012 presidential elections in the US, and the 2010 mid-term congressional elections in that country) and an unforeseen nationwide political crisis that took place in Argentina in 2008. This combination of commonalities and differences across various temporal periods allowed us to see if the gap cut across related but dissimilar sites, to ascertain the effect that different factors might have and to probe whether news choices are dynamic or not.

We followed a similar procedure across the various studies we conducted. For each of the sites and for each data collection day, we identified the top stories selected by journalists and the top stories selected by consumers. The journalists' selections consist of the first ten stories on the homepage, counting from left to right and from the top down in a grid-like manner. These are the stories usually placed on the first screen of a homepage, which are akin to above-the-fold stories on the front pages of newspapers. They represent a suitable approximation to journalists' choices of the most newsworthy stories of the day. The consumers' selections are the top four, five or ten stories in the 'most read' list made publicly available by each site. In all, we collected 50,409 news articles: 24,261 from the journalists' lists,

20,615 from the 'most clicked', 2,763 from the 'most emailed' and 2,770 from the 'most commented' lists.

A team of trained researchers evaluated each story on two variables. First, they assessed the content of the story and decided whether it dealt with either a public affairs issue (political, economic, business or international news) or a non-public affairs issue (primarily sports, weather, celebrity or crime news). Second, they looked at the storytelling format of each article to see if it was straight news, feature style, opinion, blogs or user-generated content.[2]

Assessing the news gap

We found that the content choices of journalists and consumers in the seven countries studied differed significantly. Journalists had a higher preference for public affairs news than consumers. This led to a news gap that had an average of 18 percentage points across sites. The gap was not correlated with ideological and geographical variations: it was present in sites of different ideological orientations and located in countries with quite diverse media histories, structures and traditions. On the contrary, the gap changed with variations in the political context. During periods of heightened political activity – whether it was a planned electoral event in the USA or a sudden political crisis in Argentina – it went down drastically, only to go back to the normal state of affairs during periods of routine political activity. This pattern was mostly due to changes in consumer behaviour – journalists' choices were much more stable. This context-dependent nature of news choices shows that the news gap can be dynamic.

Our research also showed that straight news is the leading storytelling alternative for journalists and consumers across all sites and periods of study. Thus, contrary to the widespread belief that the news has gone soft (Baum, 2002; Heith, 2010; Hollander, 2005; Prior, 2003; Taniguchi, 2007), our account showed that, on average, 72 percent of the ten most newsworthy articles and 61 percent of the ten most clicked articles were straight news across sites – the far distant second most popular option was feature-style narratives. Moreover, our analysis also challenged the notion that novel formats, such as blogs and user-generated content, may revitalize journalism by allowing audiences to contribute material that can counter the limitations of traditional media (Benkler, 2006; Dutton, 2009; Reese et al., 2007; Singer, 2005; Thelwall, Byrne and Goody, 2007). Web 2.0 formats like blogs and user-generated content were not popular with either journalists or consumers. Across sites, blogs accounted for four per cent of the journalists' choices and three per cent of those of consumers, and user-generated content averaged one per cent and 0.26 per cent respectively. Our analysis of the combination of content and storytelling choices indicated that journalists oversupply straight news that deals with public affairs topics and undersupply all the other combinations.

Finally, our account showed that technology matters in the news gap. Consumers most often clicked on non-public affairs stories in straight-news format, which they find interesting, and emailed non-public affairs stories told in feature style, which are bizarre or useful, to their network of friends and family. In contrast, audience members tended to comment on opinion or straight-news pieces about high profile public affairs topics, to discuss controversial topics with a larger audience composed mostly of unknown people. Thus, the news gap increased when one juxtaposed the journalists' top choices with the most emailed articles and changed in the reverse direction when journalists' top preferences were contrasted with the most commented-on stories. Technological affordances allow the users of news sites to interact with the news and with other consumers in various ways, and they took advantage of that opportunity.

Origins and evolution of the gap

These findings tell us that the news gap is a regular feature of the digital media landscape – and possibly of other platforms too – and that its magnitude is fairly large. They also suggest that it is affected by shifts in the political environment and in technological affordances, but is not affected by regional or ideological variables. But how did the news gap originate and how has it evolved in the current media context? Although there have not been any historical accounts of the news gap per se, in our view it originated from major developments in three areas in the media space: market power; occupational dynamics; and audience behaviour.

First, for most of the twentieth century, the leading media organizations usually enjoyed natural monopoly or oligopoly positions in the respective markets in which they operated (Baum and Kernell, 1999; Clemons, Gu and Lang, 2002; Frijters and Velamuri, 2009; Gurevitch, Coleman and Blumler, 2009; Kind, Nilssen and Sorgard, 2009). In the USA, for instance, by the 1980s, print newspapers had monopoly positions in 97 per cent of their respective markets (Picard and Brody, 1997). Furthermore, up until the advent of cable television news, also in the 1980s, there were only a handful of broadcast network stations that disseminated audiovisual news content to the population. The strong market position of leading media organizations meant that the advertisers in the markets they operated had a major incentive to advertise with them in order to reach their target populations. This, in turn, allowed media organizations to provide high levels of public affairs content even when their publics were not as highly interested in them, since the bottom line was healthy and there were ample resources for investigative projects.

Second, during the same period, journalism evolved as an occupation marked by a public service mission centred on the provision of news that could improve the quality of democratic life. The apex of this image was the Watergate case, which has subsequently emerged as an icon in public discourse not only in the USA, but also in many other countries (Schudson, 1993). Furthermore, journalists were relatively unchallenged in their jurisdictional space since they were seen as the natural purveyors of news about the polity. Even though there were other providers of that information, journalists working for leading, mainstream media organizations emerged as the independent and reliable sources (Boczkowski, 2004; Deuze, 2007; Sousa, 2006; Waisbord, 2013).

Third, the public's longstanding tendency to gravitate towards stories about leisurely aspects of daily life rather than news about the polity was partly mitigated by the affordances of print and audiovisual media. The combination of the linearity of these media and the relatively low levels of interactivity that they afford made it more difficult for their consumers to avoid the news they were not interested in and focus on the rest. In other words, there was a significant level of accidental exposure to public affairs news that took place while flipping the pages of a newspaper for a sports story or waiting for the fifth segment of a newscast for the weather story (Downs, 1957; Prior, 2007; Schoenbach, 2004; Schoenbach, de Waal and Lauf, 2005).

The past few decades have seen massive changes in each of these three dimensions. The advent of cable television and especially the internet altered the dynamics of market power and the competitive landscape for news. The level of competition for audience attention, subscription revenue and advertising dollars has increased exponentially. The days of enjoying natural monopoly or oligopoly positions are a distant memory of the past for leading media organizations who see the economic health of their enterprises suffer year after year. Massive lay-offs, closing of foreign bureaus and unpopular beats, and decreased levels of resources for investigative projects are some of the common signs of the systemic deterioration that has affected the leading media organizations in many countries. In this context, ignoring the news preferences of consumers has become much harder to do than in the past.

The jurisdictional space of journalism has also seen significant modifications in recent years. Bloggers, citizen journalists, amateurs and algorithms have been vying for a slice of the news production territory that journalists once dominated with minimal challenges (Bruns, 2008; Gillmor, 2004; Lowrey, 2006; Robinson, 2007; Williams and Delli Carpini, 2000). This has eroded the audience, funding and necessity of traditional journalism one story at a time. Tied to this, and also to the issues noted in the previous paragraph, is the fact that journalists have much more access to information about audience behaviour than in the past (Ashuri, 2016; Boczkowski, 2010; MacGregor, 2007; Nguyen, 2013). Quite often inside newsrooms, this serves as an insidious reminder of the audience's preferences for non-public affairs reportage and, together with the market trends mentioned before, make it less appealing to 'write for one another' (Darnton, 1975, p. 176).

The increased centrality of digital media as a primary vehicle for the consumption of news has upended the assumptions about linearity, unidirectionality and bundling that characterized print and broadcast media. Either on the web or via mobile devices, the public has a much greater ability to consume the news they want, how they want it and when they want it than before (Dutta-Bergman, 2004; Mutz, 2006; Sheehan, 2002). This has also meant a significantly increased capacity to avoid the news they are not interested in. This has directly eroded the access to public affairs news on leading news sites.

Taken together, the trends in these three dimensions suggest that even if the gap existed as strongly yesterday as it exists today, its meaning in both periods is quite different. Yesterday's gap meant a capacity for leading media organizations to communicate the type of news that they thought their publics needed to know as informed members of society; this could occur irrespective of whether or not there was a very high level of interest in those stories. Today's gap means growing challenges to the provision of public affairs reportage by these organizations and the economic viability of their public service mission in the medium-term future. The news gap also threatens the jurisdiction of journalists in general and public affairs reportage in particular, and could potentially erode journalism's relevance as a political actor and as a cultural form. Should mainstream news outlets privilege what the public must know about, as they have done in the past, or should they cater more closely to audiences' preferences, even if that means forgoing the traditional democratic mandates of journalism? Whatever course journalism undertakes, its role in the democratic polity will likely be transformed.

Conclusion: making sense of the news gap

On the basis of these findings, we offer two levels of theorizing. First, we conceptualize on the factors that affect the gap and those that do not. Second, we reflect on the implications of the gap for broader theoretical debates at the nexus of media, technology and society.

First, contextual and technological variables shape the news gap, and geographical and ideological ones do not. The role of contextual and technological variables has to do with the ability of news consumers to enact diverse informational practices in contexts characterized by varying levels of political activity, and in relation to the different affordances of websites. The absence of a major effect having to do with geographical and ideological variables is, at least partly, a function of the convergence of media systems and the globalization of popular taste among the public of leading and mainstream media organizations (Pfetsch and Esser, 2004; Reese, 2001; Swanson, 2004).

Second, our findings regarding the news gap have implications for the following theoretical discussions: agenda setting (McCombs and Shaw, 1972), monitorial citizenship (Schudson, 1998) and the role of storytelling formats in media reception. Regarding issues of agenda setting, we contend that the gap implies that the media have a fairly reduced power to set the agenda for the mass public during times of relatively routine levels of political activity – the elite public composed of politicians, business leaders and other related actors might behave differently. Things do change during periods of heightened political activity, which in turn suggests that the agenda-setting power of the media is highly contextually dependent. News media have been central in allowing large complex democratic societies to reach common ground. The reduced agenda-setting power of mainstream media could thus entail both a deterioration of a cohesive social agenda marked by matters of the polity and shared by major segments of the public, as well as a rising disconnect between policy makers and the citizenry.

On the second theoretical debate, political communication scholars have recently been engaged in a normative debate about whether citizens want the media to provide comprehensive information about public affairs continually (the 'full information' thesis) (Bennett, 2003) or only when critical dynamics of the polity are at stake (the 'monitorial citizenship' thesis) (Zaller, 2003). Our account of variations in the size of the gap between periods of routine and heightened political activity contributes a unique perspective to this debate and supports the monitorial citizenship thesis. Audiences are somewhat unaware of public affairs topics until something – such as an election or a government crisis – attracts their attention. In contrast, the supply of public affairs news remains mostly constant, due to organizational and professional factors. The difference between the variability in audience demand and the stability in news supply also challenges the established form of journalism.

Finally, despite much popular and academic discourse that 'the news has gone soft' and that peer-to-peer production systems are the way of the future, our findings indicate that when we look at what people actually click on, rather than what the pundits say they do, journalists gravitate to straight-news treatments of public affairs subjects and consumers to straight-news focused on non-public affairs subjects. Content rules in an era of information abundance and a multiplicity of storytelling formats, so we see each group falling back on what we could consider the 'basics' of journalism.

The existence, magnitude and widespread character of the news gap have important consequences for the role of media in a liberal democracy. In addition to a decreased ability to set the public's agenda around news on politics, international affairs, business and economics, these consequences touch upon the watchdog role of journalism and the dynamics of the public sphere. Performing a vibrant watchdog role is a major contribution of media organizations to the health of the body politic that requires significant investment of investigative resources on their part (Coronel, 2010; Donohue, Tichenor and Olien, 1995; Skidmore, 1993; Waisbord, 2000). Our findings on the news gap suggest that the audience is not massively interested in the outcomes of these investigations. Therefore, if the economic hardships of mainstream media organizations continue, it is possible that their investment on watchdog journalism might decrease even more than it has in the past couple of decades. Finally, mainstream media also contribute to the health of the body politic by providing information on public affairs that aids democratic deliberation and decision making (Barber, 1984; Dewey, 1946; Habermas, 1989; Page, 1996; Papacharissi, 2002). As with the outcome of watchdog investigations, the news gap might signal a disincentive for mainstream media organizations to continue contributing with the same level of intensity to a robust public sphere. Taken together, these potential consequences for agenda setting, watchdog journalism and the public sphere raise major concerns for the quality of democratic life in the current media age.

Acknowledgements

This is a revised version of the keynote presentation that the first author gave at the conference 'Rethinking Journalism II: The Societal Role and Relevance of Journalism in a Digital Age', held at the University of Groningen on 23 and 24

January 2014. The work in this chapter summarizes ideas and findings contained in *The News Gap: When the Information Preferences of the Media and the Public Diverge* (Cambridge, MIT Press, 2013). We want to acknowledge the feedback received from the conference organizers, Marcel Broersma and Chris Peters, and other participants.

Notes

1 The first data collection process included Chicagotribune.com, CNN.com, News. yahoo.com and Seattlepi.com. Data were gathered on 21 randomly selected days (three for each day of the week) during this period, for a total of three composite weeks between April and June 2007. On each coding day, research assistants collected data at 10 am, 4 pm and 10 pm Central Time, yielding 63 distinct data collection shifts (21 days × 3 times per day) for each site. The second data collection process included Clarin. com, Nacion.com; Folha.com, Welt.de, Tagesspiegel.de, Eluniversal.com.mx, Reforma. com, Elmundo.es, Elpais.es, Guardian.co.uk and Times.co.uk. Data were collected on 92 randomly selected days during 25 weeks (approximately four days for each of the weeks) from 10 November 2007 to 5 May 2008, from Monday to Saturday. The third data collection process included Abcnews.com, Cbsnews.com, CNN.com, Foxnews. com, Usatoday.com and Washingtonpost.com. Data were collected on 79 days during 19 weeks from 1 August to 1 December 2008. Data were also collected in 2009 (14 days surrounding Election Day) two weeks surrounding the mid-term congressional elections of 2010, the corresponding 14 days in 2011 and 89 days from August 1 to December 2, 2012. For description of sites, including online viewing figures, please see explanations in *The News Gap*.
2 Intercoder reliability averaged 90 per cent and Cohen's Kappa averaged .8 across all data coding iterations. The minimum kappa coefficient was .75 and the maximum was .88.

References

Ashuri, T. (2016). When online news was new: Online technology use and constitution of structures in journalism. *Journalism Studies, 17*(3), 301–318.

Barber, B. (1984). *Strong democracy.* Berkeley: University of California Press.

Bartels, L. M. (1993). Messages received: The political impact of media exposure. *American Political Science Review, 87*(2), 267–285.

Baum, M. A. (2002). Sex, lies, and war: How soft news brings foreign policy to the inattentive public. *American Political Science Review, 96*(1), 91–110.

Baum, M. A., & Kernell, S. (1999). Has cable ended the golden age of presidential television? *American Political Science Review, 93*(1), 99–114.

Benkler, Y. (2006). *The wealth of networks: How social production transforms markets and freedom.* New Haven, CT: Yale University Press.

Bennett, W. L. (2003). The burglar alarm that just keeps ringing: A response to Zaller. *Political Communication, 20*(2), 131–138.

Bennett, W. L., Lawrence, R. G., & Livingston, S. (2007). *When the press fails: Political power and the news media from Iraq to Katrina.* Chicago: University of Chicago Press.

Berkowitz, D. (1992). Routine newswork and the what-a-story: A case study of organizational adaptation. *Journal of Broadcasting & Electronic Media, 36*(1), 45–60.

Berkowitz, D. (2000). Doing double duty: Paradigm repair and the Princess Diana what-a-story. *Journalism, 1*(2), 125–143. doi: 10.1177/146488490000100203.

Bird, S. E. (2003). *The audience in everyday life: Living in a media world.* New York: Routledge.

Boczkowski, P. J. (2004). *Digitizing the news: Innovation in online newspapers*. Cambridge, MA: MIT Press.

Boczkowski, P. J. (2010). *News at work: Imitation in an age of information abundance*. Chicago: University of Chicago Press.

Bogart, L. (1989). *Press and public: Who reads what, when, where, and why in American newspapers*. Hillsdale, NJ: Lawrence Erlbaum Associates.

Boyle, M. P., Schmierbach, M., Armstrong, C. L., McLeod, D. M., Shah, D. V., & Pan, Z. D. (2004). Information seeking and emotional reactions to the September 11 terrorist attacks. *Journalism & Mass Communication Quarterly, 81*(1), 155–167.

Bruns, A. (2008). The active audience: Transforming journalism from gatekeeping to gate-watching. In C. A. Paterson & D. Domingo (Eds.), *Making online news: The ethnography of new media production* (pp. 171–184). New York: Peter Lang.

Clemons, E. K., Gu, B., & Lang, K. R. (2002). Newly vulnerable markets in an age of pure information products: An analysis of online music and online news. *Journal of Management Information Systems, 19*(3), 17–41.

Cook, T. (1998). *Governing with the news: The news media as a political institution*. Chicago: University of Chicago Press.

Coronel, S. (2010). Corruption and the watchdog role of the news media. In P. Norris (Ed.), *Public sentinel: News media and governance reform* (pp. 111–136). Washington, DC: World Bank.

Darnton, R. (1975). Writing news and telling stories. *Daedalus, 104*(2), 175–194.

Davis, R. (1995). *The press and American politics: The new mediator*. White Plains, NY: Longman.

Dean, W., Pertilla, A., & Belt, T. (2007). The myths that dominate local TV news: The X-structure, and the fallacy of the hook-and-hold method of TV news. In T. Rosenstiel, M. Just, T. Belt, *et al.* (Eds.), *We interrupt this newscast: How to improve local news and win ratings, too* (pp. 51–93). New York: Cambridge University Press.

Deuze, M. (2007). *Media work*. Cambridge: Polity Press.

Dewey, J. (1946). *The public and its problems*. Chicago: Gateway Books.

Donohue, G. A., Tichenor, P. J., & Olien, C. N. (1995). A guard dog perspective on the role of media. *Journal of Communication, 45*(2), 115–132. doi: 10.1111/j.1460-2466.1995.tb00732.x.

Downs, A. (1957). *An economic theory of democracy*. New York: Harper & Row.

Druckman, J. N. (2005). Does political information matter? *Political Communication, 22*(4), 515–519.

Dutta-Bergman, M. J. (2004). Complementarity in consumption of news types across traditional and new media. *Journal of Broadcasting & Electronic Media, 48*(1), 41–60.

Dutton, W. H. (2009). The fifth estate emerging through the network of networks. *Prometheus, 27*(1), 1–15.

Fishman, M. (1980). *Manufacturing the news*. Austin: University of Texas Press.

Frijters, P., & Velamuri, M. (2009). Is the internet bad news? The online news era and the market for high-quality news. *Review of Network Economics, 9*(2), 2.

Gans, H. J. (2004). *Deciding what's news: A study of CBS Evening News, NBC Nightly News, Newsweek, and Time* (25th anniversary edition). Evanston, IL: Northwestern University Press.

Gillmor, D. (2004). *We the media: Grassroots journalism by the people, for the people*. Sebastopol, CA: O'Reilly Media, Inc.

Gitlin, T. (1980). *The whole world is watching*. Berkeley: University of California Press.

Graber, D. (1984). *Processing the news: How people tame the information tide*. New York: Longman.

Graber, D. A. (2006). *Mass media and American politics*. Washington, DC: CQ Press.

Gurevitch, M., Coleman, S., & Blumler, J. (2009). Political communication: Old and new media relationships. *ANNALS of the American Academy of Political and Social Science, 625*(1), 164–181.

Habermas, J. (1989). *The structural transformation of the public sphere.* Cambridge, MA: MIT Press.

Habermas, J. (1996). *Between facts and norms: Contributions to a discourse theory of law and democracy.* Cambridge, MA: MIT Press.

Hamilton, J. (2004). *All the news that's fit to sell: How the market transforms information into news.* Princeton, NJ: Princeton University Press.

Heith, D. J. (2010). Reaching women: Soft media in the 2004 presidential election. *Journal of Women, Politics & Policy, 31*(1), 22–43.

Holbrook, T. M. (1996). *Do campaigns matter?* Thousand Oaks, CA: Sage.

Hollander, B. A. (2005). Late-night learning: Do entertainment programs increase political campaign knowledge for young viewers? *Journal of Broadcasting & Electronic Media, 49*(4), 402–415.

Huang, E. (2009). The causes of youths' low news consumption and strategies for making youths happy news consumers. *Convergence: The International Journal of Research into New Media Technologies, 15*(1), 105–122.

Jensen, K. (1990). The politics of polysemy: Television news, everyday consciousness and political action. *Media, Culture and Society, 12*(1), 57–77.

Jones, A. S. (2009). *Losing the news: The future of the news that feeds democracy.* Oxford: Oxford University Press.

Kind, H. J., Nilssen, T., & Sorgard, L. (2009). *Business models for media firms: Does competition matter for how they raise revenue?* CESifo, Center for Economic Studies & Ifo Institute for Economic Research.

Lee, A. M., Lewis, S. C., & Powers, M. (2014). Audience clicks and news placement: A study of time-lagged influence in online journalism. *Communication Research, 41*(4), 505–530.

Lowrey, W. (2006). Mapping the journalism-blogging relationship. *Journalism, 7*(4), 477–500.

MacGregor, P. (2007). Tracking the online audience: Metric data start a subtle revolution. *Journalism Studies, 8*(2), 280–298.

McCombs, M., & Shaw, D. (1972). The agenda setting function of mass media. *Public Opinion Quarterly, 36*(2), 176–187.

Mindich, D. T. Z. (2005). *Tuned out: Why Americans under 40 don't follow the news.* New York: Oxford University Press.

Mutz, D. (2006). How the mass media divide us. In D. W. Brady & P. S. Nivola (Eds.), *Red and blue nation?* Washington, DC: Brookings Institution Press.

Nguyen, A. (2013). Online news audiences. In K. Fowler-Watt & S. Allan (Eds.), *Journalism: New challenges* (pp. 146–161). Bournemouth: Centre for Journalism & Communication Research Bournemouth University.

Page, B. I. (1996). *Who deliberates?: Mass media in modern democracy.* Chicago: University of Chicago Press.

Papacharissi, Z. (2002). The virtual sphere: The internet as a public sphere. *New Media & Society, 4*(1), 9–27.

Park, R. (1981 [1940]). Introduction. In H. Hughes (Ed.), *News and the human interest story.* Herndon, VA: Transaction Publishers.

Patterson, T. (1994). *Out of order.* New York: Vintage Books.

Pfetsch, B., & Esser, F. (2004). Comparing political communication: Reorientations in a changing world. In F. Esser & B. Pfetsch (Eds.), *Comparing political communication* (pp. 3–22). New York: Cambridge University Press.

Picard, R. G., & Brody, J. H. (1997). *The newspaper publishing industry.* Boston: Allyn & Bacon.

Price, V., & Zaller, J. (1993). Who gets the news: Alternative measures of news reception and their implications for research. *Public Opinion Quarterly, 57*, 133–164.

Prior, M. (2003). Any good news in soft news? The impact of soft news preference on political knowledge. *Political Communication, 20*(2), 149–171.

Prior, M. (2007). *Post-broadcast democracy: How media choice increases inequality in political involvement and polarizes elections*. New York: Cambridge University Press.

Reese, S. D. (2001). Understanding the global journalist: A hierarchy-of-influences approach. *Journalism Studies, 2*, 173–187.

Reese, S. D., Rutigliano, L., Hyun, K., & Jeong, J. (2007). Mapping the blogosphere: Professional and citizen-based media in the global news arena. *Journalism, 8*(3), 235–261. doi: 10.1177/1464884907076459.

Robinson, S. (2007). 'Someone's gotta be in control here'. *Journalism Practice, 1*(3), 305–321.

Schoenbach, K. (2004). A balance between imitation and contrast: What makes newspapers successful? A summary of internationally comparative research. *Journal of Media Economics, 17*(3), 219–227.

Schoenbach, K., de Waal, E., & Lauf, E. (2005). Research note: Online and print newspapers – Their impact on the extent of the perceived public agenda. *European Journal of Communication, 20*(2), 245–258.

Schramm, W. (1947). Measuring another dimension of newspaper readership. *Journalism Quarterly, 24*, 293–306.

Schudson, M. (1993). *Watergate in American memory: How we remember, forget, and reconstruct the past*. New York: Basic Books.

Schudson, M. (1998). *The good citizen: A history of American civic life*. New York: Martin Kessler Books.

Schudson, M. (2003). *The sociology of news*. New York: Norton.

Sheehan, K. B. (2002). Of surfing, searching, and newshounds: A typology of internet users' online sessions. *Journal of Advertising Research, 42*(5), 62–71.

Shoemaker, P. J., & Cohen, A. A. (2006). *News around the world: Content, practitioners, and the public*. New York: Routledge.

Singer, J. B. (2005). The political j-blogger: 'Normalizing' a new media form to fit old norms and practices. *Journalism, 6*(2), 173–198. doi: 10.1177/1464884905051009.

Singer, J. B. (2011). Community service: Editor pride and user preference on local newspaper websites. *Journalism Practice, 5*(6), 623–642.

Skidmore, T. E. (1993). Politics and the media in a democratizing Latin America. In T. E. Skidmore (Ed.), *Television, politics, and the transition to democracy in Latin America* (pp. 1–22). Baltimore, MD: Johns Hopkins University Press.

Sousa, H. (2006). Information technologies, social change and the future: The case of online journalism in Portugal. *European Journal of Communication, 21*(3), 373–387.

Stone, G., & Boudreau, T. (1995). Comparison of reader content preferences. *Newspaper Research Journal, 16*, 13–28.

Swanson, D. (2004). Transnational trends in political communication. In F. Esser & B. Pfetsch (Eds.), *Comparing political communication: Theories, cases, and challenges* (pp. 45–63). New York: Cambridge University Press.

Taniguchi, M. (2007). Changing media, changing politics in Japan. *Japanese Journal of Political Science, 8*(1), 147–166.

Tewksbury, D. (2003). What do Americans really want to know? Tracking the behavior of news readers on the internet. *Journal of Communication, 53*(4), 694–710.

Thelwall, M., Byrne, A., & Goody, M. (2007). Which types of news story attract bloggers? *Information Research, 12*(4).

Thompson, J. B. (1995). *The media and modernity: A social theory of the media*. Cambridge: Polity Press.

Thorson, E. (2008). Changing patterns of news consumption and participation: News recommendation engines. *Information, Communication & Society, 11*(4), 473–489.

Tuchman, G. (1978). *Making news*. New York: Free Press.

Waisbord, S. R. (2000). *Watchdog journalism in South America: News, accountability, and democracy.* New York: Columbia University Press.

Waisbord, S. (2013). *Reinventing professionalism: Journalism and news in global perspective.* Hoboken, NJ: John Wiley & Sons.

Williams, B. A., & Delli Carpini, M. X. (2000). Unchained reaction: The collapse of media gatekeeping and the Clinton-Lewinsky scandal. *Journalism: Theory, Practice & Criticism, 1*(1), 61–85.

Williams, B. A., & Delli Carpini, M. X. (2012). *After broadcast news: Media regimes, democracy, and the new information environment.* New York: Cambridge University Press.

Zaller, J. (1999). Market competition and news quality. Paper presented at: *The American Political Science Association, Atlanta, GA.*

Zaller, J. (2003). A new standard of news quality: Burglar alarms for the monitorial citizen. *Political Communication, 20*(2), 109–130.

12

THE RHETORICAL ILLUSIONS OF NEWS

Chris Peters and Marcel Broersma

Imagine for a moment – a thought experiment if you will – that journalism as we have come to know it would disappear overnight. What would happen in terms of the informational flows in society? What would we miss and what would be the risk, if any? Instinctively, the answers likely proffered to such a hypothetical scenario are predictable: people would lose crucial information for engaging civically; unfettered from investigative oversight, governments, businesses and other powerful institutions would become less accountable; the fodder for public discussion on prominent issues of the day would be lost, and so on and so forth. In sum, the conditioned reaction on questions about 'what journalism is good for' tends to lead back towards familiar rhetorics and rationales.

Journalism's normative claims rely heavily upon these established modernist discourses which serve to affirm its essential role within a democracy and assert its relevance to the public (see McNair, 2012; Schudson, 2008). However, the reality is that most journalism is not a public good, at least not in the traditional economic sense. Publishers in print and online as well as commercial broadcasters are typically companies with all the drawbacks and market susceptibilities this implies, no matter how much journalists, journalism studies scholars and audiences alike frequently place expectations of public service upon journalism *tout court*. Even public broadcasting, for that matter, is obliged by law to cater for and reach certain audiences. Given this context, it is intriguing to consider the possible disconnect between journalism's normative assertions, its day-to-day activities and its actual resonance.

The perseverance and ubiquity of time-honoured notions to define journalism's worth (in the face of rapidly shifting practices in the digital era) seems evidence of, if nothing else, a rhetorical entrenchment fostered by the 'objective' journalistic ethos established over the course of the twentieth century (Broersma, 2007). And while easy to empathize with, embracing such normative thinking evidently raises challenges. For one thing, it tends to restrict the scope of what we consider to be proper journalistic practice (Josephi, 2013), which may blind us to both the historical and future functions of 'the news' (Zelizer, 2013). It also conflates news discourse, the claim to represent social 'reality' through the daily production of 'factual' stories, with journalism's performative discourse, the different sets of routines and conventions enacted on a daily basis to achieve this, which must be accepted by the public in various contexts to achieve an intended social function (Broersma, 2010). In other words, while people may hold the central claims of journalism's societal value to be true in an abstract sense, they may also simultaneously reject its performance in their everyday lives. This could be because they simply feel it is not a necessity to satisfy their informational needs or are just uninterested, both of which are somewhat damning in light of the rhetoric of journalism's worth.

Moreover, the taken-for-granted positioning of journalism as a central and necessary institution in democratic societies, its public relevance seemingly self-evident, appears to lend itself to a perpetual 'crisis' discourse. This limits the opportunities to think through the contingent and differentiated possibilities of journalism(s)' futures (Zelizer, 2015). So if we want to construct arguments for why journalism matters – or indeed what journalism 'is' – what might we do rather than retread familiar discursive ground? This chapter argues that reverse engineering the process and switching the emphasis might offer a better way. In other words, in a world without journalism, what would make it appear afresh? What would this new 'journalism' look like? Would audiences (as consumers or citizens) demand it? Or would the functions that journalism has traditionally fulfilled in everyday life be taken over by other institutions that do not label themselves as journalism? These questions are somewhat akin to the entrepreneurial mindset currently being demanded of many journalists. Having lost their careers in legacy media or having never been able to latch on to a job in the first place, they now attempt to launch media start-ups that engage in something that lays claim to the territory of journalism. We believe that such strategic thinking is not only productive at this level, but is equally vital when scaled up to larger media outlets as well.

This chapter accordingly explores the possible disparities between journalism's claim of being essential to democracy and the actual news and informational preferences of (digital) news consumers. Through the lens of the informational habits of citizens, we set out to critically investigate journalism's democratic worth anew, something the industry and many observers leave largely unquestioned. This dogmatism, we argue, potentially stifles the reflexivity needed for transformations ranging from possible adaptation to disruptive change. In this regard, this chapter argues that a bottom–up approach to begin rethinking (digital) journalism's possible futures is more fruitful than to depart from grand normative theories; it is more constructive to start with, in Jay Rosen's (2006) well-known phrase, 'the people formerly known as the audience'.

While audience-centred research has experienced something of a resurgence in recent years (see COST Action, 2014), we feel further efforts to unpack how people experience and evaluate journalism can help to align citizens' needs with journalism's offerings. Such understandings potentially provide both economic benefits as well as a public rationale for cross-subsidizing (news) media. Furthermore, we maintain that when it comes to journalism, which is well-established both as a public and a private enterprise, these values should not be viewed as distinct. People use news on different platforms and devices for different reasons, at different places and times of the day, but this does not make certain uses worthwhile and others worthless. Rather, it speaks to the fact that news use is a cultural practice that orders and interrelates with other practices, from starting one's workday or commuting to work to speaking with colleagues or connecting with issues and other people.

By investigating such patterns from the perspective of the audience, we can begin to discuss journalism's potential civic – and possibly democratic – function concretely, as these must be anchored in everyday life, either through familiar presence or by signalling the exceptional (see Highmore, 2002). Establishing these dynamics is central to scholarship wishing to understand the impact of the current shifts transforming the media landscape and to make democratic claims on digital journalism's behalf. Therefore, the latter part of this chapter employs an exploratory study of social media use to illustrate what such an approach might tell us about the actual informational preferences and civic engagement beget by new media technologies. If we want to think through what types of journalism are wanted and potentially needed in a digital age, audience-based studies matter significantly if for no other reason than without them, the purpose of producing journalism in any era is somewhat meaningless, whether or not one is speaking economically, democratically or socioculturally.

Digital culture, communication and democracy

While other formal institutions such as policing, education or healthcare certainly also face public criticism and budget cuts amidst challenging economic times, few professions that claim to serve and be central to society are consistently exposed to a forecast as bleak as journalism. Recent changes in the ways that journalism can be delivered imply that people (at least in a Western context) increasingly have the means to access 'news' at any moment without much hassle, which likely changes the experience of journalism for many. One might even argue that beyond this, the way in which we interact with information on a daily basis transforms. Yet despite these paradigmatic changes, the profession tends to hold on to conventional norms that guide its outlook on what is considered newsworthy (Boczkowski and Mitchelstein, 2013), direct the approach it takes to generate authority (Broersma, 2013; Carlson, 2012) and greatly influence how it visualizes the relationship with the public (Jönsson and Örnebring, 2011). It does seem that quantifiable audience metrics – the power of clicks – have had an influence on story selection, placement and follow-up (Anderson, 2011), and that the birth of online and mobile news has impacted workflows and journalistic priorities (Usher, 2014). However, this has not necessarily altered how newsrooms conceptualize their foundational journalistic remit.

In spite of ongoing economic problems and issues of public legitimacy – challenges that surely erode claims of representing 'the people' – journalism holds on to the paradigms it successfully developed at the end of the nineteenth century (see Hampton, 2004). This is understandable, for these paradigms helped underwrite the industry's central claim of relevance and democratic necessity, and dovetailed with the successful rise of the mass press (Broersma and Peters, 2013). In this vein, contemporary discussions around the threats to journalism rarely pose journalism's core function as the problem; instead, outside forces, whether they are technological developments, the worldwide economic crisis or new competitors on the information market, are seen to threaten its existence and must be accounted for.

How one interprets the changes journalism is facing is often quite telling. It reveals marked and meaningful philosophical differences about how one views different recurring debates, such as the role of technology, perceptions of citizenship and 'the public', and journalism's appropriate social role. For instance, many of the current issues facing journalism are lamented by those we might consider 'techno-pessimists'. They claim that the rise of digital culture causes a de-ritualization of news use that potentially undermines civic engagement. Conversely, 'techno-optimists' laud the rise of new platforms that de-industrialize news production and potentially democratize public debate (Broersma and Peters, 2013; Fenton, 2010). Yet despite this apparent opposition, both strands are rooted in the same normative rhetoric – whether one views digital transformations as 'good' or 'bad', the importance of journalism for democracy and society is taken for granted and at face value.

Of course, this is not to claim that notions of democracy have not shifted at all in a digital era (see Dahlberg, 2011). When we think back to the dominant, established discourses that successfully connected journalism and democracy over the course of the nineteenth and twentieth centuries, these featured grand narratives and strong notions of democracy (and consequently high demands of journalism and high expectations of citizens). Many of these notions stand firm, but in the current era we have also seen the rise of an emphasis that shies away from this to stress the participatory possibilities afforded by digital and networked media. Although democracy does not feature as the main aim in this new wave of digital journalism, it is still an important part of the discourse surrounding it: democracy in journalism rather than through it (Peters and Witschge, 2015). This newer focus – often prioritizing derivative concepts such as interaction or openness – is increasingly espoused by and coupled with mainstream professional journalism through its various user-based initiatives, and tends to stress the potentiality of the individual and/or the technological. Academic studies thus typically focus upon what empowerment of audiences means for journalism (Chung, 2007; Lewis, 2012, Tandoc, 2014), and how news organizations incorporate and perceive their (possible) contributions (Heinrich, 2011; Singer *et al.*, 2011; Williams, Wardle and Wahl-Jorgensen, 2011; Witschge, 2012).

We thus continue to learn an increasing amount about how journalists view audiences, their contributions and the impact of social media on newsrooms, and it would overstate the point to claim that the rhetoric of journalism as a democratic resource for citizens remains completely unchanged. There is no doubt evidence of an inchoate collaborative ethic associated with emerging practices such as citizen journalism, crowdsourcing and user-generated content, and this has consequences for the institutional and societal position envisioned for journalism in a digital age as well as corresponding associations with ideas of democracy, publics and citizenship (Allan and Peters, 2015; Hermida and Thurman, 2008). However, in both 'thick' and 'thin' visions of journalism's democratic role, the main motivations for and value from news and informational use are often sketched along familiar contours. We think it unlikely the experiences of audiences perfectly reflect this potent and robust discourse, meaning that such assumptions bear closer scrutiny.

An emerging emphasis on news audiences

The changing relationship between media producers and consumers is quickly becoming a foundational trope for a journalism studies scholarship increasingly concerned with digital culture, communication and democracy. This seems obvious since the public remains the key stakeholder in various recurring debates, as the framework of many contemporary studies is based upon seeing how journalism can remain democratically relevant, promote civic engagement and facilitate robust business models that adapt to the economic realities of a digital age. It would thus be somewhat of a rhetorical flourish to claim that we know very little about contemporary news audiences. Yet for a number of very valid reasons – the challenge and cost of audience research, the ethical conundrums it raises, the research design issues involved in capturing the depth of mediated experience but also being able to make wider claims – it nonetheless remains true that we have far less profound knowledge about the preferences and experiences of audiences, or 'users', than we do of emerging digital newsroom practices and their associated produced content.

While understandable, this seems not only strange but also somewhat misguided. The public appears far more often as either a potentiality or a rhetorical justification for research rather than as an object of empirical study. Partly this is because a loss of (paying) readers and declining subscriptions are simply at the centre of the current troubles in the newspaper industry, and partly it is because – in a networked communication infrastructure – it is easy to view audiences as partiality-formed or potential publics, readily measured by clicks, shares and the like. But this notion of an imagined public should not be immediately equated to a 'more democratic' journalism or to the lived materiality of journalism in people's everyday lives. In this respect, the (socially desirable) attitudes towards news consumption in an increasingly wired world may be remnants of longstanding societal discourses about the purpose of the press rather than being grounded in possible transformations in people's lived experiences of media (Peters, 2016).

Disavowing ourselves of these long-held assumptions is challenging and familiar themes on journalism and democracy creep into research designs almost without notice. For instance, a Pew Research Center (2011) study on attitudes of American audiences towards news from 1985 to 2011 – a period which saw the rise of cable news, online news and social media – found that the 'watchdog' orientation towards the press was still largely supported and consistent over time. Yet possibly more intriguing was the design of the survey itself; many questions were organized along traditional binaries such that the 'positive' responses were inscribed with traditional journalistic norms, such as being independent, fair to both sides, accurate and politically neutral, while 'negative' indicators of public sentiment were simply the opposite. Such choices are oversimplifications, albeit powerful and telling ones. Although this is but one example, it is not a stretch to say that journalists, academics and audiences themselves are quick to trot out standard descriptions of why people need news (Peters, 2015). Almost unconsciously, many studies start from conventional assumptions on what journalism *should* be and use these as the basis of defining what makes for 'quality' journalism (see Christians *et al.*, 2009; Zaller, 2003). The implicit claim is that we naturally know why audiences need journalism (all the familiar normative democratic reasons) and our attention should accordingly be focused on figuring out where audiences now go to get it, how often, and their judgements over how well different outlets are doing it.

Similarly, inspired by the economic downfall of journalism and the rise of a somewhat chaotic and hybrid media landscape, there is a burgeoning strand of (mostly quantitative) research on the behavioural shifts, preferences of audiences and expectations thrust upon new technology. The Reuters Institute survey on digital news use, for instance, has now been running since 2012 and finds that people increasingly expect to be able to get news anytime and anywhere they want, with smartphones and tablets being ever-more embraced (Newman, Levy and Nielsen, 2015). The Pew Research Center also conducts a number of specific studies focusing on the use of 4th generation mobile communication technologies by audiences as well as covering a breadth of consumption and use-based statistics in its wide-ranging annual *State of the News Media* report. In many Western countries, we increasingly have access to vast data sets which tell us how often people are accessing news on different devices, and the news industry itself also employs a large number of in-house researchers to keep abreast of shifting audience metrics. These studies indicate that in a relatively short timeframe, mobile devices have gone from having limited appeal for news consumption in digitally advanced countries (see Schrøder and Larsen, 2010; Westlund, 2010) to being increasingly used to access news as the technology has become cheaper and easier to use (Chan-Olmsted, Rim and Zerba, 2013; Wei *et al.*, 2013). Dimmick, Feaster and Hoplamazian (2011) found that news consumption practices on mobile technology generally occurred at the interstices of everyday life, slotting into gaps in daily routines, while Costera Meijer and Groot Kormelink (2014) found evidence of a 'checking cycle' associated with mobile devices, in which a familiar pattern of news and other social and informational apps were quickly consulted at points in the day to keep abreast of both personal and traditional news.

This emphasis on technologies has not only remained at the level of device – another prominent and growing emphasis is on news and information consumption via social media platforms. Such research usually talks about users, but (far) less often with them, mainly analysing tweets and – to a far lesser extent – Facebook posts to indicate which topics are trending and how users engage in, for example, political activism. There is also a growing emphasis on large-scale self-report surveys, which increasingly want to know how often people get news via social media, follow breaking news, potentially click through to a 'traditional' news company, and which topics they encounter (Barthel *et al.*, 2015). Studies that do focus on user experiences similarly tend to ask why different groups adapt various platforms (Hargittai and Litt, 2011, 2012) or how people try to obtain social capital by interacting with others (Jiang and De Bruijn, 2014; Vitak and Ellison, 2013). A survey among Canadian users of social networking sites (Hermida *et al.*, 2012) found that users tended to see social media as an addition to their news diet, but not as a replacement of the traditional news outlets they trusted. They particularly liked the possibility of social interaction with friends and relatives through the recommendation of news.

From this brief overview, what becomes evident is that the predominant research focus in most emerging studies is on the visible transformation in the object of study, namely the changing ways of obtaining 'news' from established news institutions and of participating in the production of it. While informative, such an approach fails to anticipate more fundamental transformations witnessed as we shift from mass communication to hybrid media systems (Chadwick, 2013). Moreover, the increasing prominence of this 'participation paradigm' in media and communication research should not go unchecked. It obliges researchers to move beyond mapping changes in user behaviour. Research should be more attuned not only to the modes of participation afforded to audiences but also to the actual experiences people have (or choose not to have) through mediated engagement (Livingstone, 2013). If we want to understand to what extent, if any, news audiences' practices bear affinity to notions of democratic and civic engagement, we would benefit ourselves greatly by casting aside the presumption of public attention (Couldry, Livingstone and Markham, 2007). Furthermore, it behoves us not only to question what 'journalism' and 'news' are, but also to interrogate to what extent acts of public connection based on encountering informational flows (including but not limited to journalism) should be considered to fulfil the traditional democratic ethos of news, and to what extent these discourses need to be questioned.

Instead of criticizing from afar, the remainder of this chapter attempts to take up this challenge, albeit in a preliminary manner. We briefly discuss what we found when crafting an exploratory approach to media use that tried to get away from the established rhetoric of journalism to see how behaviour, attitudes, expectations and experiences overlapped with habits and rituals of everyday use. Rather than taking for granted what news is and how people consume it from traditional journalistic organizations, we tried to focus on what constitutes the object ('news') itself now that the technologies of journalism and the corresponding media ecology are changing so rapidly. This is increasingly important now that news organizations have lost their monopoly on the distribution of news. They are only one information supplier among many that are avowedly non-journalistic, although this should not be considered akin to being uninformative or 'not news'.

Exploratory study: social media and the everyday experience of news

Our lack of understanding about possibly shifting definitions of familiar categories such as 'news' and 'journalism', or reluctance to question foundational tropes around its democratic relevance, stems largely from the limitations of many instruments typically used to address research questions about audiences. Surveys and (online) content analysis can only give us fairly basic insights when we try to go beyond dominant attitudes and behaviours. If we want to understand more complex relationships, such as how the use of social media for news consumption interweaves with the experience of journalism or whether there is any dialectic process between practices of news consumption and the broader rhetoric surrounding its societal role, we need to adopt complementary methods. To this end, there has recently been a growing emphasis on the changing experiences of audiences in the contemporary digitalized age. This 'audience turn', if you will, posits the necessity of going beyond highly informative, but essentially descriptive, quantitative foci on changing patterns of use (e.g. Mitchell and Rosenstiel, 2012) to consider novel meanings and experiences people associate with journalism (see Groot Kormelink and Costera Meijer, 2014; Heikkilä and Ahva, 2015; Madianou, 2009).

The problem with trying to understand changing news use and preferences starting from established discourses on journalism, as surveys typically do, is that audiences generally end up evaluating based upon a spectrum we already know, or describing behavioural patterns and usage rates that are difficult to situate in terms of everyday practices. A similar problem occurs with qualitative methods that pre-define the terms of discussion.[1] In attempting to avoid this, our exploratory study established a foundation based on emergent definitions of news. We allowed the participants to self-define what information they found important and relevant, aiming to investigate how interacting with and encountering these informational flows was situated within everyday life (i.e. habituated and circuitous consumption). A related concern was building up a research design that tried to account for the fundamentally interwoven nature of online and offline words in an age of ubiquitous media. By employing subjects' pre-existing social networks as a starting point, we hoped to allow them to express news preferences that were not externally or artificially imposed. Embracing the idea of 'linking' or 'meshing' data across research phases (Mason, 2006), each subsequent stage of this project was generated out from this original starting point.

Our study analysed the news preferences and online media habits of eight graduate-level Dutch university students who participated in a journalism studies research seminar. An obvious limitation was that journalism students were more likely to be heavy news consumers than other young adults and might be more attuned to common conceptions of news and journalism. Yet this limitation was also a strength. Utilizing such a 'knowledgeable' population presented almost a best-case scenario for analysing journalism's claim of democratic relevance and any possible disjuncture this had from practice and perception. Simply put, if we found that journalism students didn't experience civic value in their everyday news use, we should exercise caution towards assuming this for the general populace.

Using a combination of experimental reflection, semi-structured interviews, media diaries and self-reflective assessments on all phases of the research design, each participant provided approximately 20 hours of their time, generating some 160 hours' worth of research data dedicated to exploring questions of news consumption and the role of social media within this equation. We took their use of the two main social media platforms, Twitter and Facebook, as points of departure for our study, arguing that on these social networks, different types of messages circulate and are aggregated: posts of individual users and (news) institutions, links to all kinds of websites, and conversations between users. Social network sites thus not only connect individual users or institutions to one another, but also connect them to a broad range of news and information that circulates. Conventional news organizations are in this network structure just one source among many possible feeds, and using this approach allowed us to explore the place and relevance that conventional and emerging journalism retained in the everyday lives of a digital generation.

The research process consisted of six instruments which together provided a layered and comprehensive impression of the participants' news use and their attitudes towards this. First, we asked the participants to document their Facebook 'news' and Twitter 'home' feed for seven days to show which information they received on their accounts. Furthermore, they were asked to select ten tweets and ten Facebook items from their Twitter and Facebook feeds every day based upon what they felt was 'interesting information to know' and to briefly reflect upon their selection. Consecutively, they ranked the five most 'relevant' tweets and Facebook items and briefly explained their ranking. In phrasing these questions we carefully avoided wording relating to 'news' and 'journalism' so that participants' assessment of information would not be guided by their existing perceptions of what news is or should be. In these first two phases, participants had not yet been told about the subsequent phases of the research or its leading questions; they were merely informed we wanted to see how they were using social media.

In the following week, we asked the participants to write a brief reflection on what logging their feeds made them realize about their own social media use. Furthermore, they developed and conducted a semi-structured interview with another participant. This interview covered the themes of: media habits; social media, news and information use; reflections on Facebook and Twitter; and the profession of journalism. The final phase involved a research diary which the participants filled out for each media platform they used, even when used simultaneously with other platforms, noting starting time and duration of use, whether different content (i.e. channels, websites, apps) were used during the session (yes/no variable), the types of content (entertainment, news site, video portal, Facebook, etc. – multiple entries possible), location of use, interaction (yes/no variable) and reason for use (socializing, passing the time, etc. – multiple entries possible). Participants were asked to complete these diaries on a Monday, Wednesday, Friday and Sunday. It is intriguing to note that this proved overwhelming for most of them, despite the fact that they were responsible for crafting this part of the research design themselves and selected the relevant categories to be charted. Notwithstanding their control over this phase of the project, many gave up after one to two days. A week after they completed this assignment, participants were asked for a short follow-up reflection on cross-media use.

What is news on Facebook and Twitter?

The study showed just how integrated media consumption is with other social practices and individual routines which are not (or are only very loosely) related to journalism's normative claims and its perceived function in democracy. At the same time, participants were very aware of what journalism 'should be'. In the remainder of this chapter, we briefly touch upon some key findings in terms of what reflections on social media use and content revealed about news as a democratic resource. In interviews and self-reflections, participants indicated that the two platforms had different functions in their lives. Most indicated that they started to use Facebook to establish or maintain social relations and now also used it to structure their social activities, communicate with closer friends and keep track of their lives. Most had been active on Facebook much longer than Twitter and indicated that they only signed up for the latter when they started their journalism education and realized it could potentially be a useful tool to acquire information. Most did not associate Twitter that much with their social life; they considered it a medium for practical and work-related reasons, for example, to 'follow journalists and politicians, in order to find out what their statements are and what articles they recommend to read' (respondent: Saminna).

As a result, Facebook was far more integrated in the daily lives of the participants and all of them checked their news feed multiple times a day, at least every hour, mainly on their mobile phones. It's remarkable that almost all participants stated that they used Facebook as a 'distraction' from work or simply when they were 'bored' or needed a 'mental break'. Participants used Twitter far less regularly and mainly for professional activities when they had a practical reason, mostly when researching and writing articles. It functioned as an awareness system (Hermida, 2010) which they checked 'if something is really booming or something is happening, or someone finds something really important' (respondent: Saminna). On both platforms they limited themselves in most cases to quickly scanning the headlines and seldom clicked on links.

When it came to discussing these habits and their relation to news, the answers and reflections of the participants indicated that standard understandings were quite stable and well-entrenched in their cognitive frames. When reflecting on what they perceive as 'news', most argued along familiar lines: it is something 'important' that one 'should know', produced and distributed by a news organization. They also emphasized that journalism should give citizens background information to understand what is going on in the world and that it is important to be informed to be a 'good citizen'. While the fact the participants studied journalism probably indicates that they were (being) socialized in this professional rhetoric, it appeared that these conceptions were already deeply entrenched. Some showed awareness of how difficult it is to avoid the established definition of news:

> In terms of news, it depends on how one defines news how much I use Facebook for that. I do get links from a news broadcaster and work from colleagues, which offers me news in the more traditional way. But I also get different news via Facebook, in the form of upcoming events or practical information about school. That can be news for me too.
>
> (Respondent: Amanda)

Our research design anticipated this phenomenon by asking them at the very start of the research project to rank items on Twitter and Facebook that they considered 'interesting information to know', thus avoiding common interpretations of what news is or should be. Consecutively, we asked them to rate the five items they considered most relevant. In reflecting on this task, respondents pointed out it provoked them to use social media in a very different way than normal. While they regularly skimmed the headlines of tweets and posts in their timeline without thinking about their relevance, they now read them more closely and actually followed the links to websites and news stories. About half of them indicated that this made them realize that social media contained more interesting information than they were otherwise aware of:

> Normally, I wouldn't really do that, I would think 'oh yeah', but now, because I was spending an amount of time on it anyway, I was opening things and like 'oh, wow, that's interesting'!
>
> (Respondent: Leonie)

It seems that consulting Facebook and – to a lesser extent – Twitter almost functions on an unconscious level, quickly checking 'what happened' or 'what is new'. This was a repetitive and integral part of their daily lives, as opposed to watching television or reading the newspaper, which were deliberate, purposeful activities according to students.

A more detailed picture of what participants considered 'interesting' and 'relevant' information on Facebook and Twitter can be illustrated by the discrepancy in rankings on a given day in the middle of the research week. Classifying the stories they mentioned indicated that the posts they value on Facebook and Twitter had a different character: the former being more social and the latter more business-like. Stories on Facebook were mainly generated by friends, with about 55 per cent of the rated stories consisting of personal updates or comments. They valued them because they wanted to keep up with their friends' lives and experiences or because they personally related to something they were involved in themselves. As one student wrote: 'the news that affects me most is most relevant' (respondent: Bert). The following rationale illustrates these mechanisms clearly:

The top ranked post is the most relevant to me because the information gives me an opportunity to meet up with a friend who I haven't seen for quite a while because he now lives abroad. The second two posts are quite relevant to me because they keep me informed on what my friends are working on. The fourth ranked post is relevant to me because it gives me the chance to do something I like with [a] discount. The fifth ranked post is relevant to me because it relates to two organizations I regularly have had contact with.

(Respondent: Anne-Floor)

More than Facebook, Twitter resembles traditional patterns of news consumption. About 53 per cent of the participants' top tweets were links to news items, mainly from mainstream news organizations, while 8.5 per cent linked to entertainment sites and 11.5 per cent to comments on current affairs. Students used Twitter to obtain information from organizations or people they do not know personally but whom they consider authoritative and credible. Only 10 per cent of the ranked tweets were comments, updates or links from friends.

While the declared preferences indicated different use values for the platforms, our findings also pointed towards another fairly noteworthy discrepancy. When we considered the top-ranked 'interesting' and 'relevant' stories for our participants, these preferences deviated sharply from the mainstream Dutch news outlets. On the day we mention above, the two main national broadcasters and newspapers were quite consistent, selecting new figures about the decline of the Dutch economy and a report about a 2010 plane crash in Tripoli that caused the death of 103 (mainly Dutch) people for prominence. News about the resignation of the pope and doping allegations against Dutch cyclist Michael Boogerd also dominated mainstream news. Our participants – aspiring journalists – barely mentioned these topics. Just two (satirical) tweets about the pope and one tweet of a journalist about the air crash were listed. Instead, students valued news that touched them personally, because it was news about the town they live in, a topic of interest or personally useful information (for example, a local housing agency increasing rents). As one student remarked, 'the most relevant news is close to home' (respondent: Bert).

In sum, while students in the interviews pointed to traditional definitions of news and emphasized its importance for democracy, their personal news preferences and patterns of consumption told a much different story. They were not that interested in stories that had an impact on society, but merely those that impacted their personal situation. Facebook was mainly used to engage with friends and relatives about personal experiences, recommended reads and practical information, and thus to gain social capital. On Twitter, participants followed mainstream (news) organizations and people they respected to learn about information. However, the worth of this input was digested in a very personalized way. While mainstream news outlets told 'the' news that was also deemed hypothetically important by the students, their reflections on their own social media feeds was that what counted was 'their' news, and it was this that they actually engaged with and valued.

Conclusion: a discourse detached from practice?

The changing patterns of news consumption in the current era bring about new configurations between audiences, information, the devices upon which they consume it, and the different (mobile) places and (shiftable) times when and where this is possible. Coupled with the rapid proliferation of news and informational sources arising alongside this, trying to keep up with what 'news' and 'journalism' exactly are, or may become, perplexes even the most avid and insightful observers. What we do seem to know fairly unequivocally is that much of the confusion and concern wrought by the changing media landscape is less about what journalism 'is' anymore, but – quite crucially – what uses people still have for it, which functions are reconfigured or being created anew, and whether or not journalism 'as we knew it' will remain financially viable. Journalism studies, and media and communication studies more broadly, have tried – and are still in the process of trying – to come to grips with these changing dynamics (e.g. Peters and Broersma, 2013; Zelizer, 2009) and special issues have been produced to interrogate fundamental questions about the relationship of journalism and democracy (Josephi, 2013) as well as theories of a newfound digital journalism (Steensen and Ahva, 2015). In these and other accounts, we see an emergent emphasis on what audiences 'do' with news and the various possibilities afforded by technology.

This chapter continues further down this path by critically reflecting on how the uses and feelings about the information potentially available to users in a digital era interacts with our dominant conceptions of journalism and its rhetoric of democratic necessity and civic empowerment. It points to the robustness of this discourse, but its exploratory study also indicates the possibility of a notable disconnect, at least in terms of two dominant social networking platforms of this era, namely Facebook and Twitter, and people's informational preferences and personal patterns of news use. Methodologically, we feel this study, while admittedly modest and not representative, nonetheless indicates the value of developing innovative approaches to bridge the analytic dichotomy that treats online and social media news use as something separate from everyday life. Furthermore, it points to the need to contextualize and critically reflect upon research designs that frequently begin from – and circulate back to – an analytic starting point rooted in conventional discourses.

To be clear, our aim in this chapter has not been to substitute some form of behaviourism to understand the 'real' value of news, and we hope our analysis and claims are not misinterpreted. Just because our respondents do not seem to actively use journalism via social media in a politically involved way does not mean that it is not democratically useful to them. Knowing it is there to fulfil many of the traditional goals of providing information and acting as a watchdog seems to provide comfort and was noted in the interviews. Similarly, it would be foolhardy to ignore the apparent correlation between a historically robust 'free' press within a country and its citizens' civil liberties and democratic voice; indeed, much of the modernist rhetoric about journalism is closely tied to the establishment of many foundational human rights as well as societal cohesion in general, and we would not suggest otherwise.

However, what we do want to point out is that journalists, scholars, politicians and citizens alike are putting a great deal of faith in the inherent potential of journalism to promote civic engagement. While we do not expect everyone to take to the streets, some of the grandiose claims about journalism providing a foundation for a well-informed, civically engaged populace seem naïve. This is even more the case in an age where social media is increasingly used – albeit often in a sporadic, superficial manner – and yet the personal importance of journalistic information through these channels does not necessarily resonate. To draw a parallel, we would not expect children to be well educated if they only attended school irregularly throughout the day and without any structure. So we should be wary of lauding the impact of the civics lessons journalism imparts when it is only attended to haphazardly, and then often only as an afterthought to more immediate personal uses of social media. While testing our suspicions has only so far been done through an exploratory study with some obvious limitations, our fairly 'elite' core of respondents cast enough doubt on the tangible democratic worth of everyday news consumption that it presents a cautionary tale for unquestioningly assuming journalism's value for the populace in this regard. This parallels other studies which have noted that there is a notable disconnect between media availability and consumption and actual civic engagement (see Couldry, Livingstone and Markham, 2007; Swart, Peters and Broersma, 2016). Although the modernist rhetoric of journalism is largely familiar, this chapter reflects the inchoate realizations we are starting to gain about the practices and preferences of digital news consumption. The tendency seems to be towards more shallow and sparse rituals forming and more (opportunities to gratify) personalized news preferences.

It is questionable to what extent this acts as a substitute for the more sustained interactions we associate with traditional platforms for news – the 30-minute or hour-long television newscast and the daily newspaper. The technological affordances of online media certainly allow for greater diversity of, control over and interaction with news and information. Accordingly, understanding the significance of these changes demands multi-faceted approaches that bridge these distinctions and attempt to integrate the experience with daily use amidst ever-increasing possibilities. Our exploratory study tried to do just this, using our participants' (pre-existing) online social networks as an analytic starting point and then integrating their ongoing input and feedback to adapt the research design. It points to important differences between journalism's normative claims about its function in society and democracy in particular, what news consumers say they consider important, and what they actually consume and prefer in daily practice.

Note

1   The hegemonic position of the survey as the preferred instrument for quantitative audience studies is mirrored by the status of the interview in qualitative accounts.

References

Allan, S., & Peters, C. (2015). Visual truths of citizen reportage: Four research problematics. *Information, Communication & Society*, *18*(11), 1348–1361.

Anderson, C. (2011). Between creative and quantified audiences: Web metrics and changing patterns of newswork in local US newsrooms. *Journalism*, *12*(5), 550–566.

Barthel, M., Shearer, E., Gottfried, J., & Mitchell, A. (2015). *The evolving role of news on Twitter and Facebook*. Pew Research Center. Retrieved from http://www.journalism. org/2015/07/14/the-evolving-role-of-news-on-twitter-and-facebook/.

Boczkowski, P., & Mitchelstein, E. (2013). *The news gap: When the information preferences of the media and the public diverge*. Cambridge, MA: MIT Press.

Broersma, M. (2007). Form, style and journalistic strategies: An introduction. In M. Broersma (Ed.), *Form and style in journalism: European newspapers and the representation of news, 1880–2005* (pp. ix–xxix). Dudley, MA: Peeters.

Broersma, M. (2010). Journalism as performative discourse: The importance of form and style in journalism. In V. Rupar (Ed.), *Journalism and meaning-making: Reading the newspaper* (pp. 15–35). Cresskill, NJ: Hampton Press.

Broersma, M. (2013) A refractured paradigm: Journalism, hoaxes and the challenge of trust. In C. Peters & M. Broersma (Eds.), *Rethinking journalism: Trust and participation in a transformed news landscape* (pp. 28–44). London: Routledge.

Broersma, M., & Peters, C. (2013). Introduction: Rethinking journalism: The structural transformation of a public good. In C. Peters & M. Broersma (Eds.), *Rethinking journalism: Trust and participation in a transformed news landscape* (pp. 1–12). London: Routledge.

Carlson, M. (2012). Rethinking journalistic authority: Walter Cronkite and ritual in television news. *Journalism Studies*, *13*(4), 483–498.

Chadwick, A. (2013). *The hybrid media system: Politics and power*. Oxford: Oxford University Press.

Chan-Olmsted, S., Rim, H., & Zerba, A. (2013). Mobile news adoption among young adults: Examining the roles of perceptions, news consumption, and media usage. *Journalism & Mass Communication Quarterly*, *90*(1), 126–147.

Christians, C., Glasser, T., McQuail, D., Nordenstreng, K., & White, R. (2009). *Normative theories of the media: Journalism in democratic societies*. Champaign, IL: University of Illinois Press.

Chung, D. (2007). Profits and perils: Online news producers' perceptions of interactivity and uses of interactive features. *Convergence*, *13*(1), 43–61.

COST Action. (2014). *Transforming audiences, transforming societies*. EU and European Science Foundation. Retrieved from http://www.cost-transforming-audiences.eu.

Costera Meijer, I., & Groot Kormelink, T. (2014). Checking, sharing, clicking and linking: Changing patterns of news use between 2004 and 2014. *Digital Journalism*, *3*(5), 664–679.

Couldry, N., Livingstone, S., & Markham, T. (2007). *Media consumption and public engagement: Beyond the presumption of attention*. Basingstoke: Palgrave Macmillan.

Dahlberg, L. (2011). Re-constructing digital democracy: An outline of four 'positions'. *New Media & Society*, *13*(6), 855–872.

Dimmick, J., Feaster, J., & Hoplamazian, G. (2011). News in the interstices: The niches of mobile media in space and time. *New Media & Society*, *13*(1), 23–39.

Fenton, N. (Ed.). (2010). *New media, old news: Journalism and democracy in the digital age*. London: Sage.

Groot Kormelink, T., & Costera Meijer, I. (2014). Tailor-made news: Meeting the demands of news users on mobile and social media. *Journalism Studies*, *15*(5), 632–641.

Hampton, M. (2004). *Visions of the press in Britain, 1850–1950*. Champaign, IL: University of Illinois Press.

Hargittai, E., & Litt, E. (2011). The sweet smell of celebrity success: Explaining variation in Twitter adoption among a diverse group of young adults. *New Media & Society, 13*(5), 824–842.

Hargittai, E., & Litt, E. (2012). Becoming a tweep: How prior online experiences influence Twitter use. *Information, Communication & Society, 15*(5), 680–702.

Heikkilä, H., & Ahva, L. (2015). The relevance of journalism: Studying news audiences in a digital era. *Journalism Practice, 9*(1), 50–64.

Heinrich, A. (2011). *Network journalism: Journalistic practice in interactive spheres*. New York: Routledge.

Hermida, A. (2010). Twittering the news: The emergence of ambient journalism. *Journalism Practice, 4*(3), 297–308.

Hermida, A., Fletcher, F., Korell, D., & Logan, D. (2012). Share, like, recommend: Decoding the social media news consumer. *Journalism Studies, 13*(5–6), 815–824.

Hermida, A., & Thurman, N. (2008). A clash of cultures: The integration of user-generated content within professional journalistic frameworks at British newspaper websites. *Journalism Practice, 2*(3), 343–56.

Highmore, B. (2002). *Everyday life and cultural theory: An introduction*. London: Routledge.

Jiang, Y., & De Bruijn, O. (2014). Facebook helps: A case study of cross-cultural social networking and social capital. *Information, Communication & Society, 17*(6), 732–749.

Jönsson, A. M., & Örnebring, H. (2011). User-generated content and the news: Empowerment of citizens or interactive illusion?. *Journalism Practice, 5*(2), 127–144.

Josephi, B. (2013). How much democracy does journalism need? *Journalism, 14*(4), 474–489.

Lewis, S. (2012). The tension between professional control and open participation: Journalism and its boundaries. *Information, Communication & Society, 15*(6), 836–866.

Livingstone, S. (2013). The participation paradigm in audience research. *Communication Review, 16*(1–2), 21–30.

Madianou, M. (2009). Audience reception and news in everyday life. In K. Wahl-Jorgensen & T. Hanitzsch (Eds.), *The handbook of journalism studies* (pp. 325–340). London: Routledge.

Mason, J. (2006). Mixing methods in a qualitatively driven way. *Qualitative Research, 6*(1), 9–25.

McNair, B. (2012). *Journalism and democracy: An evaluation of the political public sphere*. London: Routledge.

Mitchell, A., & Rosenstiel, T. (2012). *Mobile devices and news consumption*. Pew Research Center. Retrieved from http://stateofthemedia.org/2012/mobile-devices-and-news-consumption-some-good-signs-for-journalism/.

Newman, N., Levy, D., & Nielsen, R. K. (2015). *Reuters Institute digital news report 2015*. Retrieved from http://www.digitalnewsreport.org/.

Peters, C. (2015). Evaluating journalism through popular culture: HBO's The Newsroom and public reflections on the state of the news media. *Media, Culture & Society, 37*(4), 602–619.

Peters, C. (2016). Spaces of news audiences. In T. Witschge, C. W. Anderson, D. Domingo & A. Hermida (Eds.), *Sage handbook of digital journalism* (pp. 354–369). *London: Sage.*

Peters, C., & Broersma, M. (Eds.). (2013). *Rethinking journalism: Trust and participation in a transformed news landscape*. London: Routledge.

Peters, C., & Witschge, T. (2015). From grand narratives of democracy to small expectations of participation: Audiences, citizenship, and interactive tools in digital journalism. *Journalism Practice, 9*(1), 19–34.

Pew Research Center. (2011). *Views of the news media: 1985–2011*. Retrieved from http://www.people-press.org/files/legacy-pdf/9-22-2011%20Media%20Attitudes%20Release.pdf.

Rosen, J. (2006). *The people formerly known as the audience*. Retrieved from http://archive. pressthink.org/2006/06/27/ppl_frmr.html.

Schrøder, K., & Larsen, B. (2010). The shifting cross-media news landscape: Challenges for news producers. *Journalism Studies, 11*(4), 524–34.

Schudson, M. (2008). *Why democracies need an unlovable press*. Cambridge: Polity Press.

Singer, J., Domingo, D., Heinonen, A., Hermida, A., Paulussen, A., Quandt, T., Reich, Z., & Vujnovic, M. (2011). *Participatory journalism: Guarding open gates at online newspapers*. Oxford, UK: John Wiley & Sons.

Steensen, S., & Ahva, L. (2015). Theories of journalism in a digital age: An exploration and introduction. *Digital Journalism, 3*(1), 1–18.

Swart, J., Peters, C., & Broersma, M. (2016). Navigating cross-media news use: Media repertoires and the value of news in everyday life. *Journalism Studies* (ahead-of-print). doi: 10.1080/1461670X.2015.1129285.

Tandoc, E. (2014). Journalism is twerking?: How web analytics is changing the process of gatekeeping. *New Media & Society, 16*(4), 559–575.

Usher, N. (2014). *Making news at the New York Times*. Ann Arbor, MI: University of Michigan Press.

Vitak, J., & Ellison, N. B. (2013). 'There's a network out there you might as well tap': Exploring the benefits of and barriers to exchanging informational and support-based resources on Facebook. *New Media & Society, 15*(2), 243–259.

Wei, R., Lo, V., Xu, X., Chen, Y., & Zhang, G. (2013). Predicting mobile news use among college students: The role of press freedom in four Asian cities. *New Media & Society, 16*(4), 637–654.

Westlund, O. (2010). New(s) functions for the mobile: A cross-cultural study. *New Media & Society, 12*(1), 91–108.

Williams, A., Wardle, C., & Wahl-Jorgensen, K. (2011). 'Have they got news for us?': Audience revolution or business as usual at the BBC? *Journalism Practice, 5*(1), 85–99.

Witschge, T. (2012). Changing audiences, changing journalism? In P. Lee-Wright, A. Philips & T. Witschge (Eds.), *Changing journalism* (pp. 117–134). London: Routledge.

Zaller, J. (2003). A new standard of news quality: Burglar alarms for the monitorial citizen. *Political Communication, 20*(2), 109–130.

Zelizer, B. (2009). *The changing faces of journalism: Tabloidization, technology and truthiness*. London: Routledge.

Zelizer, B. (2013). On the shelf life of democracy in journalism scholarship. *Journalism, 14*(4), 459–473.

Zelizer, B. (2015). Terms of choice: Uncertainty, journalism, and crisis. *Journal of Communication, 65*(5), 888–908.

AFTERWORD

Crisis? What crisis?

Silvio Waisbord

The chapters in the first part of this collection, focusing on 'Journalism and its societal role', confirm that journalism has experienced major transformations in recent years, a familiar point of departure and arrival that characterizes recent academic analysis and popular commentary (Franklin, 2014). The collapse of old business models, increased market pressures, and the proliferation of digital news and information have redrawn journalistic practices and news in the West and other regions of the world. Although the intensity and depth of the changes are not identical everywhere, similar dynamics are under way. These developments have fuelled the sense that journalism is at a historical turning point of re-invention, as news, information and communication are being completely transformed.

It often seems as if everything we knew about journalism has undergone dramatic changes and needs to be revisited. Just as the current circumstances are challenging for journalists and the news business, they have also forced journalism scholarship to re-assess standard arguments. Tectonic shifts in journalistic practices have disrupted old arguments about gatekeeping, sources, skills, values, ethics, audiences and economics. This is why 'rethinking' fundamental issues in journalism studies, as this collection sets out to do, is necessary.

The concept of 'crisis' has been frequently used to characterize the current situation (Alexander, 2015; Reinardy, 2011; Siles and Boczkowski, 2012; Starr, 2012). If crisis describes when 'the old is dying and the new cannot be born', in Antonio Gramsci's classic definition, its analytical appeal is understandable. Amid existential anxieties about journalism and news, one thing is certain: the old regime has crumbled and it is not self-evident that it will be replaced by anything resembling a coherent, well-defined regime of news.

In the reflexive and critical spirit of this collection – inspired by the various observations and assertions raised within the six chapters that comprise its first thematic section – my interest here is to rethink the concept of 'the crisis of journalism'.

Can we convincingly categorize journalism's current predicament as a crisis? Is everything about journalism in crisis? In my mind, the label has been hastily applied, lacking sufficient nuance to comprehend the situation. 'Crisis' is too broad of a conclusion to capture uneven changes. Concepts used to classify the current situation in journalism should be used carefully (Zelizer, 2015). Changes are not transitions, and transitions are not crises. Recent developments affect multiple dimensions of journalism in different ways. Not everything has experienced massive shifts. Not all boundaries are blurred inside journalism or between journalism and other institutions and forms of news production. Characterizing the current situation as 'liquid' (Deuze, 2008) is too broad to capture the multiple dimensions of journalism. Not everything is as fluid and blurred as it seems or some would like it to be. Nor is it clear whether specific assessments are normative desires for specific changes or, instead, are basically descriptive. What is needed, then, is to carefully examine the reach and intensity of the 'crisis' in journalism with a fine analytical brush, otherwise we run the risk of missing essential aspects of the current situation and paving over important differences across contexts.

News business and labour conditions

By all accounts, the news business is in crisis. At the core of the situation is the dire condition of the newspaper industry. Despite some bright spots around the world (Nielsen, 2012), it has gone through rocky times recently. It has suffered the blunt of the damage of the process of 'creative destruction' unleashed by the multiplication of news outlets, shrinking advertising and the migration of readers to digital platforms. Because newspapers have historically been the main producer of original news, their situation is concerning. Fears abound about significant reductions in the amount of original content, particularly those news forms viewed as essential for democratic life in that they scrutinize power, stimulate critical reasoning, provide insights to know and understand public problems, and emphasize humanity and solidarity. The longstanding paradox of democratic news has become obvious: journalism, long seen as a central institution of democracy, has been largely funded by the self-interest of the market. Although news is widely seen as an essential public good for democratic life, it has been largely produced by private companies that are, expectedly, more concerned with profit than public virtue. For a long time, democracy rode on the assumption that the market-based press handsomely functioned on Adam Smith's premises of doing social good while pursuing private gain. Despite promising offshoots, we are still far from having convincing evidence about viable alternatives to replace the old order (Conboy and Eldridge, 2014; Schlesinger and Doyle, 2014).

The upheaval in the news business has profoundly changed working conditions. Massive lay-offs, closings and employment uncertainty have been common, particularly in the newspaper industry. Between 2000 and 2012, the journalistic workforce shrunk by 18,400 people in the USA (Pew Research Center, 2014). In the UK, about a third of the workforce was laid off between 2001 and 2010. Job precariousness is rampant. Freelance and part-time work have become common-place. Leading online news sites and aggregation services ride on low-pay or no-pay jobs (Bakker, 2012). Job prospects continue to remain bleak even after recovery from the 2008 recession (Taibi, 2015). Furthermore, unpredictable conditions and slashed budgets discourage newsrooms from investing massive resources on quality reporting (Ekdale *et al.*, 2015).

No doubt, these conditions suggest more than just a transition. This is what crisis looks like: the collapse of old business models, uncertainty about new funding mod-els, massive loss of traditional news jobs and limited employment growth.

The social standing of journalism

It is less obvious that other aspects of journalism have experienced a similar crisis. Consider its social standing in the circulation of news and opinion. Journalism is no longer the pre-eminent, all-dominant purveyor of news and information, sitting atop news systems as it has for the past two centuries. It now competes with other forces – from citizens to organizations routinely engaged in producing and dissemi-nating news and information. Its traditional wares are no longer the exclusive prop-erty of one single institution. News, opinions, data, information, headlines, updates and conversation are everywhere. Journalism's once unique output is now the air in today's digital life suffused with news and information. Consequently, journalism does not toil in barren, information-poor landscapes, but is nestled within multilay-ered and dynamic networks of communication (Russell, 2013).

Because journalism used to be the gravitational point of news flows, it enjoyed unmatched power to decide news. No institution could contest, let alone com-pete, with its towering position to decide what information came in and news came out, for how long and in what way. Only governments and corporations with deep pockets were sufficiently powerful to wrestle with journalism in shaping news. Today, instead, journalism does not stand alone in the news ecology. This is why, as Nick Couldry argues in his chapter, contemporary democracies lack a single insti-tution that dominates the public circulation of news and communication. We have barely explored the implications of this unprecedented shift. Just as it is mistaken to completely discount journalism, it is equally wrong to insist that it continues to control news flows like during the heyday of the mass media.

Although one could reasonably argue that the transition from news scarcity to news abundance has shifted the position of journalism, this does not mean that its social standing is in crisis. Certainly, multiple actors perform social functions that used to be unique to journalism. Journalism is not the only or the dominant news gatekeeper. In his chapter, Rasmus Kleis Nielsen dissects the concept of 'audience gatekeeping' and raises important questions. Are there gatekeepers when audiences/public, social media platforms and virtually any individual and organization con-trol the outflow of news and information? The fact that social networks increas-ingly filter people's experience with news and journalism puts in evidence the mosaic structure of news gatekeeping. Google, Facebook, Twitter and other online platforms are mediating channels of the 'news experience', which reflects the complexity of gatekeeping. Just as journalism has traditionally mediated the relationship between publics and reality, the interaction between journalism and publics is mediated by social media and other platforms. Users do not need to be directly exposed to news websites or legacy broadcast and print media to access original news.

Although the proliferation of 'news gates' means that journalism does not tightly control the flow of news and information, it is worth discussing whether journalism remains a significant gatekeeper. After all, this was its unmatched social function in the past. How does it compare to audience gatekeeping? Considering that legacy news organizations have continued to lead the daily preferences of news users, as web analytics demonstrate, it is not obvious that the social standing of journalism has completely changed (Newman, Dutton and Blank, 2012). It is too soon to count journalism out in terms of attracting substantial amounts of users, influencing news agendas and framing the way citizens think about specific issues. The circulation of news is not completely flattened. Huge disparities in terms of news production capacity, reach and presence still persist. Readers increasingly rely on social media to consume news, but this does not mean that legacy news organizations are irrelevant. Understanding why conventional journalism commands readers' attention is necessary to assess its roles in fast-changing information ecologies. Do traditional journalistic brands still command trust among users to provide comprehensive and curated news? Are they perceived to provide convenient shortcuts to navigate complex and fragmented news ecologies?

The persistent influence of traditional journalism is linked to another aspect of its social standing – the claim to be the news authority. Again, in principle, such a claim is harder to sustain when news flows lack an identifiable centre or pyramidal structure. In today's noisy and chaotic world of news, it is impossible for journalism, or for that matter any other institution, to occupy a central role in fluid news ecologies. If there is not a clearly demarcated centre, then, the authority of journalism suffers, as Karin Wahl-Jorgensen observes in her chapter. Holding social authority demands the ability to monopolize a certain area of expertise. If anyone could diagnose and cure, design and build, or represent citizens in courts, then medical doctors, architects and lawyers would not command similar social authority. Maintaining firm boundaries between experts and non-experts is central to professional authority. Blurred boundaries make it difficult to wield similar power.

The contestation of the professional boundaries of journalism challenges the traditional relationship between journalism and expertise, as Zvi Reich and Yigal Godler explore in their chapter. Confronted with the complexity of reality, journalism has resorted to 'primary definers' (Hall *et al.*, 1978) to determine news. In this respect, it more closely aligns with Walter Lippmann's well-known view of journalism's social role, as reporters felt more comfortable with the notion that democracy demands information served up by experts rather than active citizen involvement. Journalism's credibility has been linked to this prominent position within the political and economic establishment. Therefore, cementing expertise had little to do with engaging citizens in news decision making or mobilizing popular discourse, but instead was associated with presenting the voices of experts and authorities.

Dependence on 'authoritative' sources has not only been a handy, expeditious shortcut for journalism to distil information into news; it has also been a deliberate strategy to bolster its credibility and social standing. Just as journalism presents itself as the expert of news, it submits particular sources as trusted, legitimate assessors of reality. By doing so, it has failed to problematize the supposed authority of sources. The reason is rather simple: questioning the authority of sources implicitly raises questions about the legitimacy of journalism. It would tear the veil of opacity that surrounds news decisions. The unproblematic presentation of authoritative sources has been central to how journalism has built its social standing as a credible institution.

Has the social standing of journalism completely changed? What is the social standing of journalism when apparently 'everyone is a journalist'? The fact that multiple sources are able to contest, complement and correct journalism's 'self-proclaimed authority' (Bogaerts and Carpentier, 2013) does not necessarily mean that journalism completely losses credibility. Nor does it mean that it has become just one among many voices in a competitive news environment. Further research on this question is needed to assess the social standing of journalism when its performance and claims are more likely to be questioned.

Participatory news

Another area to explore the question of crisis is the incorporation of citizen participation in news making. In the footsteps of the 'public journalism' movement and on the cusp of the digital explosion in the 2000s, there was interest and hope in revitalizing journalism by bringing newsrooms closer to citizens. Journalism seemed ripe for participatory news (Deuze, Bruns and Neuberger, 2007). Such a position was premised in critical views according to which mainstream journalism had betrayed its democratic mission by cutting off its ties to the public, the true protagonist of public life. Dominated by commercial interests and professional norms antithetical to democratic debate, journalism was seen to have turned its back on the public. It perpetuated the views of dominant political and economic interests, and it embraced professional ideals that were contrary to its democratic obligations. It minimized tasks essential to democracy such as holding power accountable, foregrounding citizens' voices, and promoting public understanding and solutions to myriad problems. Journalism could only be redeemed if it were reconnected to citizens.

Digital technologies were seen as opportunities to strengthen the public mission of journalism. Digital platforms and equipment could facilitate the twinning of professional reporters and ordinary people in news reporting and distribution, leading to significant shifts in the overall orientation of journalism (Borger *et al.*, 2013). Citizens could be tirelessly engaged in news making in multiple capacities – reporters, eyewitnesses, curators, sources, correctors, photo/videographers, fact-checkers and copyeditors. Closer engagement with citizens could broaden the focus of news, enrich perspectives, and bring out issues and views generally absent in journalism (Bruns, 2011).

What happened? Scores of studies have produced valuable insights to answer this question (see Singer *et al.*, 2011). Undoubtedly, newsrooms have incorporated citizens in multiple capacities. Journalists regularly rely on citizens for story tips, checking information, first-person testimonies and images. They resort to collective wisdom and citizen participation, particularly when newsrooms lack access to sites and sources such as during wars (Wall and El Zahed, 2015) and humanitarian emergencies. Online editions typically feature comments sections.

Other studies, however, suggest that journalism has not opened all its doors to citizens. It has generally remained comfortable with the usual routines rather than turning news into opportunities for the voices of ordinary citizens and public platforms. Journalists have generally approached participatory tools gingerly, concerned that citizens' input lowers standards of quality (Carlsson and Nilsson, 2015). They have controlled participation according to conventional ways of deciding news and content quality. The managed uses of participatory news have neither challenged dominant power hierarchies in news decisions nor blurred the distinction between reporters and publics. Collaborations cement existing relations instead of overhauling traditional divisions in news production. Reporters have not fundamentally changed the way they view publics or news practices. They have not rushed to engage with citizens as sources or experts (Reich, 2015). Only circumstantially (and strategically perhaps) do journalists tap into 'collective wisdom' and crowdsourcing to gain citizens' insights, get story tips or assess interests (Hermida, 2012; Loke, 2012; Paulussen and Harder, 2014). Such uses, however, do not imply that newsrooms have consistently involved citizens in several aspects of their work or that they introduced fundamental changes to reform conventional practices and news values (Robinson and DeShano, 2011). Changes have been minimal as newsrooms remained stuck in traditional norms and practices.

How can we explain the fact that developments fell short of normative expectations about a revolution in participatory news? Citizens may no longer be conventionally considered 'audiences', passively waiting for news content pushed out by news organizations, yet it is questionable whether they have been generally willing to become engaged in the news-making process. Although 'news audiences' have been reconceptualized as 'produsers' (Bruns, 2011), the evidence does not suggest that citizens have rushed to become full-time contributors or lead actors in news or that newsrooms have welcomed them with open arms (Karlsson *et al.*, 2015; Örnebring, 2013; Scott, Millard and Leonard, 2015). Selected experiences do suggest that citizens have an interest in news reporting and novel forms of blending different forms of professional and citizen expertise, but they hardly amount to a complete overturn in the traditional division of news labour. Although plenty of examples feature citizens' work, they should not be considered conclusive evidence of revolutionary changes in the nature of journalism.

How do we explain the uneven integration of citizens in newsrooms and the record of participatory news? Participatory platforms may burnish some of journalism's democratic credentials, namely as a catalyst of public expression, yet they raise questions about conventional professional conceptions of trust and quality. The poor quality of amateur images negatively reflects on professional standards (Andén-Papadopoulos and Pantti, 2013; Nilsson and Wadbring, 2015). Rumours, lies and unconfirmed assertions negatively reflect on news sites hosting commentary and debates. Loose, unmoderated participation potentially challenges journalism's longstanding ambition to provide authoritative, credible news. This is why news organizations have tried to control news commentary by moderating interventions in order to promote 'civil' discourse and preserve conventional ethics (Zion and Craig, 2014).

Furthermore, news companies and journalists have used digital participation to bolster their position and advance typical goals such as profit making and producing predictable news. The widespread use of web analytics monitoring readers' preferences attests to this phenomenon (Tandoc, 2014). Although certain news outlets may seem 'participatory' because they cull information from audiences, they are hardly democratic for they do not redress power hierarchies in news decisions or stimulate diversity in news representations. In fact, they are functional to the constant search for audiences and profits. More than overhauling the traditional division of news work, instances of so-called participatory news are blatant attempts to capture clicks and shares with free or low-cost labour (Hellmueller and Li, 2015).

In summary, it is questionable whether participatory news has contributed to the kind of democratic goals some had in mind bringing citizens into key decisions, changing the nature of news content, and shifting the relationship between journalists and publics. Evidence suggests the incorporation of a 'minimalist' view of participation (Peters and Witschge, 2015; Witschge, 2013). There has not been a professional rupture or a paradigm shift – a major reconsideration of traditional news values to embed participatory news. Instead, journalism has tried to limit interaction and integrate citizen-produced information seamlessly into conventional routines without introducing major transformations. However, collaborations between reporters and citizens are not deliberately set up to undo traditional dynamics. Such a shift would demand a complete epistemological overhaul – turning journalism from the arbiter of news into the catalyst of public conversation.

No doubt, there has been experimentation and innovation in past years, but they neither consistently resulted in more participatory news making nor were they primarily tied to the search for expanding democratic life. The incorporation of citizen journalism is perfectly compatible with a non-political, professional view of journalism that leaves its ideological and epistemic foundations untouched. As long as the commercial logic remained central in mainstream media, particularly at a time of unprecedented uncertainty about business models and the economic viability of news, the push for experimentation was conditioned by strong pressures to deliver audiences and advertisers. One could suggest that the tension between 'professional control and open participation' (Lewis, 2012) was ultimately settled in favour of professional control or, worse, the enhancement of economic logics.

Should the record of participatory news be surprising? Hardly. Optimistic hopes were analytically simplistic for they failed to address basic questions. Why would journalism voluntarily share power with citizens? Why would it unilaterally revisit hierarchical structures and support horizontal decision making? Ambitious, normative expectations were not properly grounded in sociological theories of institutions, specifically how organizations and professions approach innovations. Just because opportunities arise, it does not mean that they willingly incorporate changes that potentially threaten established norms and hierarchies. Organizations, workplaces and professions are generally cautious about new developments that may potentially undermine existing hierarchies or introduce significant changes. Journalism is no exception in its ambition to control boundaries (Waisbord, 2013). Merely fulfilling democratic expectations is not sufficient to drive transformations. Without a nuanced institutional analysis of the reaction of journalism to challenges and complexity, it is difficult to comprehend the dynamics between established newsrooms and participatory opportunities (Broersma and Peters, 2013).

What should we conclude? It is not obvious that the core values of the professional culture of journalism have undergone significant changes or that they are in a crisis. If professionalism entails 'boundary work', as Matt Carlson reminds us in his chapter, the record of participatory news suggests that journalism has been inclined to do what professions typically do: patrol boundaries to re-assert authority and spheres of competence. Journalism remains embedded in traditional professional ethics. It has not wholeheartedly embraced deliberative politics in the way that many had hoped. Embedding journalism in communitarian and participatory politics would have required jettisoning the whole institutional and ideological apparatus underpinning mainstream news – certainly not a small endeavour, particularly given that it was not obvious why journalism would relinquish social privileges in order to share practices and decisions with ordinary citizens. Receptiveness to user-generated content and adopting social media to check and verify news alone do not drive a paradigm shift. They are perfectly compatible with traditional professional ethics.

Conclusion: changes and continuities

To be clear, I am not suggesting that nothing has changed. Journalism has undergone plenty of transformations over the past decade. The proliferation of digital tools, the rise of new expectations about news-gathering and production skills, and the uses of audience data have impacted newsrooms. The news business, particularly the newspaper industry, has also been transformed. News habits continue to experience unprecedented changes, too.

My argument is different: recent conclusions about the crisis of journalism need to be refined in order to examine changes and continuities. Only then can we assess the condition of journalism in a changing environment grounded in theoretically nuanced and rich explanations. The conservatism of newsrooms vis-à-vis developments and changes is hardly surprising. Bureaucratic organizations are resistant to change and tend to adapt slowly to innovations. Preserving power and hierarchy is not unexpected. Commercial pressures further narrow the potential of reshaping reporting. Actually, it would have been truly astounding if journalism had given up its prerogative to 'make news' and embraced participatory news altogether or completely changed professional norms. Notwithstanding economic uncertainty and major transformations in public communication, not everything about journalism is in question. A careful dissection of the current situation is necessary to refine our understanding of what is (and what is not) in crisis.

What seems to be in crisis is the notion of journalism as a single institution. Can we persuasively continue to talk about journalism in singular given centrifugal dynamics? The balkanization of journalism seems inevitable, driven by the multiplication of business models, gatekeeping dynamics and normative visions. The erosion of the common core, which characterized journalism in democracies in the West, raises questions about whether we should continue approaching journalism as a unified, coherent institution and/or a profession with shared norms, structures and dynamics. Just as we need to question the relevance of other collective nouns inherited from the heyday of mass communication such as 'the media' or 'the audience', it is worth revisiting the appropriateness of talking about 'journalism' in light of the heterogeneity of institutional and non-institutional forms of producing and consuming news.

Also, it is necessary to chart out ways in which a journalism imbued by a broad vision of citizenship is possible amid fluid economic situations and uncertain labour conditions. Persuading myriad institutions to fund journalism, as Couldry urges in his chapter, is necessary considering the fact that the economic foundations of quality news have been shaken up. For a long time, the prospects of mainstream journalism rode on the profitability of news and organizational cross-subsidies in commercial systems as well as the commitment of public broadcasting and public support. That old order is sagging, to say the least. Self-evident market failures demand new actions and visions for democratic journalism.

Criticizing journalism for remaining stuck in its old ways is also necessary. Calling journalism to be set up on new premises, as John Steel argues in this book, is important, too. Questioning the ethical norms of professionalism and the negative impact of market forces remains as important as ever. The analysis, however, should do more than castigate neo-liberalism and conventional professional ethics, especially if scholars are interested in engaging in conversations with journalists and shaping discussions about practice. There is no obvious path to link ideal democratic ethics and real existing journalism. To promote specific ethics divorced from changes as if journalism remains a single institution is misguided. To continue to pile up expectations on a beleaguered journalism is unlikely to result in positive changes without grounding the analysis in the present conditions. Such perspective is important, particularly if journalism studies aims to be influential in shaping changes in practice and the news industry by engaging with editors and journalists in fruitful discussions about the present and the future of news (Blumler and Cushion, 2014).

References

Alexander, J. C. (2015). The crisis of journalism reconsidered: Cultural power. *Fudan Journal of the Humanities and Social Sciences*, *8*, 9–31.

Andén-Papadopoulos, K., & Pantti, M. (2013). Re-imagining crisis reporting: Professional ideology of journalists and citizen eyewitness images. *Journalism*, *14*, 960–977.

Bakker, P. (2012). Aggregation, content farms, and Huffinization: The rise of low-pay and no-pay journalism. *Journalism Practice*, *6*, 627–637.

Blumler, J. G., & Cushion, S. (2014). Normative perspectives on journalism studies: Stock-taking and future directions. *Journalism*, *15*, 259–272.

Bogaerts, J., & Carpentier, N. (2013). The postmodern challenge to journalism: Strategies for constructing a trustworthy identity. In C. Peters & M. Broersma (Eds.), *Rethinking journalism: trust and participation in a transformed news landscape* (pp. 60–71). London: Routledge.

Borger, M., van Hoof, A., Costera Meijer, I., & Sanders, J. (2013). Constructing participatory journalism as a scholarly object: A genealogical analysis. *Digital Journalism*, *1*, 117–134.

Broersma, M., & Peters, C. (2013). Introduction: Rethinking journalism: The structural trans-formation of a public good. In C. Peters & M. Broersma (Eds.), *Rethinking journalism: Trust and participation in a transformed news landscape* (pp. 1–12). London: Routledge.

Bruns, A. (2011). News produsage in a pro-am mediasphere: Why citizen journalism mat-ters. In G. Meikle & G. Redden (Eds.), *News online: Transformations and continuities* (pp. 132–147). Basingstoke: Palgrave Macmillan.

Carlsson, E., & Nilsson, B. (2015). Technologies of participation: Community news and social media in Northern Sweden. *Journalism* (ahead-of-print). doi: 10.1177/1464884915599948.

Conboy, M., & Eldridge II, S. A. (2014). Morbid symptoms: Between a dying and a re-birth (apologies to Gramsci). *Journalism Studies*, *15*, 566–575.

Deuze, M. (2008). The changing context of news work: Liquid journalism for a monitorial citizenry. *International Journal of Communication*, *2*, 848–865.

Deuze, M., Bruns, A., & Neuberger, C. (2007). Preparing for an age of participatory news, *Journalism Practice*, *1*, 322–338.

Ekdale, B., Tully, M., Harmsen S., & Singer, J. B. (2015). Newswork within a culture of job insecurity: Producing news amidst organizational and industry uncertainty. *Journalism Practice*, *9*, 383–398.

Franklin, B. (2014). The future of journalism: In an age of digital media and economic uncer-tainty pages. *Journalism Practice*, *8*, 469–487.

Hall, S., Critcher, C., Jefferson, T., Clarke J., & Roberts, R. (1978). *Policing the crisis*. London: Macmillan.

Hellmueller, L., & Li, Y. (2015). Contest over content: A longitudinal study of the CNN iReport effect on the journalistic field. *Journalism Practice*, *9*, 617–633.

Hermida, A. (2012). Tweets and truth: Journalism as a discipline of collaborative verification. *Journalism Practice*, *6*, 659–668.

Karlsson, M., Bergström, A., Clerwall, C., & Fast, K. (2015). Participatory journalism – the (r)evolution that wasn't. Content and user behavior in Sweden 2007–2013. *Journal of Computer-Mediated Communication*, *20*, 295–311.

Lewis, S. C. (2012). The tension between professional control and open participa-tion: Journalism and its boundaries. *Information, Communication & Society*, *15*, 836–866.

Loke, J. (2012). Old turf, new neighbors: Journalists' perspectives on their new shared space. *Journalism Practice*, *6*, 233–249.

Newman, N., Dutton, W., & Blank, G. (2012). Social media in the changing ecology of news: The fourth and fifth estates in Britain. *International Journal of Internet Science, 7*, 6–22.

Nielsen, R. K. (2012). *Ten years that shook the media world: Big questions and big trends in international media developments.* Oxford: Reuters Institute for the Study of Journalism.

Nilsson, M., & Wadbring, I. (2015). Not good enough? Amateur images in the regular news flow of print and online newspapers. *Journalism Practice, 4*, 484–501.

Örnebring, H. (2013). Anything you can do, I can do better? Professional journalists on citizen journalism in six European countries. *International Communication Gazette, 75*, 35–53.

Paulussen, S., & Harder, R. A. (2014). Facebook, Twitter and YouTube as sources in newspaper journalism. *Journalism Practice, 8*(5), 542–551.

Peters, C., & Witschge, T. (2015). From grand narratives of democracy to small expectations of participation: Audiences, citizenship, and interactive tools in digital journalism. *Journalism Practice, 9*, 19–34.

Pew Research Center. (2014). *Newspaper newsroom workforce continues to drop.* Retrieved from http://www.journalism.org/media-indicators/newsroom-workforce.

Reich, Z. (2015) Why citizens still rarely serve as news sources: Validating a tripartite model of circumstantial, logistical, and evaluative barriers. *International Journal of Communication, 9*, 22.

Reinardy, S. (2011). Newspaper journalism in crisis: Burnout on the rise, eroding young journalists' career commitment, *Journalism, 11*, 33–50.

Robinson, S., & DeShano, C. (2011). Anyone can know: Citizen journalism and the interpretive community of the mainstream press, *Journalism, 12*, 1–20.

Russell, A. (2013). *Networked: A contemporary history of news in transition.* Cambridge: Polity Press.

Schlesinger, P., & Doyle, G. (2014). From organizational crisis to multi-platform salvation? Creative destruction and the recomposition of news media, *Journalism, 16*(3), 305–323.

Scott, J., Millard, D., & Leonard, P. (2015). Citizen participation in news: An analysis of the landscape of online journalism, *Digital Journalism, 3*, 737–758.

Siles, I. & Boczkowski, P. J. (2012). Making sense of the newspaper crisis: A critical assessment of existing research and an agenda for future work. *New Media and Society, 14*, 1375–1394.

Singer, J. B., Domingo, D., Heinonen, A., Hermida, A., Paulussen, S., Quandt, T., ... Vujnovic, M. (2011). *Participatory journalism: Guarding open gates at online newspapers.* Malden, MA: Wiley.

Starr, P. (2012). An unexpected crisis: The news media in postindustrial democracies. *International Journal of Press/Politics, 17*, 234–242.

Taibi, C. (2015). Employment rates are improving for everyone but journalism majors. *Huffington Post.* Retrieved from http://www.huffingtonpost.com/2015/02/23/unemployment-journalism-major-college-graduate_n_6737496.html.

Tandoc, E. C. Jr. (2014). Journalism is twerking? How web analytics is changing the process of gatekeeping. *New Media & Society, 16*, 559–575.

Waisbord, S. (2013). *Reinventing professionalism: Journalism and news in global perspectives.* Cambridge: Polity Press.

Wall, M., & El Zahed, S. (2015). Embedding content from Syrian citizen journalists: The rise of the collaborative news clip. *Journalism, 16*, 163–180.

Witschge, T. (2013). Digital participation in news media: 'Minimalist' views versus meaningful interaction. In R. Scullion, R. Gerodimos, D. Jackson, & D. Lilleker (Eds.), *The media, political participation and empowerment (pp. 103–115).* London: Routledge.

Zelizer, B. (2015). Terms of choice: Uncertainty, journalism and crisis. *Journal of Communication, 65*, 888–908.

Zion, L., & Craig, D. (Eds.). (2014). *Ethics for digital journalists: Emerging best practices.* New York: Routledge.

AFTERWORD

Revisioning journalism and the 'pictures in our heads'

Stuart Allan

> In order then that the distant situation shall not be a gray flicker on the edge of attention, it should be capable of translation into pictures in which the opportunity for identification is recognizable. Unless that happens it will interest only a few for a little while. It will belong to the sights seen but not felt, to the sensations that beat on our sense organs, and are not acknowledged. We have to take sides.
>
> (Lippmann, 1922, p. 165)

'It started as a sudden, stunned hush', Jamie Fahey (2015) of *The Guardian* recalled. 'Once a few seemingly eternal seconds had shifted us into the realm of prolonged silence – with a few heads shaking with empathic resignation – it was abundantly clear that this was a huge moment.' Fahey, a production editor on the news desk, described *The Guardian*'s lunchtime meeting on 2 September 2015 when colleague Roger Tooth, head of photography, revealed 'the shocking pictures that were about to become a symbol for an outpouring of condemnation'. The pictures in question depicted the tragic scene on a beach in Turkey, where the corpses of drowned Syrian refugees had washed ashore. In one, three-year-old Alan Kurdi was shown face down on the sand, while in another, a Turkish police officer, who had recovered the child's lifeless body, tenderly cradled it in his arms.[1] While *The Guardian* had expended considerable effort to report on the emergent immigration and refugee crisis in Europe over previous weeks, these photographs – already viral across social media platforms – were of an altogether different order, the potential to ignite global consternation readily apparent. 'It felt like the moment a crisis defined by abstract debates over ideology, statistics and terminology suddenly shifted to one about people', Fahey observed.

The power of imagery to galvanize public opinion has long been recognized, particularly when it disrupts journalism's tacit presuppositions about the world around us (such unspoken rules being all the more apparent when transgressed). This rapidly proved to be the case where the Kurdi imagery was concerned, with sharply differing views regarding how best to handle such upsetting material engendering significant controversy for news organizations. In the absence of agreed conventions over visual parameters, questions regarding the acceptable limits of representation were frequently framed as revolving around stereotypes, specifically their perceived influence on public awareness of the growing refugee crisis (see Berry, Garcia-Blanco and Moore, 2016; White, 2015). Once a mainstay of journalism scholarship, the concept 'stereotype' has seen its explanatory power steadily diminish over recent years, typically yielding to a more semiologically rich vocabulary in its place. And yet, sometimes timeworn concepts can surprise us by prompting counter-intuitive insights, encouraging us to reconsider how everyday assumptions guide our ways of seeing, not only on the basis of subtle projections of inclusivity, but equally by the exclusions we calmly disregard. To be self-reflexive about our status as researchers is to acknowledge the accustomed normativity of our position – our preferred inflections, intentional or otherwise, of how the world ought to be – in the wider discursive fields we inhabit.

Accordingly, this Afterword will revisit this rather old concept – the stereotype – to consider its potential for future efforts to further elaborate modes of inquiry inspired by the chapters in Part II of *Rethinking Journalism Again*. Here I have chosen to re-inflect the remit typically associated with this genre – ordinarily written with a view to invoking closure on the preceding chapters' discussion – in order to advance this forward-looking agenda. Impressed by the diverse ways in which the respective authors have characterized journalism's evolving relationships with its publics (recognizing that what is rendered an explicit question for some is left implicit by others), it occurred to me that the social relations of stereotyping might usefully serve as an impetus for a critical revisioning of journalism's social responsibilities, especially when distressing imagery is at stake. Prior to returning to the specifics of the Kurdi photographs below, then, our attention will turn to the journalist and political commentator Walter Lippmann's (1922) initial formulation of the stereotype as a concept in its own right. It is my objective to show that a close reading of his book *Public Opinion* helps us to pinpoint how analyses of stereotyping can facilitate efforts to disrupt journalism's prefigurements of 'the audience' and corresponding presumptions about public aptitudes towards the plight of distant others. To read the news image's visual language of othering from such a vantage point, I will argue, is to begin discerning how and why such imagery can work to reaffirm – and, on occasion, challenge – what Lippmann so aptly called the 'casual cruelty of our prejudices' (1922, p. 256).

Journalism's publics

Before we proceed to develop this Afterword's alternative trajectory, let us clarify its point of departure. Each of the six chapters in Part II of this edited collection urges us to rethink journalism for different, yet compelling reasons. What I have perceived to be a shared thematic across their breadth – that is, a commitment to envisaging anew journalism's relationships with its publics – underscores the importance of recognizing that there is no one 'journalism' to be illuminated by the spotlight of reform. This section's contributors provide the rationale for their approach with care, signalling analytical priorities that can be briefly overviewed here. Mark Deuze and Tamara Witschge elucidate several of the institutional imperatives at issue in their examination of how – and why – journalists are adopting new tactics to cope with evolving organizational pressures, including where self-conceptions of prescribed roles and responsibilities to audiences within wider democratic cultures are concerned. Jane B. Singer's chapter purview includes scrutinizing several new forms of collaboration journalists are setting in motion with their audiences, revealing how traditional source relations may be renegotiated as partnerships with the rise of social media. In her chapter, Kaori Hayashi considers how journalism needs to enrich its civic cultures to better support an ethic of care, and thereby offer enhanced forms of empathy and solidarity for citizens struggling to exercise their right of free speech.

The chapter co-authored by Seth C. Lewis, Avery E. Holton and Mark Coddington makes the case for theorizing reciprocity – 'a principle of mutual exchange and giving in community that is linked with the core social attributes of trust and social capital' – in order to show why, in their view, it 'offers a useful new lens for imagining what the journalist–audience relationship could be, not only in reconceiving it broadly, but also in evaluating what participatory journalistic initiatives might work and why'. Pablo J. Boczkowski and Eugenia Mitchelstein assess current debates regarding whether there is a 'news gap' between the news media and their publics in various Western media systems, drawing upon empirical evidence to assess its relative magnitude as well as the variables possibly affecting it. And, lastly, Chris Peters and Marcel Broersma critically investigate journalism's implicit democratic worth, contending that 'in spite of ongoing economic problems and issues of public legitimacy – challenges that surely erode claims of representing "the people" – journalism holds onto the paradigms it successfully developed at the end of the nineteenth century', even when these paradigms are looking increasingly anachronistic in the age of digital media ecologies.

Taken together, these chapters cast journalism's relationships with its publics in a fascinating light, effectively revealing an array of informed – and suitably provocative – vantage points from which to rethink familiar issues, problems and questions. In my case, reading these chapters at the same time as the controversy over the Alan Kurdi photographs was unfolding proved beneficial in numerous ways, helping me to come to grips with the stratified politics of othering being perpetuated by media stereotypes of immigrants, refugees and asylum seekers in the weeks beforehand. Overt instances of inflammatory prejudice had not been restricted to news organizations editorially opposed to higher levels of immigration (in the UK, the majority of national newspapers), which meant that even the more balanced treatments frequently belied forms of stigmatization which the Kurdi imagery was suddenly exposing, at least in the short term. Time and again, I was struck by how often the concept of 'stereotype' appeared in the ensuing news coverage, including references to social media sites where members of the public were mocking certain newspapers' dramatic reversal away from stereotypes generating antipathy. While only one of the six chapters in the second part of this collection mentions stereotypes directly, all of them encouraged me to re-assess certain theoretical and methodological commitments towards journalism's public resonance and responsibilities, specifically as it pertains to visual news cultures, and with the considerable benefit of their fresh perspectives. Beginning in the next section, then, I will strive to extend this agenda, in the first instance by revisiting the concept of 'stereotype' as its tenets were formulated almost a century ago.

'The habits of our eyes'

Walter Lippmann's *Public Opinion*, first published in 1922, opens with an intriguing tale. Lippmann sets the scene by describing a remote island where British, French and German expatriates live together in a harmonious community. In the absence of telegraphic cables connecting them with the outside world, the islanders rely on a mail steamer to visit every 60 days with the latest newspaper to keep them abreast of what is happening beyond their shores. In September 1914, however, the steamer is delayed, making everyone even more anxious for news than usual, not least because coverage of a celebrated murder trial is the talk of the island. 'It was, therefore, with more than usual eagerness that the whole colony assembled at the quay on a day in mid-September to hear from the captain what the verdict had been' Lippmann (1922, p. 3) writes. Instead, what they learn comes as a shock. Britain and France, they discover, are waging war against Germany. What were the islanders to think? 'For six strange weeks they had acted as if they were friends', he observes, 'when in fact they were enemies' (1922, p. 3).

In describing the islanders' quandary, Lippmann remarks that it was not that different from what most people in Europe experienced at the time. Whether it was six weeks or a mere six hours, there was 'a moment when the picture of Europe on which men [and women] were conducting their business as usual, did not in any way correspond to the Europe which was about to make a jumble of their lives' (1922, p. 3). Each person had a 'picture of Europe' in their heads, one which they trusted and held to be true, and yet which pertained to an environment that no longer existed. From this example, then, Lippmann proceeds to elaborate a general theoretical position. 'We can see that the news of [this environment] comes to us now fast, now slowly', he writes, 'but that whatever we believe to be a true picture, we treat as if it were the environment itself' (1922, p. 4). In order to open up for analysis this space between people's perceptions, on the one hand, and their 'real' environment where action eventuates, on the other, Lippmann introduces the concept – with a gesture to Freud – of a 'pseudo-environment'. This pseudo-environment is the individual's 'interior representation of the world', a representation that necessarily shapes his or her thoughts, feelings and conduct. Lippmann states:

the real environment is altogether too big, too complex, and too fleeting for direct acquaintance. We are not equipped to deal with so much subtlety, so much variety, so many permutations and combinations. And although we have to act in that environment, we have to reconstruct it on a simpler model before we can manage with it. To traverse the world [women and] men must have maps of the world.

(Lippmann, 1922, p. 11)

To understand public opinion, therefore, it is important to recognize this triangular relationship between the real environment ('the scene of the action'), the individual's mental picture of that environment, and the individual's response to that picture as it impacts upon the real environment. 'The pictures inside the heads of these human beings, the pictures of themselves, of others, of their needs, purposes, and relationship, are their public opinions', Lippmann maintains. 'Those pictures which are acted upon by groups of people, or by individuals acting in the name of groups, are Public Opinion with capital letters' (1922, p. 18).

Discerning this disjuncture between the 'pictures in our heads' and 'the world outside', Lippmann draws attention to what he considers to be the main set of issues at stake for journalism in the USA at the time. It is recurrently the case, he argues, that these internal pictures serve to mislead individuals in their dealings with the external world. A range of factors are involved which, taken together, constrain the individual's access to necessary facts. These factors, he writes, 'are the artificial censorships, the limitations of social contact, [and] the comparatively meager time available in each day for paying attention to public affairs'. Furthermore, he adds, there is also 'the distortion arising because events have to be compressed into very short messages, the difficulty of making a small vocabulary express a complicated world, and finally the fear of facing those facts which would seem to threaten the established routine of men's [and women's] lives' (1922 p. 18; see also Lippmann, 1920). For Lippmann, these factors invite a larger question, namely how 'this trickle of messages from the outside is affected by the stored up images, the preconceptions, and prejudices which interpret, fill them out, and in their turn powerfully direct the play of our attention, and our vision itself' (1922, pp. 18–19). It is by taking account of these factors, it follows, that it becomes possible to theorize the process by which 'a pattern of stereotypes' is formed, effectively encouraging the individual to identify these 'limited messages from outside' with their own interests as 'he [or she] feels and conceives them' (1922, p. 19).

Here it is important to note that Lippmann did not proffer an explicit definition of 'stereotype', let alone a single, unified theory of its effectuality (previously the term referred to a printer's use of a solid plate of type-metal). Rather, he intended it to help illuminate how our feeling about an event outside the realm of direct experience is aroused by our mental image of that event. In other words, beyond what we can directly observe, our opinions have to be 'pieced together out of what others have reported and what we can imagine' (1922, p. 53). News of a distant scene may therefore be recognized as 'the joint product of the knower and known', one where the 'facts we see depend on where we are placed, and the habits of our eyes' (1922, p. 54). This phrase 'the habits of our eyes' is telling, signalling as it does our predisposition to make sense of 'the great blooming, buzzing confusion of the outer world' in particular ways shaped by our previous apprehension of the familiar and the strange. 'For the most part we do not first see, and then define, we define first and then see', Lippmann writes, thereby succinctly pinpointing how accustomed norms and beliefs consistent with our picture of the world – which he likens to a repertory of stereotypes, by which he means our evolving stock of accepted impressions – recurrently effect inchoate, yet pervasive influence (1922, pp. 54–5, 59). Our preconceptions govern the process of perception, such that when '[a]roused, they flood fresh vision with older images, and project into the world what has been resurrected in memory' (1922, pp. 59–60). Stereotypes, then, condition what will be accepted as true – and thereby what is to be publicly acknowledged as good or evil – in ways that are all the more formidable to the extent they seem perfectly obvious or commonsensical, even when they are inevitably partial, selective and contingent.

Imagery, not surprisingly, warranted particular attention in this regard. At the time of Lippmann's intervention, the reportorial forms and practices of what was increasingly being termed 'photographic journalism' were in early stages of consolidation, yet he recognized the power of imagery to transfigure news events through the act of representation. 'Photographs have the kind of authority over imagination today, which the printed word had yesterday, and the spoken word before that', he contends. 'They seem utterly real. They come, we imagine, directly to us without human meddling, and they are the most effortless food for the mind conceivable' (1922, p. 61). However, in contrast with the 'inert' news photograph requiring conscious effort to interpret, the 'moving picture' was capable of 'steadily building up imagery which is then evoked by the words people read in their newspapers' (1922, p. 60). On the cinema screen, he argued, 'the whole process of observing, describing, reporting, and then imagining, has been accomplished for you', leading him to express his anxiety over how vague, hazy notions can take vividly compelling shape, even though they may be wholly inaccurate or morally pernicious (1922, p. 61). In any case, an idea conveyed by either a still or moving image will not be 'fully our own until we have identified ourselves with some aspect of the picture', which requires at least a degree of empathy, even though it 'may be almost infinitely subtle and symbolic' (1922, p. 105). It is through our personal attachment of feelings in this regard, Lippmann believed, that we make the significance of a given image our own.

Stereotypical visions

Commentators from the early reviews of *Public Opinion* onward praised Lippmann's conception of how newspapers furnish a 'picture of reality' influencing public perceptions (Holcombe, 1922; Park, 1922), with some noting the importance of stereotypes 'in determining the attitudes of men [and women] in regard to the system of political control' (Merriam, 1923, p. 210; Dewey, 1922). Several academic researchers were motivated to confirm the existence of stereotypes on the basis of statistical evidence, including audience reception studies using photographs (Litterer, 1933; McGill, 1931; Rice, 1928; see also Katz and Braly, 1933). Over the following decades, Lippmann's formative ideas about stereotypes were widely hailed as constituting a major theoretical advance, prompting intense debate across multiple disciplines – not least with respect to fledgling developments in news and journalism studies – that were concerned with furthering understanding of the factors involved in shaping the formation of public opinion (see also Eulau, 1956; Fishman, 1956; LaViolette and Silvert, 1951).

Some critics expressed scepticism, however, particularly with regard to the continuing relevance of these elaborations in the age of electronic media. 'Lippmann's description of stereotypes was helpful in its day', Daniel J. Boorstin conceded, but 'he wrote before pseudo-events had come in full flood' (1961, p. 38). Boorstin's book *The Image: A Guide to Pseudo-events in America* (a classic study of the emergent visual politics of celebrity culture, advertising, public relations and related forms of publicity in the post-war years) points out that photographic journalism was 'still in its infancy' when Lippmann's *Public Opinion* was published, with wire-photo technology yet to be widely adopted by news organizations. Viewed with the benefit of hindsight, stereotypes may have 'made experience handy to grasp', he argued, but they 'dulled the palate for information' (1961, p. 38). Pseudo-events, in marked contrast, 'make experience newly and satisfyingly elusive', effectively washing away the distinction between hard and soft news, leaving in its wake news events amounting to little more than 'dramatic performances' in which 'men in the news' simply act out a 'prepared script' in the service of vested interests (1961, p. 38). 'Recent improvements in vividness and speed, the enlargement and multiplying of news-reporting media, and the public's increasing news hunger', Boorstin maintained, 'now make Lippmann's brilliant analysis of the stereotype the legacy of a simpler age' (1961, p. 38).

Putting to one side the question of whether or not life was any simpler in the 1920s, few would dispute that the notion of the 'stereotype' continues to resonate in both scholarly and public debate. James W. Carey's (1989, 1997) thought-provoking assessments of Lippmann's contribution noted a pivotal turn, namely his redefining of 'the problem of the press from one of morals and [partisan] politics to epistemology' (1989, p. 76). More specifically, in Carey's reading, *Public Opinion* extended a metaphor of communication revolving around vision and representation; that is, the view that reality is 'picturable' (Carey's term, not Lippmann's), where 'truth can be achieved by matching an independent, objective, picturable reality against a language that corresponds to it' (1989, p. 77). Carey took issue with Lippmann's stance at several levels, claiming that he effectively 'took the public out of politics', rendering it subservient to experts better placed to make critical choices. In this 'depoliticized world', Carey surmised, news can approximate truth 'only when reality is reducible to a statistical table' (economic data, court decisions, elections, sports scores and the like) supplied by 'a good machinery of record', which meant – in what he regarded as Lippmann's overly pessimistic view – that it was much more likely to provide a 'pseudo-reality of stereotypes' instead. Moreover, Carey considered Lippmann's proffered solution for news organizations to be unfeasible, namely that they employ independent 'cadres of social scientists' using 'the latest statistical procedures' to secure 'veridical representations of reality' so as to ensure the newspaper will correctly inform public opinion (1989, pp. 78, 81). Models of news and communication, Carey insisted, must initiate a break with Lippmann's conception of vision in order to place a more pragmatic emphasis on hearing, preferably in the manner espoused by the philosopher John Dewey. It was the latter who argued: 'Vision is a spectator, hearing is a participator' (Dewey, 1927, p. 219; on the oft-labelled 'Lippmann–Dewey debate', see also Allan, 2013; Frosh, 2011; Jansen, 2008; Rakow, 2015; Schudson, 2008; Tell, 2013).

While this distinction between vision (information) and hearing (conversation) risks overstatement, it nevertheless usefully underscores the importance of attending to the complications besetting any presumed relationship between 'pictures in our head' and democratic ideals. In his review of *Public Opinion*, Dewey drew attention to the heuristic value of stereotypes in this regard, crediting Lippmann's discussion with 'a more significant statement of the genuine "problem of knowledge" than professional epistemological philosophers have managed to give' (1922, p. 286). Stereotypes, in this analysis, amount to 'traditions and habits of mind that form the standing "categories" through which facts are received, illusions that have to do with defence, prestige, morality; deficiencies in recognition of extended space and enduring time spans', such that real, lived connections manifest in action are lost, effectively – and here Dewey uses Lippmann's phrase – 'clipped and frozen in the stereotype' (1922, p. 286). He similarly admires Lippmann's trenchant criticism of how 'stereotypes are called into play and emotions enlisted by use of appeals and symbols', particularly 'the ways in which politicians currently secure this needed dramatic identification – methods which are anything but conducive to clearness and justice of thought' – to advance their interests (1922, pp. 286–7). Still, where Lippmann's proposed remedy is concerned, the organization of expert intelligence to provide leaders with the necessary data for policy making, Dewey expresses serious reservations. 'Mr. Lippmann seems to surrender the case for the press too readily – to assume too easily that what the press is it must continue to be', he writes. Consequently, for Dewey, journalism must rise to the challenge of 'supplying to the whole people an objective record of the news' rather than being focused on the concerns of the privileged few. 'The enlightenment of public opinion', he maintains, 'still seems to me to have priority over the enlightenment of officials and directors' (1922, p. 288).

A central feature of current efforts to compare and contrast Lippmann's convictions with those of Dewey revolves around their respective viewpoints regarding the normative role of the press in a participatory democracy. Much is made of attendant differences in opinion (to my mind, more a question of relative emphasis than stark polarities), yet both occupy common conceptual ground concerning the debilitating effects of stereotypes on public life, if disagreeing over how best to ameliorate them. Interestingly, Lana F. Rakow (2015) observes that Dewey employed the term 'stereotyped' several years before Lippmann's *Public Opinion* appeared, when he wrote in his book *How We Think*:

> Certain men or classes of men come to be the accepted guardians and trans-
> mitters – instructors – of established doctrines. To question the beliefs is to
> question their authority; to accept the beliefs is evidence of loyalty to the
> powers that be, a proof of good citizenship. Passivity, docility, acquiescence,
> come to be primal intellectual virtues … Beliefs that perhaps originally were
> the products of fairly extensive and careful observation are *stereotyped* into
> fixed traditions and semi-sacred dogmas accepted simply upon authority, and
> are mixed with fantastic conceptions that happen to have won the acceptance
> of authorities.
>
> (Dewey, 1910, p. 149, emphasis added)

Rakow rightly points out that Lippmann acknowledges having read Dewey's book
in *Public Opinion*, but proceeds to argue that not only did he fail to mention this
earlier usage of 'stereotyped', but also that his conception of stereotype 'stripped' it
'of the context of power and authority provided by Dewey [thereby] fueling beliefs
in the irrational and inevitably fallible nature of the public' (Rakow, 2015, p. 15). As
I trust my discussion above makes apparent, I would suggest this is an unfair criticism of Lippmann, who was alert to precisely these questions of power and authority, but this is not to deny Dewey makes the point in compelling terms. As to the
lineage of the concept, as Rakow notes, Dewey himself praised Lippmann's formulation, writing in his essay 'Education and Politics': 'What Mr Lippmann has so well
called stereotypes are more responsible for confusion and error in the public mind
than is consciously invested and distorted news' (1983, p. 331). Both Lippmann and
Dewey, I would suggest, were calling for journalism to find new ways to disentangle
the pressing issues of the day from deleterious stereotypes ostensibly legitimized as
popular beliefs and, in so doing, to make apparent the means by which these 'stored
up images' frequently impose untenable constraints upon our knowledge of reality
and capacity to act.

Alternative visions

In recognizing, after Lippmann, that stereotypes may prove to be 'blind spots' with
the potential to undermine reasoned evaluation and judgement, critical analyses
of news imagery may proceed to interrogate common perceptions by opening up
alternative spaces for divergent readings. Returning to the refugee crisis discussed
at the outset of this Afterword, we may ask the following question: to what extent
have typical forms of news imagery recurrently cultivated 'pictures in our heads'
misrepresenting the lived realities of those caught-up in such misery? Further, have
such systems of stereotypes worked to close off or foreclose possible options for
humane responses to such suffering?

In the days leading up to the harrowing events involving Alan Kurdi and his
family, certain news organizations – particularly the right-wing tabloid press in the
case of the UK – proclaimed Europe was under 'siege', facing an 'invasion' from
a 'horde', its coasts likened to a 'war zone' with 'marauding' foreigners trying to

'swarm' the borders (Taylor, 2015). Columnist Katie Hopkins (2015), writing in the Murdoch-owned *The Sun*, insisted: 'Make no mistake, these migrants are like cockroaches', before advocating: 'Bring on the gunships, force migrants back to their shores and burn the boats.' A front-page *Daily Mail* (31 July 2015) headline read: 'The "Swarm" on Our Streets', with the subheading: 'As police seize stowaway migrants across South, [Prime Minister] Cameron is attacked for "likening them to insects".' Contrary voices striving to challenge such rhetoric pointed out that the plight of tens of thousands of refugees and asylum seekers in need of sanctuary – many from war-torn Syria, Iraq and Afghanistan – was being compounded by hurtful stereotypes. Desperately vulnerable people were labelled 'frauds' and 'cheats', even 'terrorists' in some instances, effectively inviting the popular acceptance of an 'us' versus 'them' dichotomy ratified by a pernicious politics of othering. Stereotypes, Lippmann writes, afford us – which is to say, not them – 'an ordered, more or less consistent picture of the world, to which our habits, our tastes, our capacities, our comforts and our hopes have adjusted themselves' (1922, p. 63). In this world, 'people and things have their well-known places, and do certain expected things', he continued. 'We feel at home there. We fit in. We are members. We know the way around.' It is there 'we find the charm of the familiar, the normal, the dependable; its grooves and shapes are where we are accustomed to find them' (1922, p. 63).

It is this sense of consistency that is taken for granted, these ritualized normalcies imperceptibly sustained by timeworn conventions. 'No wonder, then, that any disturbance of the stereotypes seems like an attack', Lippmann contends:

> It is an attack upon the foundations of our universe, and, where big things are at stake, we do not readily admit that there is any distinction between our universe and the universe. A world which turns out to be one in which those we honor are unworthy, and those we despise are noble, is nerve-racking. There is anarchy if our order of precedence is not the only possible one.
>
> (1922, p. 63)

No pattern of stereotypes is neutral, representing as it may 'the core of our personal tradition', and as such amounting to normative expectations corresponding to our preferred social position:

> It is the guarantee of our self-respect; it is the projection upon the world of our own sense of our own value, our own position and our own rights. The stereotypes are, therefore, highly charged with the feelings that are attached to them. They are the fortress of our tradition, and behind its defenses we can continue to feel ourselves safe in the position we occupy.
>
> (1922, p. 64)

Such comfort is illusory in that 'it censors out much that needs to be taken into account', but it makes good its promise to hold us to a moralized rendering of apparent facts – until, that is, 'the day of reckoning comes, and the stereotype is shattered' (1922, p. 74).

The heart-rending images of Alan Kurdi worked in precisely this way, shattering prevailing stereotypes of the 'European migrant crisis' by opening them up to contest, and thereby helping to mobilize resistant readings calling into question the reassuring values promoted in so many official statements (the word 'migrant', with its connotations of a voluntary decision to relocate, almost always privileged over 'refugee'). The photographer of the 'world shaking picture', Nilüfer Demir of Turkey's Dogan News Agency (DHA), later recalled the tragic scene on the Bodrum coast. 'At that moment', she told an interviewer, 'I was petrified.' Kurdi was 'lying lifeless face down in the surf, in his red t-shirt and dark blue shorts folded to his waist', Demir said. 'The only thing I could do was to make his outcry heard.' In that instant, she added: 'I believed I would be able to achieve this by clicking the shutter of my camera and took his picture' (cited in DHA, 2015). Little could she have imagined how far and wide this outcry would be heard, her images igniting across social media platforms an extraordinary outpouring of support for refugees, as well as concerted appeals to governments to intervene on their behalf. News headlines included:

- Brutal images of Syrian boy drowned off Turkey must be seen, activists say (*New York Times*, 2 September 2015)
- A dead baby becomes the most tragic symbol yet of the Mediterranean refugee crisis (*Washington Post*, 2 September 2015)
- If these images don't change Europe, what will? (*Al Jazeera*, 2 September 2015)
- Humanity washed ashore (*Gulf News*, 3 September 2015)
- Shocking images of Syrian toddler who drowned off Turkey cause widespread outrage (*Today's Zaman* [Turkey], 3 September 2015)
- The tragic picture that moved the world: Why it took Aylan to make us take notice (*The Age* [Melbourne], 3 September 2015)
- Images of drowned Syrian child spark horror over Europe migrant crisis (*Hindustan Times*, 3 September 2015)
- Image that made the world sit up and take notice (*The Star* [South Africa], 5 September 2015)
- The photographs that moved the world to tears – and to take action (*The Observer* [London], 6 September, 2015)

Intense disagreements were negotiated in many newsrooms over how to handle the imagery in an appropriately sensitive manner, with some editors fearful of criticism that journalistic boundaries – particularly the social taboo where the depiction of dead children is concerned – were being crossed. Others disagreed, believing they had a professional duty to make such imagery available (including Demir herself, who told CNN: 'I thought, "This is the only way I can express the scream of his silent body"' (cited in Griggs, 2015)), recognizing its potential to serve as a catalyst for civic engagement. It 'is not offensive, it is not gory, it is not tasteless – it is merely heartbreaking, and stark testimony of an unfolding human tragedy that is playing out in Syria, Turkey and Europe, often unwitnessed', Kim Murphy of the *Los Angeles Times* maintained. 'We have written stories about hundreds of migrants dead in capsized boats, sweltering trucks, lonely rail lines', she continued, 'but it took a tiny boy on a beach to really bring it home to those readers who may not yet have grasped the magnitude of the migrant crisis' (cited in Mackey, 2015).

Conclusion

End-of-year retrospectives of 2015's most memorable news images recurrently highlighted the 'iconic' photographs of Alan Kurdi, with commentators joining what was an ongoing debate regarding the reasons why they resonated so profoundly with such diverse publics. 'Part of what touched people about this picture is that it is shocking but it isn't graphic', Nicole Itano of Save the Children told the BBC. 'He isn't maimed, he isn't bloodied, he looks like he could be sleeping except for the context. He looks like he could be any of our children' (cited in Gunter, 2015). For Peter Bouckaert of Human Rights Watch, the child's ethnicity was an important factor. 'This is a child that looks a lot like an European child', he explained to *TIME*. 'The week before, dozens of African kids washed up on the beaches of Libya and were photographed and it didn't have the same impact. There is some ethnocentrism [in the] reaction to this image, certainly' (cited in Laurent, 2015). Over and again, commentators stressed how the images 'humanized' a crisis that previously seemed remote and abstract, somehow not involving 'real people' like 'us'. The words 'this could have been my child' featured repeatedly, while the remediation of the imagery captured and relayed via social media platforms – bricolages of Kurdi's prone body Photoshopped into alternative scenes, depicted in artwork, caricatures, graffiti murals and so forth – provoked ideological reflection and critique, as well as parody or satire, to pinpoint perceived inconsistencies, contradictions or outright hypocrisies in public responses.

Demands for social reform (not least for journalists to scrupulously avoid discriminatory stereotypes that condone or, worse, encourage prejudice) were articulated across the mediasphere, where debate raged over Europe's ethical responsibilities to refugees, particularly those from Syria. Confident assertions that the Kurdi images would prove to be a 'tipping point' in 'awakening' public consciences, much like politicians' assurances that their governments would respond compassionately, were greeted with considerable scepticism (see Berry, Garcia-Blanco and Moore, 2016; Vis and Goriunova, 2015; White, 2015). Others maintained the flipside of negative stereotypes – where every refugee is a virtuous, saint-like victim anxious to assimilate – was similarly shorn of understanding. Views on whether or not policy making would adequately address the structural violence underpinning the refugee crisis were hotly contested, with more progressive visions of social integration contingent upon 'a radical enlargement of the range of attention', to borrow Lippmann's (1922, p. 257) phrase. When persistent stereotypes of displaced populations derive their strength from fear and ignorance, news organizations are obliged to delve beneath the surface of events to challenge repertoires of stereotypical visions in order to ensure the right of the dispossessed to have their voices heard. The Kurdi images played a vital instigatory role in this regard, but it was obvious that much more needed to be done. Responding to concerns that these images would not sustain collective action over time, Tima Kurdi, who was Alan's aunt, expressed her worry that her family's tragedy would be soon forgotten. 'They're not terrorists. They're human beings', she said in a newspaper interview, before making a plea poignant in its simplicity: 'I want the world to remember that picture' (cited in Omand, 2015).

To close, this Afterword has sought to set a forward-looking agenda by revisiting the concept of 'stereotype' in light of certain insights the contributors to this section of *Rethinking Journalism Again* have shared into journalism's evolving relationships with its publics. Of particular interest to me has been the importance of elaborating a critical revisioning of journalism's social responsibilities, especially when pejorative imagery – indifferent to human dignity – risks being normalized as reasonable, even legitimate in authenticating the realities it claims to represent. It has not been my aim to simply reclaim the concept of 'stereotype' for critical research into news imagery, but rather to invite further explorations into the complexities its more traditional usages tend to gloss over for the purposes of analytical convenience (or to facilitate strategic intervention by various stakeholders). Due care needs to be taken to avoid treating it as a static, totalizing concept, ostensibly impervious to the nuance of cultural specificity and its lived contingencies. Echoing familiar debates about 'frames', I would suggest that it is more productive to focus less on stereotypes and more on stereotyping, recognizing the latter to be a fluidly multi-faceted process of signification; that is, a process uneven in its materialities, provisional in its ideological purchase and constantly open to contestation in the very intimacy of its imbrications. However, just as certain journalists have propagated hurtful 'images in our heads' about the refugee crisis, we must recognize our own unintentional complicities – the 'casual cruelty of our prejudices', to repeat Lippmann's (1922) telling words. Identifying and then reversing the potentially devastating implications of this culture of intolerance is difficult, unsettling work, and an exigent moral priority.

Note

1 Alan Kurdi's first name was misspelled Aylan in early news reporting. He was one of 16 on an inflatable dinghy (designed for a maximum of eight) minutes into a journey towards the Greek island of Kos when it capsized in rough seas. Amongst those who perished were Alan's mother, Rehanna, and his five year-old brother, Ghalib. 'I grabbed my sons and wife and we held onto the boat', Abdullah Kurdi told Syria's opposition Radio Rozana in an interview. 'We stayed like that for an hour', he said, 'then the first [son] died and I left him so I could help the other, then the second died, so I left him as well to help his mom and I found her dead ... what do I do.' He continued, 'I spent three hours waiting for the coast guard to come. The life jackets we were wearing were all fake' (cited in MacKinnon, 2015).

References

Allan, S. (2013). *Citizen witnessing: Revisioning journalism in times of crisis.* Cambridge: Polity Press.

Berry, M., Garcia-Blanco, I., & Moore, K. (2016). Press coverage of the refugee and migrant crisis in the EU: A content analysis of five European countries. Report for the Office of the United Nations High Commissioner for Refugees, Geneva, Switzerland.

Boorstin, D. J. (1961). *The image: A guide to pseudo-events in America.* New York: Atheneum.

Carey, J. W. (1989). *Communication as culture: Essays on media and society.* London: Unwin Hyman.

Carey, J. W. (1997). The Chicago School and the history of mass communication research. Reprinted in E. S. Munson & C. A. Warren (Eds.), *James Carey: A critical reader* (pp. 14–33). Minneapolis: University of Minnesota Press.

Dewey, J. (1910). *How we think.* London: D.C. Heath.

Dewey, J. (1922, 3 May). Review of *Public opinion. The New Republic,* 286–288.

Dewey, J. (1927). *The Public and its problems.* Athens, OH: Swallow Press.

Dewey, J. (1983). Education as politics. Reprinted in J.A. Boydston (Ed.), *John Dewey: The middle works, 1899–1924* (pp. 329–334). Carbondale: Southern Illinois University Press (original work published 1922).

DHA. (2015, 3 September). Photographer of the world shaking picture of drowned Syrian toddler: 'I was petrified at that moment'. *Dogan News Agency.* Retrieved from http://www.dha.com.tr/photographer-of-the-world-shaking-picture-of-drowned-syrian-toddler-i-was-petrified-at-that-moment_1017371.html.

Eulau, H. (1956). From public opinion to public philosophy: Walter Lippmann's classic reexamined. *American Journal of Economics and Sociology, 15*(4), 439–451.

Fahey, J. (2015, 8 November). *The Guardian*'s decision to publish shocking photos of Aylan Kurdi. *The Guardian.*

Fishman, J. A. (1956). An examination of the process and function of social stereotyping. *Journal of Social Psychology, 43*(1), 27–64.

Frosh, P. (2011). Framing pictures, picturing frames: Visual metaphors in political communications research. *Journal of Communication Inquiry, 35*(2), 91–114.

Griggs, B. (2015, 3 September). Photographer describes 'scream' of migrant boy's 'silent body'. *CNN.* Retrieved from http://edition.cnn.com/2015/09/03/world/dead-migrant-boy-beach-photographer-nilufer-demir/.

Gunter, J. (2015, 4 September). Alan Kurdi: Why one picture cut through. *BBC News.*

Holcombe, A. N. (1922). Review of *Public opinion. American Political Science Review,* 16(3), 500–501.

Hopkins, K. (2015, 16 April). Rescue boats? I'd use gunships to stop migrants. *The Sun.*

Jansen, S. C. (2008). Walter Lippmann, straw man of communication history. In D. W. Park & J. Pooley (Eds.), *The history of media and communication research: Contested histories* (pp. 71–112). New York: Peter Lang.

Katz, D., & Braly, K. (1933). Racial stereotypes of one hundred college students. *Journal of Abnormal and Social Psychology, 28*(3), 280–290.

Laurent, O. (2015, 4 September). What the image of Aylan Kurdi says about the power of photography. *TIME.*

LaViolette, F., & Silvert, K. H. (1951). A theory of stereotypes. *Social Forces, 29*(3), 257–262.

Lippmann, W. (1920). *Liberty and the news.* New York: Harcourt, Brace and Howe.

Lippmann, W. (1922). *Public opinion.* New York: Free Press.

Litterer, O. F. (1933). Stereotypes. *Journal of Social Psychology, 4*(1), 59–69.

Mackey, R. (2015, 2 September). Brutal images of Syrian boy drowned off Turkey must be seen, activists say. *New York Times.*

MacKinnon, M. (2015, 3 September). 'I was only hoping to provide a better life for my children', father of drowned migrant boy says. *Globe and Mail*.

McGill, K. H. (1931). The school-teacher stereotype. *Journal of Educational Sociology, 4*(10), 642–650.

Merriam, C. E. (1923). Review of *Public opinion. International Journal of Ethics, 33*(2), 210–212.

Omand, G. (2015, 26 December). Alan Kurdi's aunt: 'I want the world to remember that picture'. *Toronto Star*.

Park, R. E. (1922). Review of *Public opinion. American Journal of Sociology, 28*(2), 232–234.

Rakow, L. F. (2015). The world outside and a debate inside our heads: Duped by Carey or Lippmann? Paper presented at *The International Communication Association conference*. San Juan, Puerto Rico.

Rice, S. A. (1928). *Quantitative methods in politics*. New York: Knopf.

Schudson, M. (2008). The 'Lippmann–Dewey debate' and the invention of Walter Lippmann as an anti-democrat 1986–1996. *International Journal of Communication, 2*, 1031–1042.

Taylor, A. (2015, 24 August). Is it time to ditch the word 'migrant'? *Washington Post*.

Tell, D. (2013). Reinventing Walter Lippmann: Communication and cultural studies. *Review of Communication, 13*(2), 108–126.

Vis, F., & Goriunova, O. (Eds.) (2015). *The iconic image on social media: A rapid research response to the death of Aylan Kurdi*. Sheffield: University of Sheffield.

White, A. (2015) *Moving stories: International review of how media cover migration*. London: Ethical Journalism Network.

INDEX